Business Writing For Dummies®

Cheat Sheet

Start Up Sheet

Before you commit one word to paper (or your computer), you must identify three issues that are critical to all business writing: your audience, purpose, and key issue.

No matter what writing challenges you face, the following Start Up Sheet is the first step in successful business writing. Feel free to make a copy of these questions as you work on each new project. With a little practice, you can write with the confidence and competence to propel your career!

Audience

1. Who is my primary reader? Do I have multiple readers?

2. What does my reader *need to know* about the topic?

3. What's in it for my reader?

4. Does my writing need a special *angle* or *point of view?* (Managerial? Technical? Other?)

5. What's my reader's attitude toward the topic?

Purpose

6. My purpose is to _____ so that my reader will _____.

Key Issue

7. What's the one *key point* I want my reader to remember?

Delivery

8. Who should receive a copy of this message?

9. What's the best way to deliver this message? Hard copy? E-mail. Fax? Phone? Personal meeting? Other?

10. When is the best time to deliver the message? When is too early? When is too late?

Editing Checklist

Use the following Editing Checklist to experience the sense of pride and accomplishment that comes with sending a document that's as good as it can get.

❑ My subject line and/or headlines are informative and spark my reader's interest.

❑ My document includes a key word(s).

❑ My document tells a story.

❑ My message has visual impact, including

    ❑ Ample white space

    ❑ Bulleted and numbered lists, and charts and tables, where appropriate

    ❑ Sentences limited to 25 words

    ❑ Paragraphs limited to 7 lines

❑ My message is clear, well-organized and properly formatted.

❑ The message is sequenced to keep the reader interested and moving forward. The action I want the reader to take is clearly spelled out.

❑ The tone reflects my personality on paper, including the active voice and *you* approach.

❑ The spelling, grammar, and punctuation are correct.

Praise For Business Writing For Dummies

"*Business Writing For Dummies* is an important resource that will find its way to everyday use by the people in business today who intend to be the leaders in business tomorrow. It is an excellent blend of practical basics, advanced concepts, and skilled insight that will make better communicators of us all."
> — Gary Sullivan, electronic commerce consultant and university lecturer

"*Business Writing For Dummies* really means business. From job-hunting to sales-pitching, from e-mail to snail mail, Sheryl Lindsell-Roberts gives you the verbal tools to build your career with confidence and competence."
> — Richard Lederer, author of *The Write Way*

"Sheryl combines great knowledge and experience with a very readable style. This book will be an excellent resource for writers everywhere."
> — Bard Williams, Ed.D., author of *The Internet for Teachers, Web Publishing for Teachers, AOL for Teachers,* and *The World Wide Web for Teachers*

"This book presents, in an extremely readable style, the essentials of the subject in a way that is direct, creative, and helpful. It will be useful to a spectrum of readers, from large company managers and home office denizens to newly-minted graduates just entering the business world. Both new technology and new techniques are covered. A wealth of suggestions, tips, and tools for use are offered. The reader comes away with a new understanding of usage, style, and what the new jargon means. Buy this book for a full education on the subject—keep it handy to review for answers to questions. Share it with someone you know: a colleague, a family member, a student. This is easy reading that is truly profitable!"
> — William C. Noz, Principal, The ISO 9000 Network

"Concise business writing is more essential today than when I entered the workplace 30 years ago. Ms. Lindsell-Roberts's book is must-reading for those entering today's business world or for those who rely on the written word for success!"
> —Carl Lekander, Dealer Operations Manager, Ford Motor Company

"*Business Writing For Dummies* glides you through the writing process with lots of terrific tips to get you past "writer's block" and make your writing more effective."
> — Tony Giannelli, Vice President, Silknet Software

 ™

References for the Rest of Us!™

BESTSELLING BOOK SERIES

Do you find that traditional reference books are overloaded with technical details and advice you'll never use? Do you postpone important life decisions because you just don't want to deal with them? Then our *...For Dummies*® business and general reference book series is for you.

...For Dummies business and general reference books are written for those frustrated and hard-working souls who know they aren't dumb, but find that the myriad of personal and business issues and the accompanying horror stories make them feel helpless. *...For Dummies* books use a lighthearted approach, a down-to-earth style, and even cartoons and humorous icons to dispel fears and build confidence. Lighthearted but not lightweight, these books are perfect survival guides to solve your everyday personal and business problems.

> *"More than a publishing phenomenon, 'Dummies' is a sign of the times."*
>
> — The New York Times

> *"...you won't go wrong buying them."*
>
> — Walter Mossberg, Wall Street Journal, on IDG Books' ...For Dummies books

> *"A world of detailed and authoritative information is packed into them..."*
>
> — U.S. News and World Report

Already, millions of satisfied readers agree. They have made *...For Dummies* the #1 introductory level computer book series and a best-selling business book series. They have written asking for more. So, if you're looking for the best and easiest way to learn about business and other general reference topics, look to *...For Dummies* to give you a helping hand.

BUSINESS WRITING FOR DUMMIES®

BUSINESS WRITING FOR DUMMIES®

by Sheryl Lindsell-Roberts

IDG Books Worldwide, Inc.
An International Data Group Company

Foster City, CA ◆ Chicago, IL ◆ Indianapolis, IN ◆ New York, NY

Business Writing For Dummies®

Published by
IDG Books Worldwide, Inc.
An International Data Group Company
919 E. Hillsdale Blvd.
Suite 400
Foster City, CA 94404
www.idgbooks.com (IDG Books Worldwide Web site)
www.dummies.com (Dummies Press Web site)

Library of Congress Catalog Card No.: 99-61119

ISBN: 0-7645-5134-5

Printed in the United States of America

10 9 8 7 6 5 4 3 2 1

1B/RV/QT/ZZ/IN

Distributed in the United States by IDG Books Worldwide, Inc.

Distributed by CDG Books Canada Inc. for Canada; by Transworld Publishers Limited in the United Kingdom; by IDG Norge Books for Norway; by IDG Sweden Books for Sweden; by Woodslane Pty. Ltd. for Australia; by Woodslane (NZ) Ltd. for New Zealand; by TransQuest Publishers Pte Ltd. for Singapore, Malaysia, Thailand, Indonesia, and Hong Kong; by ICG Muse, Inc. for Japan; by Norma Comunicaciones S.A. for Colombia; by Intersoft for South Africa; by Le Monde en Tique for France; by International Thomson Publishing for Germany, Austria and Switzerland; by Distribuidora Cuspide for Argentina; by Livraria Cultura for Brazil; by Ediciones ZETA S.C.R. Ltda. for Peru; by WS Computer Publishing Corporation, Inc., for the Philippines; by Contemporanea de Ediciones for Venezuela; by Express Computer Distributors for the Caribbean and West Indies; by Micronesia Media Distributor, Inc. for Micronesia; by Grupo Editorial Norma S.A. for Guatemala; by Chips Computadoras S.A. de C.V. for Mexico; by Editorial Norma de Panama S.A. for Panama; by American Bookshops for Finland. Authorized Sales Agent: Anthony Rudkin Associates for the Middle East and North Africa.

For general information on IDG Books Worldwide's books in the U.S., please call our Consumer Customer Service department at 800-762-2974. For reseller information, including discounts and premium sales, please call our Reseller Customer Service department at 800-434-3422.

For information on where to purchase IDG Books Worldwide's books outside the U.S., please contact our International Sales department at 317-596-5530 or fax 317-596-5692.

For consumer information on foreign language translations, please contact our Customer Service department at 1-800-434-3422, fax 317-596-5692, or e-mail rights@idgbooks.com.

For information on licensing foreign or domestic rights, please phone +1-650-655-3109.

For sales inquiries and special prices for bulk quantities, please contact our Sales department at 650-655-3200 or write to the address above.

For information on using IDG Books Worldwide's books in the classroom or for ordering examination copies, please contact our Educational Sales department at 800-434-2086 or fax 317-596-5499.

For press review copies, author interviews, or other publicity information, please contact our Public Relations department at 650-655-3000 or fax 650-655-3299.

For authorization to photocopy items for corporate, personal, or educational use, please contact Copyright Clearance Center, 222 Rosewood Drive, Danvers, MA 01923, or fax 978-750-4470.

is a registered trademark or trademark under exclusive license to IDG Books Worldwide, Inc. from International Data Group, Inc. in the United States and/or other countries.

About the Author

My roles in life include that of wife, mother, sister, aunt, cousin, daughter-in-law, friend, author, seminar leader, marketing communications specialist, and training consultant. I grew up in "The Big Apple" and recently applied for citizenship as a Bostonian. When I say the word *coffee* (pronounced cough-ee) everyone figures out that I hail from New York.

It was in New York that I raised my two sons who truly illuminate the inner reaches of my soul. Marc Lindsell, a brilliant and talented architect, lives and has an office in San Francisco, California. Eric Lindsell, a dedicated and caring chiropractor, lives and practices in Columbia, Maryland. I'm the proudest mom in the world.

Why did I become a writer? Did I have a driving passion for writing? Did I have a craving to surpass Chaucer? Was I inspired by a muse? No, to all. My reasons were more mundane. Whenever I had something to write (even in school), I'd be willing to spend a half hour or more searching for just the right word or phrase. It was like a sculptor chipping away at the raw materials until she gets it as good as she can. So, I began to think that perhaps I could "sculpt" words and eke out a living. I'm fortunate to have a job that would be my hobby if it weren't my profession.

Between freelance writing assignments and seminars, I've written more than a dozen books for the professional and humor markets. My first publication, *The Office Professional's Quick Reference Handbook,* published by Macmillan, is in its 4th edition. My entree into the humor market was with my hot seller, *Loony Laws and Silly Statutes*, published by Sterling Publishing. *Loony Laws* continues to receive acclaim on nationwide talk shows, and in magazines and newspapers. I just finished a sequel, *Funny Laws & Other Zany Stuff.* Please look for it.

I share my love and my life with my husband, Jon. We live in Marlborough, Massachusetts (outside of Boston), in *Parnassus*—the wonderful Tudor-style home that Marc designed. In addition to writing, I love traveling, watercolor painting, gardening, photographing nature, reading, eating strawberry cheesecake, skiing, and sailing *Worth th' Wait.* (The photo shows me at the helm.) I try to live each day to the fullest!

—Sheryl Lindsell-Roberts, M.A.

ABOUT IDG BOOKS WORLDWIDE

Welcome to the world of IDG Books Worldwide.

IDG Books Worldwide, Inc., is a subsidiary of International Data Group, the world's largest publisher of computer-related information and the leading global provider of information services on information technology. IDG was founded more than 30 years ago by Patrick J. McGovern and now employs more than 9,000 people worldwide. IDG publishes more than 290 computer publications in over 75 countries. More than 90 million people read one or more IDG publications each month.

Launched in 1990, IDG Books Worldwide is today the #1 publisher of best-selling computer books in the United States. We are proud to have received eight awards from the Computer Press Association in recognition of editorial excellence and three from Computer Currents' First Annual Readers' Choice Awards. Our best-selling ...*For Dummies*® series has more than 50 million copies in print with translations in 31 languages. IDG Books Worldwide, through a joint venture with IDG's Hi-Tech Beijing, became the first U.S. publisher to publish a computer book in the People's Republic of China. In record time, IDG Books Worldwide has become the first choice for millions of readers around the world who want to learn how to better manage their businesses.

Our mission is simple: Every one of our books is designed to bring extra value and skill-building instructions to the reader. Our books are written by experts who understand and care about our readers. The knowledge base of our editorial staff comes from years of experience in publishing, education, and journalism — experience we use to produce books to carry us into the new millennium. In short, we care about books, so we attract the best people. We devote special attention to details such as audience, interior design, use of icons, and illustrations. And because we use an efficient process of authoring, editing, and desktop publishing our books electronically, we can spend more time ensuring superior content and less time on the technicalities of making books.

You can count on our commitment to deliver high-quality books at competitive prices on topics you want to read about. At IDG Books Worldwide, we continue in the IDG tradition of delivering quality for more than 30 years. You'll find no better book on a subject than one from IDG Books Worldwide.

John Kilcullen
Chairman and CEO
IDG Books Worldwide, Inc.

Steven Berkowitz
President and Publisher
IDG Books Worldwide, Inc.

WINNER

*Eighth Annual
Computer Press
Awards 1992*

IX WINNER

*Ninth Annual
Computer Press
Awards 1993*

X WINNER

*Tenth Annual
Computer Press
Awards 1994*

XI WINNER

*Eleventh Annual
Computer Press
Awards 1995*

IDG is the world's leading IT media, research and exposition company. Founded in 1964, IDG had 1997 revenues of $2.05 billion and has more than 9,000 employees worldwide. IDG offers the widest range of media options that reach IT buyers in 75 countries representing 95% of worldwide IT spending. IDG's diverse product and services portfolio spans six key areas including print publishing, online publishing, expositions and conferences, market research, education and training, and global marketing services. More than 90 million people read one or more of IDG's 290 magazines and newspapers, including IDG's leading global brands — Computerworld, PC World, Network World, Macworld and the Channel World family of publications. IDG Books Worldwide is one of the fastest-growing computer book publishers in the world, with more than 700 titles in 36 languages. The "...For Dummies®" series alone has more than 50 million copies in print. IDG offers online users the largest network of technology-specific Web sites around the world through IDG.net (http://www.idg.net), which comprises more than 225 targeted Web sites in 55 countries worldwide. International Data Corporation (IDC) is the world's largest provider of information technology data, analysis and consulting, with research centers in over 41 countries and more than 400 research analysts worldwide. IDG World Expo is a leading producer of more than 168 globally branded conferences and expositions in 35 countries including E3 (Electronic Entertainment Expo), Macworld Expo, ComNet, Windows World Expo, ICE (Internet Commerce Expo), Agenda, DEMO, and Spotlight. IDG's training subsidiary, ExecuTrain, is the world's largest computer training company, with more than 230 locations worldwide and 785 training courses. IDG Marketing Services helps industry-leading IT companies build international brand recognition by developing global integrated marketing programs via IDG's print, online and exposition products worldwide. Further information about the company can be found at www.idg.com. 1/24/99

Dedication

I dedicate this book to the memory of my mother, Ethel Lorenz. From the time I was very young, she instilled in me—by example and persistence—the importance of being a good communicator. Once I stopped rebelling, I started appreciating her efforts and following her lead.

My mother was the greatest letter writer. Throughout the years I was growing up, I remember family and friends coming to my mother with complaints about products or services. She'd sit down at something called a "typewriter" and bang out letters to the offending companies. Shortly thereafter, these people would report that they'd received an apology, a free sample, or some satisfactory action. (I can only imagine the heights my mother would have reached if e-mail and faxes were available.) A friend once said, "When Ethel writes a letter, the paper burns."

Author's Acknowledgments

Even though this book is a writer's dream, such an undertaking isn't possible without the combined efforts of lots of wonderful people. I'd especially like to thank Dr. iBard Williams, for opening this door. I'd also like to thank all the participants in my workshops whose feedback and encouragement are a great source of inspiration and wisdom. They teach me as much as I teach them. Perhaps more.

For developing and producing this book, I owe deep gratitude to

- Mark Butler, Acquisitions Editor, for endowing me with "favored nation status." He believed I was the best person to write this book and put an energetic team together to make it happen.
- Brian Kramer, Project Editor, for his feedback, encouragement, and editorial suggestions. He has great wisdom, showed incredible stamina and patience, and laughed at my jokes.
- Kathleen Dobie, Copy Editor, who made sure my *i*'s were dotted and my *t*'s were crossed. Her insights created clarity from my (sometimes) rambling thoughts.
- Lloyd Perell, Technical Editor, whom I asked to be brutally frank. I assured him this wouldn't jeopardize our relationship—personal or professional. (The jury's still out!)

And finally to my family. Without their continued love and support, I wouldn't be the person I am today.

Publisher's Acknowledgments

We're proud of this book; please register your comments through our IDG Books Worldwide Online Registration Form located at http://my2cents.dummies.com.

Some of the people who helped bring this book to market include the following:

Acquisitions and Editorial

Project Editor: Brian Kramer

Acquisitions Editor: Mark Butler

Copy Editor: Kathleen Dobie

Technical Editor: Lloyd Perell

Editorial Manager: Leah P. Cameron

Editorial Assistant: Beth Parlon

Production

Project Coordinator: Karen York

Layout and Graphics: Daniel Alexander, Maridee V. Ennis, Angela F. Hunckler, Brent Savage, Jacque Schneider, Janet Seib, Michael A. Sullivan, Brian Torwelle

Proofreaders: Christine Berman, Kelli Botta, Melissa D. Buddendeck, Nancy Price, Jennifer Mahern, Ethel M. Winslow, Janet M. Withers

Indexer: Steve Rath

Special Help

Donna Love

General and Administrative

IDG Books Worldwide, Inc.: John Kilcullen, CEO; Steven Berkowitz, President and Publisher

IDG Books Technology Publishing: Brenda McLaughlin, Senior Vice President and Group Publisher

Dummies Technology Press and Dummies Editorial: Diane Graves Steele, Vice President and Associate Publisher; Mary Bednarek, Director of Acquisitions and Product Development; Kristin A. Cocks, Editorial Director

Dummies Trade Press: Kathleen A. Welton, Vice President and Publisher; Kevin Thornton, Acquisitions Manager

IDG Books Production for Dummies Press: Michael R. Britton, Vice President of Production and Creative Services; Cindy L. Phipps, Manager of Project Coordination, Production Proofreading, and Indexing; Kathie S. Schutte, Supervisor of Page Layout; Shelley Lea, Supervisor of Graphics and Design; Debbie J. Gates, Production Systems Specialist; Robert Springer, Supervisor of Proofreading; Debbie Stailey, Special Projects Coordinator; Tony Augsburger, Supervisor of Reprints and Bluelines

Dummies Packaging and Book Design: Patty Page, Manager, Promotions Marketing

◆

The publisher would like to give special thanks to Patrick J. McGovern, without whom this book would not have been possible.

◆

Contents at a Glance

Cartoons at a Glance

By Rich Tennant

page 229

page 189

page 5

page 279

page 95

Fax: 978-546-7747 • E-mail: the5wave@tiac.net

Table of Contents

Introduction

Does your business writing shout, "Read me"?

Does it get the attention it deserves?

Does it drive the action you expect?

*I*f you answered "no" to even one of these questions, this book can change your no's to yes's. Many people—even the brightest and most capable—aren't satisfied with their writing skills and would rather have root canal surgery than commit something to the (dreaded) written word. So you're not alone. The good news is that everyone—no matter how anxious—can learn to write clearly, effectively, and strategically.

About This Book

I wrote this book because I want to share with you the outgrowth of 20 years of successful business writing experience (and perhaps make enough money to retire in style). Part of my experience comes from delivering business writing workshops in the business, academic, and government arenas. It's extremely gratifying when participants get in touch with me months after a workshop to tell me how my technique helped them master what used to be one of the most frustrating parts of their job—writing. Many relate how much more confident they feel and how powerful their writing has become.

Business Writing For Dummies is chock-full of guidelines, not rules. I encourage only a few writing rules: no slurs, no obscenities, and no dishonesty. This book leads you through my Six Steps of effective, powerful, and strategic business writing—everything from getting your ideas together to drafting your document to proofreading like a pro.

How To Read This Book

Part I is the only section I recommend that you read sequentially. It contains my Six Steps, which are the core of effective writing. To get the most out of Part I, have in mind a business document you need to write—a letter or memo, report, or anything else—and try apply each of the Six Steps to your own work as you go through Part I.

The remainder of this book builds on Part I and walks you through a wide variety of writing experiences. Feel free to jump to whatever topic interests you or applies to the writing challenges that you're faced with. The book even has appendixes with simple and practical punctuation, grammar, abbreviation, and spelling guidelines. Keep this book handy for easy reference!

Preview of Coming Attractions

Here's a sneak preview of the five parts of this book:

Part I: Basically Business

Part I introduces you to my Six Steps of effective business writing. You find out how to get started, create headlines and sequence for your reader's reaction, write a draft, design for visual impact, use the proper tone, and proofread. After you go through this part, you'll never again feel as if you're trying to create a paragraph from a bowl of alphabet soup.

Part II: Business Writing in Action

After you get a handle on the Six Steps, you have the confidence to be a writer *extrordinaire* when it comes to letters and memos, reports, proposals, presentations, or just about anything else.

Part III: Energizing Your E-Mail

This part builds on the Six Steps from Part I. It talks about the issues unique to electronic messaging—the fast-growing digital wilderness of cyberspace—including e-mail netiquette and eloquence.

Part IV: The Part of Tens

The Part of Tens is a *...For Dummies* classic. Here you find a potpourri of tips, hints, and tidbits in a variety of specific areas such as letter writing, speech writing, collaborative writing, and ways to cut information overload.

Part V: Appendixes

The four appendixes give you the ability to make your written words *speak* your voice through punctuation, grammar, abbreviations, and spelling tips.

To Whom Am I Talking? (Or Whom Am I Talking To?)

I'm talking to you if . . .

- ✔ You're a business professional and need to *cut your writing time* by 30 to 50 percent.
- ✔ You want to have greater *impact* and *influence* on your readers.
- ✔ You want your documents to be *read ahead of the others* vying for the reader's attention.
- ✔ You're interested in *advancing your career.*

Icons, Icons Everywhere

To help you find the important stuff easily, I scattered icons throughout this book—somewhat like road signs. Each of the following icons pinpoints something vital to your business writing experience:

The Tip icon gives you handy hints to take on the road to effective business writing. The paragraphs next to Tip icons may be time savers, frustration savers, life savers, or just about anything else.

The Remember icon represents little tidbits to tie around your finger. For example, remember to take your umbrella during monsoon season.

The Sheryl Says icon helps you benefit from my experiences: the blissful, the painful, and everything in between.

The Six Steps icon reminds you of my Six Steps to effective business writing: 1) getting started, 2) creating headlines and sequencing for your reader's reaction, 3) writing a draft, 4) designing for visual impact, 5) using the proper tone, and 6) proofreading.

The Start Up Sheet icon reminds you to fill out the Start Up Sheet featured on the Cheat Sheet in the front of this book. You can't write effective business documents until you use the Start Up Sheet to clearly identify your *reader, purpose,* and *key issue.*

The Checklist icon reminds you that before you send a document to your reader, you should go through the Editing Checklist (also featured on the Cheat Sheet in the front of this book).

The Caution icon calls attention to a pitfall you should avoid. If you don't heed the caution, civilization as we now know it won't come to an end—but not heeding the caution may create some stressful situations.

The Success Story icon plays off the adage, "Nothing succeeds like success." You may find it helpful to hear other people's success stories.

Author's Note about Genders

With the influx of women in the workplace—more particularly in the corner office—I searched for an elegant pronoun that would cover both genders. Unfortunately, I wasn't able to find one. Rather than getting into the clumsy he/she or him/her scenario, I opted to be an equal opportunity writer. I tossed a coin, and here's how it landed: I use the *male* gender in the *even* chapters and the *female* gender in the *odd* chapters. (If this offends anyone, I sincerely apologize.)

Just Do It!

As you read this book and develop your writing skills, your mantra should be:

- ✔ Yes, I can.
- ✔ Writing beats having root canal surgery.
- ✔ Writing is essential for my career.

Regardless of what your mantra is, you've already bought this book (or you're standing in a bookstore pouring through the Introduction). As you explore further, you'll find you have the potential to improve your writing and cut your writing time dramatically, freeing you to attend to the other responsibilities that make demands on your professional time. Your readers will thank you and think you're awesome!

Part I:
Basically Business

The 5th Wave   By Rich Tennant

"It's a memo from upper management. It's either an explanation of how the new satellite communications network functions or directions for replacing batteries in the smoke detectors."

In this part. . .

Employers equate writing skills with the ability to think clearly, examine alternatives, analyze information, and make decisions. To succeed in the business world, you must write effectively, quickly, strategically, and clearly. You must create documents your readers read first, documents that drive action, documents that affect your readers as you wish.

This part leads you through my Six Steps to energize all your business writing:

- ✔ Step 1: Getting Started
- ✔ Step 2: Creating Headlines and Strategic Sequencing
- ✔ Step 3: Writing Drafts
- ✔ Step 4: Designing for Visual Impact
- ✔ Step 5: Setting the Right Tone
- ✔ Step 6: Proofreading

Chapter 1

Writing As If Your Career Depends on It. It Does!

Writing is easy. All you do is sit staring at a blank sheet of paper until the drops of blood form on your forehead.

—Gene Fowler, American Writer

As a professional, demands on your time are endless. You're constantly competing with others for support of your ideas. Writing effectively, quickly, strategically, and clearly lets you make the best use of the time you spend marshaling that support. This book is your guide to becoming a better communicator. As a skilled writer you can

✔ Advance your career

✔ Bolster your reputation

✔ Delight your clients and customers

✔ Earn profit for your company

The Importance of Powerful Writing

In 1994, the National Center on the Evaluation of Quality in the Workplace conducted a study of United States employers. The purpose was to rate the skills most critical to job performance. The results showed that employers list communication skills as the second most critical job skill. (Attitude was Number 1.)

Employers equate communication skills with the ability to think clearly, examine alternatives, analyze information, and make decisions. Everything you write must hit the mark because your career depends on it. As a skilled business writer, you

- ✔ Get results
- ✔ Inspire action
- ✔ Influence decisions
- ✔ Stimulate business
- ✔ Maintain goodwill
- ✔ Provide leadership
- ✔ Get ahead in your career

Stephen R. Covey in *The 7 Habits of Highly Effective People* sums up the importance of writing when he says, "Writing is another powerful way to sharpen the mental saw. . . communicating on the deeper level of thoughts, feelings, and ideas rather than on the shallow, superficial level of events—it also effects our ability to think, to reason accurately, and to be understood effectively."

No matter how technological the workplace may become, there will always be real power in the written word. Technology hasn't eliminated the need for people to write clearly, it's merely simplified the writing process. Regardless of whether you use an old word processor or a state-of-the-art computer, the "written word" is the end result—the document by which you're judged. For example, e-mail has become a primary means of communicating in the workplace. Yet many people use e-mail as an excuse to send sloppy messages. E-mail messages are serious business documents and should be treated as such.

Communication Frustrations

Just as it takes two to tango; it takes two to communicate. In workshops that I teach, I'm constantly reminded of the communication frustrations that both readers and writers experience. Following are some challenges you may have dealt with.

Reader frustrations

Here are some classic frustrations readers squawk about:

- ✔ My brain is fried from information overload—and then someone hands me one more thing to read.
- ✔ After reading a piece of correspondence, I scratch my head and wonder, "Where's the beef? What's the key point?"
- ✔ The text sounds somewhat condescending.
- ✔ The organization of the text is confusing. What may be obvious to the writer, isn't obvious to me.
- ✔ The paragraphs and sentences are so long; they look like something out of *War and Peace*.
- ✔ I can't figure out what the writer wants me to do. What are the requests for action? The deadlines? The next steps?
- ✔ The typos are distracting and give me a bad impression of the writer.

Writer frustrations

When you sit down in front of your computer to write something, perhaps you stare at a blank screen and experience some of these frustrations:

- ✔ I suffer from writer's block—I can't get started or plan my content.
- ✔ I concentrate only on my point of view, not the reader's.
- ✔ I don't organize ideas to present my argument effectively.
- ✔ I have difficulty stating the key issue clearly.
- ✔ My documents don't have visual oomph.
- ✔ I have trouble identifying the right tone to use. (It's not *what* I say, but *how* I say it.)
- ✔ I'm not a good poofreader, and my spilling is aweful.

Don't let your dynamic ideas be overshadowed by poor planning and lack of organization. The Six Steps that I discuss in depth—beginning in Chapter 2—can help you become a skilled writer who gets results, prompts action, influences decisions, stimulates business, maintains goodwill, and gets ahead!

Everyone Can Learn to Write Well

If you dislike writing and find it a real chore, you're not alone. Many of the world's greatest minds share your feelings. I conduct business writing workshops throughout the United States and find that business people at all levels—from neophyte professionals to articulate CEOs—experience self-doubt when it comes to writing.

When you follow the Six Steps process that I outline in Part I, writing becomes simple and effortless. After you start going through the steps (which you'll see is quite painless), writing is like filling in the blanks:

> **Step 1: Getting Started.** With the easy-to-use Start Up Sheet, writer's block is a thing of the past. You can quickly identify your audience, purpose, and key issue.
>
> **Step 2: Creating Headlines and Strategic Sequencing.** Use powerful headlines to walk your reader through your message. You can also sequence headlines for maximum impact.
>
> **Step 3: Writing Drafts.** After you do Steps 1 and 2, writing the draft is a piece of cake because the structure is already there.
>
> **Step 4: Designing for Visual Impact.** Good visual design breaks your message into manageable, bite-sized chunks, helping the reader easily find key pieces of information.
>
> **Step 5: Setting the Right Tone.** The tone of your message influences your reader as much as the message itself.
>
> **Step 6: Proofreading.** If you send a message with even one mistake, it's like going out with mismatched shoes.

Using the Skills You Already Have

Use the skills you already have and build on them. You deal with people; you solve problems; you plan projects; you market products or services; you deal with quality control. You can tap into any of these skills to write effectively.

For example, one of your strengths may be a keen eye for detail. Because of that, you're in charge of your department's quality control. You can use those keen eyes to proofread carefully, checking the quality of your writing and perhaps the writing of others.

A Tale of Two Memos

On the following pages, you find two memos. This gives you a chance to check out two approaches to sending the same message. Please don't look at either memo until after you read following the directions.

1. **Quickly scan—don't read, just scan—Examples 1-1 and 1-2. See if you can find answers to these questions instantly:**

   - What's the date of the meeting?

   - How many agenda issues are there?

   - Who's the new EEO coordinator?

   Look at Examples 1-1 and 1-2; then come back to Number 2.

2. **After you find the answers in each example, ask yourself these questions:**

   - Which is more "reader friendly"?

   - Which gives you the answers quickly?

   - Which would you rather receive?

The envelope please?

If you found answers instantly in Example 1-1, my hat's off to you. You have the kind of vision Superman would envy. If you write like this, however, I sympathize with your readers. They're victims of your writing, not beneficiaries of it.

If you found answers instantly in Example 1-2, consider why that is. This memo is a true example of a document that focuses on the reader. Some helpful aspects of Example 1-2 that make it easier to read include:

- The subject line is direct and to the point. It gives you a vivid snapshot of what's ahead.

- There's plenty of white space that provides contrast and a resting place for your eyes.

- Paragraphs are short, readable, and easy on the eyes.

- Sentences are short, simple, and easy to grasp.

- Key information pops out without having to read the entire message.

- Headlines direct your eye to key pieces of information.

- Key information is numbered for easy reading.

- Anything else you may have noticed?

Date: November 1, XXXX

To: All Employees

From: Kathy Blythe, Human Relations Director

Re: Equal Opportunity Policy

As you know, it is illegal to discriminate against any employee or applicant for employment because of race, color, religion, sex, national origin, handicap, or veteran status. I've scheduled a meeting because we need to discuss these critical issues. The meeting will be held on Thursday, November 12, in Room 205, and everyone is expected to attend. There are several questionable issues that have come to my attention, and we need to reaffirm our company's policy.

Here are some of the issues we need to discuss: We must ensure opportunities for all employees and applicants for employment in accordance with all applicable Equal Employment Opportunity/Affirmative Action laws, directives and regulations of federal, state, and local governing bodies or agencies. Promotion decisions must be in accord with the principles of equal employment. And we must ensure that all personnel actions such as compensation, benefits, transfers, layoffs, return from layoff, company-sponsored training, education, tuition assistance, and social and recreational programs will be administered fairly. Because we've added so many members to our staff in recent months, I've hired a new assistant. Her name is Barbara Chang, and she will be responsible for equal employment opportunity issues. I'll be introducing Barbara to you at the meeting.

Employees with suggestions, problems, or complaints with regard to equal employment opportunities should report their claims to their managers. If this is not comfortable for any reason, see Ms. Chang. She will monitor the program and be responsible for making quarterly reports to us on the effectiveness of the program.

Example 1-1:
Can you find the main message in this memo?

Date: November 1, XXXX

To: All Employees

From: Kathy Blythe, Human Relations Director

Re: Meeting to Reaffirm Equal Employment Opportunity Policy

Several issues regarding possible EEO violations have come to my attention. I've scheduled a meeting for the entire staff. Attendance is mandatory.

> **Date:** November 12
> **Time:** 10:30 to 11:30
> **Place:** Room 205

Agenda Issues

1. We must ensure opportunities for all employees and applicants in accordance with all applicable Equal Employment Opportunity/Affirmative Action laws, as well as directives and regulations of federal, state, and local governing bodies or agencies.

2. Promotion decisions must be in accord with the principles of equal employment.

3. We must ensure that all personnel actions such as compensation, benefits, transfers, layoffs, return from layoff, company-sponsored training, education, tuition assistance, and social and recreational programs are administered fairly.

Barbara Chang: New EEO Coordinator

At the meeting, I'll introduce Barbara, our new EEO Coordinator. Employees with suggestions, problems, or complaints with regard to equal employment opportunities should report their claims to their managers first. If this isn't comfortable for any reason, see Barbara. She'll monitor the program and be responsible for making quarterly reports to us on the effectiveness of the program.

Example 1-2: Another memo with a different layout discussing the same topic.

Learning by Doing

You too can write documents that focus on the reader. It's simply a matter of following the Six Steps that I demonstrate in Part I of this book. You'll ultimately save time, enhance your career opportunities, and delight your readers! Remember:

What I hear, I forget.
What I see, I remember.
What I do, I understand.

——Anonymous

Follow along in Part I with a document of your own. Think of a document you need to write. It can be something in your inbox, something you've been struggling with, or just something you've been meaning to get around to. Then take your document through the Six Steps.

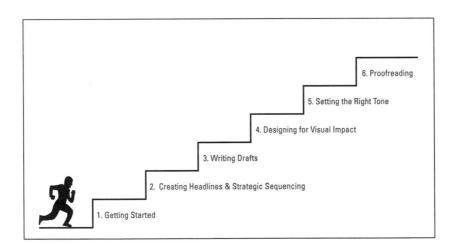

Now you're ready for Step 1: Getting Started.

Chapter 2
Step 1: Getting Started

• •

In This Chapter

▶ Understanding why getting started is tough

▶ Focusing your writing with the Start Up Sheet

▶ Kicking your writing into high gear with start up techniques

• •

A journey of a thousand miles must begin with a single step.

—Lao-Tzu, *The Way of Lao Tzu*

Everyone suffers from writer's block at some time. You sit and stare at a blank piece of paper or computer screen hoping something materializes. Even a prolific writer such as Mark Twain had trouble getting started. He'd leave a sentence unfinished, so that when he sat down for his next writing session, there'd be an easy kickoff point.

Getting started is rather simple when you have the right tools. All you need to do is use the Start Up Sheet and a few start up techniques, which I discuss in this chapter. Mark Twain would have had an easier time if he had known about these tools. You have that benefit.

Start Up Sheet

As a professional writer, I never commit a single word to my computer until I've identified three critical issues:

1. **Audience:** Is my audience (my reader) the CEO in the corner office or Quasimodo in the bell tower?

2. **Purpose:** What's my *real* motive for writing?

3. **Key Issue:** What's the one key point I want my audience to remember?

Unless these three elements are crystal clear in my mind, I can't send a clear message to my reader.

Knowing your left from your right (brain, that is)

Why can getting started be so difficult? Dr. Roger Sperry, who won the Nobel prize in medicine in 1981, discovered why. He theorized that the brain is divided into two parts; each performing a different function:

✔ **The right side** deals with logic, language, reasoning, science, and math. This is the "getting started" part, the strategic section, of your brain.

✔ **The left side** deals with visualization, creativity, and insight that you kick in later.

If you try to use the right and left sides of the brain at the same time, you may cause a cranial traffic jam. When you're trying to get started, the main thing is to engage the right side: Get the information from your brain to your paper or computer. You can deal with spelling, grammar, punctuation, or other details later. Just get started.

For each document you write, I strongly urge you to take a few minutes to put some ideas on paper by filling out a what I call a *Start Up Sheet*—like the one that follows. Try it! After the first time, it'll take you only a few minutes and save you hours.

Using the Start Up Sheet

In the front of this book is a Cheat Sheet with a copy of the Start Up Sheet. Keep it handy for all your business documents.

You'll get more out of the Start Up Sheet if you relate it to a particular document you need to write. Here's how I suggest you proceed:

1. **Read through the Start Up Sheet that follows.**

   Don't attempt to answer any of the questions yet.

2. **Think of a document you need to write.**

   It can be a letter, memo, e-mail, report, proposal, or just about anything except a note to your grandmother.

3. **Read the explanations that follow the Start Up Sheet.**

   They provide helpful clues to get you jump started.

4. **Fill out the Start Up Sheet.**

   Answer each question as it relates to your document.

Start Up Sheet

Audience

1. Who's my primary reader? Do I have multiple readers?

2. What does my reader *need to know* about the topic?

3. What's in it for my reader?

4. Does my writing need a special *angle* or *point of view?* (Managerial? Technical? Other?)

5. What's my reader's attitude toward the topic?

Purpose

6. My purpose is to _____ so my reader will _____.

Key Issue

7. What's the one *key point* I want my reader to remember?

Delivery

8. Who should receive a copy of this message?

9. What's the best way to deliver this message? Hard copy? E-mail? Fax? Phone? Personal meeting? Other?

10. When is the best time to deliver the message? When is too early? When is too late?

Understanding the Start Up Sheet

Here are the questions on the Start Up Sheet broken out in detail.

Audience

1. Who's my primary reader?

Identify your relationship with the reader. Why is it so easy to send a message to a friend or colleague you know well? Because you know him. You know his preconceived ideas, level of expertise, probable reaction to your message, reaction to slang or jargon, and so on. This same theory applies to writing any message.

When you're sending a message to someone you don't know, try imagining that you actually do know him. Take a moment, close your eyes, and ask yourself these questions: What color eyes and hair does he have? How is he dressed? Try to make him real, even if you have to invent him. Don't write to a faceless person.

I recently wrote an annual report for a company and pretended I was writing it for my brother. Although my brother is highly intelligent, he's unfamiliar with the industry. My goal was simply to give him the information I wish he would give me if our positions were reversed. If you have no siblings, it's okay to borrow mine. His name is Harry.

Do I have multiple readers?

If you're writing for multiple readers, rank your readers in order of importance. Ask yourself, "Who will take action on the basis of this message?" Now, write to that person. If you're writing a long document to a mixed audience of managers, technoids, and salespeople, consider dealing with each audience separately in clearly identified sections of your message. You may consider including

- An executive summary for those at the managerial level
- An appendix for technoids
- The body for salespeople
- A table of contents for anyone who needs the nitty-gritty

2. What does my reader *need to know* about the topic?

Think of what your reader needs to know—not what he already knows—so you won't give too much or too little information.

- What is his level of knowledge about the subject?
- Does he have any preconceived ideas?
- What are the barriers to his understanding?
- Is there anything about his style of dealing with situations that should drive your tone or content? See Chapter 6 for an in-depth discussion of tone.

During my years of experience in the field, I discovered that people with academic, scientific, or technical backgrounds tend to be process-oriented. They benefit from step-by-step explanations. Those with backgrounds in business or law are answer-oriented. They respond to quick answers. Creative types are usually visually oriented and benefit from charts, tables, and any visual representation.

3. What's in it for my reader?

When you receive a message, don't you mentally ask yourself: "What's in it for me?" or "Why is this worth my time?" Your reader will ask those same questions. Maybe what's in it for him is an opportunity to make his job easier . . . to look good to his superiors . . . to be more knowledgeable . . . to propel his career . . . to jump on a wonderful opportunity. Make it clear what's in it for him!

4. Does my writing need a special *angle* or *point of view*?

You determine the point of view by understanding the needs of your audience. Managers, for example, are big-picture people. They want to know the key issue. Technoids want the details.

5. What's my reader's attitude toward the topic?

You may not always tell the reader what he wants to hear, but you must tell him what he needs to know. Will he be responsive? Neutral? Unresponsive? The following questions can help you determine the way you need to present (or sequence) your message later on. (Check out Chapter 3 to find out more about sequencing your document for maximum impact.)

- ✔ Are you disputing existing data?
- ✔ Will your reader lose face by accepting your recommendation?
- ✔ Will your message create more work for your reader?
- ✔ Will your reader get pressure from his manager because of your message?
- ✔ Do you want to fire the reader's son?

Purpose

6. My purpose is to _____ so my reader will _____.

My purpose is to. . .

Whether you think your purpose is to communicate, to inform, to sell, or whatever, chances are you're trying *to persuade* someone to do something. For example:

- ✔ Are you writing to inform your customer of a new product offering? *Or are you trying to persuade him to make a purchase?*
- ✔ Are you writing to let your manager know of an idea that could save the company big bucks and get you a promotion? *Or are you trying to persuade him that you're worth listening to?*

So my reader will . . .

Think strategically! When your reader knows exactly what action you want him to take, he can digest your message more intelligently. Do you want him to turn the case over to the legal department? Discontinue testing? Call the bank? Refund the money? Halt shipping? Take this up with his manager? Wait to hear from you? Write a new contract? Pass the message to someone else? Send a check? Make a purchase? Do nothing?

Key Issue

7. What's the one *key point* I want my reader to remember?

Billboard advertisers, ad people, and designers know that reading is done on the fly. Kids know this too. Have you ever found (or left) a note on the table saying, "Don't forget to leave me $5—I'll explain later"?

Business readers want the key issue so that they can get to the point immediately. Put on your advertising hat. Pretend you have to write a 15-second commercial. If your reader forgets everything else, what's the one key point you want him to remember?

Delivery

8. Who should receive a copy of this message?

Are you copying people because they need to see the message or is this for CYA purposes? (You know, cover your anatomy?)

In an e-mail environment this decision should be thought through carefully. With everyone screaming about information overload, be considerate and send messages only to people who need to receive them, just as you would with paper-based mail. If you send people only the information they need to do their jobs well and don't contribute to their overload, they'll approach anything you send with respect. For more information about information overload, see Chapter 18.

9. What's the best way to deliver this message?

What's the best method of delivery: Paper? E-mail? Fax? Telephone? Face-to-face? A meeting?

There are times you should refrain from writing. Would a telephone call suffice? Does the reader have the resources to act on your request? Is the reader in the middle of a crisis? Does anyone really need this information or is it merely self-serving?

For example, if you're announcing that 10 percent of the staff is being laid off, should you hide behind paper or e-mail? Perhaps a staff meeting is more appropriate and humane.

10. When is the best time to deliver this message? When is it too early? When is it too late?

Timing is everything.

For example, if it's noon and you need to let people know about a one o'clock meeting, an e-mail message won't do. Try a phone call or leave notes on people's desks.

Think for a moment of one of the ultimate success stories—Dorothy in *The Wizard of Oz*. Dorothy's key issue was to return to Kansas. Her purpose was to find the Wizard so that he would help her. Her primary audience was the Wizard, and her secondary audience included the Scarecrow, the Tin Man, and the Cowardly Lion.

So, click your heels and look at some start up techniques.

Start Up Techniques

By filling out the Start Up Sheet, you take the first step toward being ready to write. I outline several writing methods in this section. I'm sure that one of these techniques (or a combination of several) will work for you.

Outlining

Outlining is a tried-and-tested method from high school. Some people love it; others hate it. Your computer software's outlining feature makes it easy for you to experiment with the organization and scope of information. Example 2-1 is a standard outline.

Questioning

> *I keep six honest serving-men*
>
> *(They taught me all I knew);*
>
> *Their names are What and Why and When*
>
> *and How and Where and Who.*
>
> —Rudyard Kipling

```
                              Meals for Today
        I. Lunch
                A. Heat the frozen entree I brought this morning?
                B. Go out?
                        1. Fast food?
                        2. An actual restaurant?
                                a. The rib place?
                                b. The House 'o Salads?
                                        (1) Nice Caesar salad?
                                        (2) The great Chef's salad?
                                                (a) With extra meats?
                                                (b) With extra cheeses?
                                                        i) Bleu cheese
                                                          dressing?
                                                        ii) Raspberry vinaigrette
                                                           a) Creamy?
                                                           b) Fat-free?

        II. Dinner
```

Example 2-1:
A standard
outline.

Newspapers reporters use the Who? What? When? Where? Why? How? questioning technique to guide them through stories. The answers to these questions provide the information readers want to know. Of course, not all the questions apply to your message, so decide which add to your purpose of satisfying your reader's needs. (Before you know it, you'll be questioning everything from freedom to the law of gravity.)

Be sure that the answers to your questions are specific, not vague.

Who?

> *Specific:* Feel free to call Thomas Smith, our sales manager.

> *Vague:* Feel free to call our sales manager. (Does he have a name?)

How much?

> *Specific:* You can buy our equipment for $798, which is 25 percent less than the suggested retail price.

> *Vague:* Our merchandise is not expensive. (By whose standards? And what's the price?)

When? Where?

Specific: The sales meeting will be on May 12, Room 1134, City Hall, from 7 to 9 p.m.

Vague: The meeting will be on May 12 from 7 to 9. (Which meeting? Where? a.m. or p.m.?)

When? What?

Specific: Please send us *The Secret Lives of Cats,* Volumes II and III, by September 1.

Vague: Please send us *The Secret Lives of Cats,* Volumes II and III ASAP. (As soon as possible isn't a date.)

Brainstorming

Brainstorming is the process of moving ideas from your head to your paper, such as the one in Example 2-2. (And I do strongly recommend you use paper, not your computer, for your brainstorming sessions. It's easier to draw and make connecting lines on paper.) You may be familiar with brainstorming as it relates to large groups; however, it's also a helpful technique for one person to do a brain dump. Here are a few brainstorming tips.

- ✔ Pass no judgments.
- ✔ Don't dwell on any one idea.
- ✔ Start with a circle in the center that states your purpose.
- ✔ Use branches to write your main ideas and twigs to write your sub-ideas, as shown in Example 2-2.

Freewriting

Joggers do warm-up exercises to limber up their legs and get their blood circulating. Your brain is an organ just as your heart and lungs are; you need to warm it up. Think of freewriting as a warm-up exercise for the mind. Example 2-3 shows freewriting.

If you're angry or frustrated about something and it's keeping you from getting to the task at hand, consider freewriting a good way to vent and let off steam.

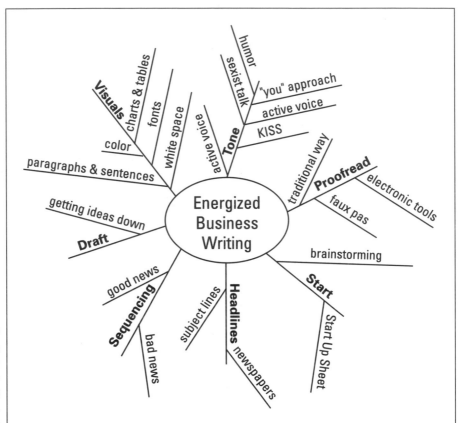

You can do freewriting on your computer or on a sheet of paper. Just start writing. Even if you can't focus on the subject at hand, write anything. After you're on target, remember your purpose is to transfer ideas from your brain to the computer or paper. Example 2-3 shows a sample freewriting exercise.

If you're using a computer, don't be distracted by typos. This is just a start up exercise. If typos are too much of distraction, try turning off the spell-checking feature on your word processor (so that those squiggly red lines don't distract you) or try simply darkening your computer screen.

I know I have to get this written. Having truble getting started. Keep checking the clokc. The weather's great.It's the first nice day wev'e had in a week. Boy would I love to be outside right now indtead of trying to concentrate on getting thie written. I h ave to tell Mitch that the computers we have ar slowing down. We need more updated stuff. I know Mitch doesn't like to spend money. The buffalo gores him before he'll part with a nickle---- I checked and for under $25,000 we can get what we need. . . I'd better remember to get my dry cleaningon the way home-----Uh, How can I convince Mitch that my suggestion is worthwhile, that we need new computers. I need to document how we're expere9ncing less revenue for because of all the computer screw ups. I seem to be rambling,,,,,better settle down. I must get myself organized in order to convince Mitch that new computers are the way to go.

Example 2-3: Freewriting sample.

Tape recording

Consider keeping a small tape recorder nearby. If you're a commuter, this is a great way to get work done.

I get some of my best writing ideas at three in the morning or while riding in my car. So I always keep a voice-activated tape recorder next to my bed or next to me in the car.

Other start up techniques

Perhaps you have some start up techniques of your own. Here are a few more of my favorites:

- ✔ **Index cards.** Put one idea on each card and move the cards around to create an outline.
- ✔ **Sticky notes.** As an alternative to index cards, try using sticky notes. (I refer to them as high-tech index cards.) You can paste them up on a board or wall and move them around to create an outline.
- ✔ **Get into the right frame of mind.** If you aren't battling a tight deadline, try reading a short magazine article on an unrelated topic. Notice the way the author gets his point across. Perhaps taking a break may help you relax and write with renewed energy.

Use the Start Up Sheet and start up techiques for the document you need to write.

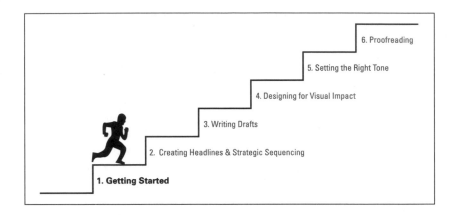

Now you're ready for Step 2: Creating Headlines and Strategic Sequencing.

Chapter 3

Step 2: Creating Headlines and Strategic Sequencing

The difficulty is not to affect your reader, but to affect him precisely as you wish.

— Robert Louis Stevenson

Headlines are used by newspapers and magazines to tell the story and direct the reader's eye to what's important. Headlines can make or break a story. Here's a perfect example: Hal Prince, the noted Broadway producer, was interviewed on *60 Minutes*. The commentator asked how Mr. Prince knew when a show is a flop or success. Mr. Prince answered something like this: The morning after the show opens, I open the newspaper and read the headlines. The headlines make or break the show. They're powerful!

You need to be able to grab your reader's attention and deliver your key point quickly and effectively. This chapter shows you how to craft powerful headlines that get results.

Writing Headlines That Shout "Read Me!"

Headlines are powerful tools. Have you ever been lured by a tabloid headline while waiting in a supermarket checkout line? Here are a few I've actually seen:

[Politician] Caught in the Act

Baseball Takes the Field

Dog-face Baby Celebrates First Birthday

Woman Gives Birth to Her Own Grandchild

How to Spice Up Your Sex Life

Newspapers are such a popular news source because they're a "quick read." Newspaper headlines are informative and tell a story. Headlines give directions, instructions, results, and recommendations. They swing voters in an election, make or break companies, and give readers an honest or false sense of what's important.

One of the most popular newspapers in the United States is *USA Today*. The appeal of *USA Today,* and newspapers in general, lies in its attention-grabbing headlines. When I travel, I don't always have time to read a newspaper thoroughly. But I do have time to pick up a copy of *USA Today,* which magically appears under the door of my hotel room. The headlines give me a snapshot of the day's news. Even if I don't get a chance to read the articles, I can sound like an informed person. If someone asks wether I've heard the latest news, I can say, "Yes, I read that."

Harnessing the Power

You can apply the power of dynamic headlines to your business writing.

> ✔ **As a writer,** you can direct your reader's attention to what's important and direct the flow of information.

> ✔ **As a reader,** you can get the gist of the message and find key information quickly.

Scenario: You've just returned from a balmy, relaxing two-week Hawaiian vacation—far away from the hustle 'n' bustle of the office. Now, it's back to the real world. Immediately after you walk into the office, your supervisor calls. He needs immediate answers to questions that were sent to you in an e-mail message while you were away.

Check out the two versions of the same message in Examples 3-1 and 3-2. Ask yourself which message would be more helpful if you were in a rush to answer the following questions:

✔ When will the evacuation drill take place?

✔ How will I know?

✔ What should I do?

Example 3-1: Long-winded memo. Notice there are no headlines, and the message is unreadable.

Beginning next month, ABC Security will be conducting evacuation drills throughout the building. The drills will require us to vacate our department, proceed to the nearest stairway, and wait for security to give us the all-clear signal. We won't be required to vacate the building. The evacuation drill for our floor is scheduled for Monday, June 10 at 9:00 AM. The drill will commence with sounding the alarm, followed by notification by Security that: "This is a drill. Employees are to evacuate to their designated areas." We will then evacuate the department and proceed to the nearest stairway and wait for the all clear. In the event of an actual emergency, it's important for you to be familiar with alternate stairway routes out of the area. Notices will be posted on bulletin boards around the building. Please take a moment to familiarize yourself with the floor's layout and routes that are available. If you have any questions regarding the drill, please contact me at extension 223.

Example 3-2: A headline-driven and very readable memo.

Subject: Evacuation drills
Beginning next month, ABC Security will be conducting evacuation drills throughout the building. You'll be asked to proceed to the nearest stairway, but not to leave the building.

When and How
On <u>Monday, June 10 at 9 AM</u>, a slow whooping alarm will sound and you'll hear: "This is a drill. Employees are to evacuate to their designated areas."

Action
Proceed to the nearest stairway and wait for the all-clear signal.

Where to find emergency routes
Maps of our floor are posted on bulletin boards around the building.

Questions?
If you have any, please call me at extension 223.

Crafting Attention-Getting Headlines

Headlines come from a variety of sources. For example, revisit your start up techniques in Chapter 2 to locate key words or phrases that would make good headlines. Then fashion these ideas into attention-grabbing headlines. Here are some specific ways to do this:

- ✔ **If you use the outlining technique,** the roman numerals can be headlines.

- ✔ **If you use the questioning technique,** circle the word or words that can be appropriate headlines. Check out Example 3-3 to see how you can use a questioning technique to write a meeting announcement.

- ✔ **If you use the brainstorming technique,** circle the branches that can be appropriate headlines as shown in Example 3-4.

- ✔ **If you use the freewriting technique,** circle, highlight, or underscore the word or words that may be appropriate headlines, as demonstrated in Example 3-5.

- ✔ **If you use another start-up technique,** take a look at the key issues you identified.

Check out these direct, attention-grabbing headlines that direct the reader's eye to key information. Use these headlines verbatim or tweak them to enhance your document. For example, you can expand "Action Requested" to read "Action Requested: Call Immediately."

- ✔ Action requested
- ✔ Action required
- ✔ Urgent *(Use only when it is.)*
- ✔ Deadline: <date>
- ✔ Effective date: <date>
- ✔ Meeting information

    When:

    Where:

- ✔ Advantage(s)
- ✔ Disadvantage(s)
- ✔ Next step(s)
- ✔ Any questions?

SHERYL SAYS

After you craft your headlines, they become the framework for your draft. (For more on writing drafts, check out Chapter 4.) After you write the draft, you can change, tweak, or replace any of your headlines. They're not carved in granite until you send your document.

Example 3-3: Questioning headlines help readers find key information quickly.

Subject:	XYZ Executives' Meeting
When:	April 10 at 8 AM
Where:	Plaza Hotel, Marlborough, Massachusetts
Purpose:	To finalize the budget for the coming year.
Agenda:	8 - 9 Breakfast (We'll provide)
	9 - 12 Meeting
	12 - 1 Lunch (We'll provide)
	1 - 5 Meeting
RSVP:	(508) 222-1234

Example 3-4: Headlines generated from a brainstorming session. The twigs and branches may make good headlines.

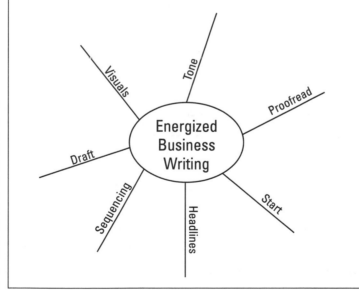

> I know I have to get this written. Having truble getting started. Keep checking the clokc. The weather's great. It's the first nice day wev'e had in a week. Boy would I love to be outside right now indtead of trying to concentrate on getting thie written. I h ave to tell Mitch that the <u>computers we have ar slowing down. We need more updated stuff</u>. I know Mitch doesn't like to spend money. The buffalo gores him before he'll part with a nickle—— I checked and for <u>under $25,000</u> we can get what we need. . . I'd better remember to get my dry cleaningon the way home———Uh, How can I convince Mitch that my suggestion is worthwhile, that <u>we need new computers.</u> I need to document how <u>we're expere9ncing less revenue</u> for because of all the computer screw ups. I seem to be rambling,,,,,better settle down. I must get myself organized in order to convince Mitch that new computers are the way to go.

Example 3-5: Headlines generated from a freewriting session. Notice how the writer transitioned from random thoughts to the task at hand. You can identify some good headlines from the latter.

Writing Dynamic Subject Headlines

The subject line of a letter, memo, or e-mail message is *the most important headline* because it gives your reader the big picture. Sometimes you can let your subject line tell the story. Here are a few that do:

✔ **Subject:** Sales soar 25%

✔ **Subject:** Yes, we can honor your request

✔ **Subject:** Staff meeting 2/15 in Room 100 at noon

Look at Question 7 on your Start Up Sheet. Why not make your subject line the reader's key issue?

Subject lines can be the most important line of an e-mail. Be sure to check out Part III for writing tips when dealing with e-mail.

Sequencing Headlines for Maximum Impact

We all learned to write when we were in school. We filled our document with a lot of information, yet the reader didn't read the key issue until she reached the end, much like the funnel in Example 3-6.

Example 3-6: Avoid using a "funnel of babble" when you write. No one has time to sift through the details before reaching the main point. Put the key issue at the document's beginning.

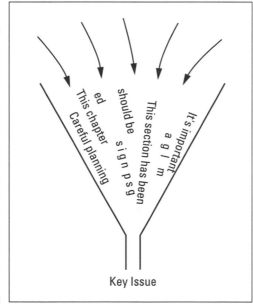

Key Issue

Our school experiences taught us to *babble* at the beginning of the document—write a lot of information before getting to the key issue in the final paragraph. Business people don't have time for babble. They want the key issue *at the beginning of the document*. That's where you should put it. The supporting information should filter down *from* the key issue.

Being mindful of where to put your key issue is one of your challenges as a writer. The secret to effective communication is to sequence your ideas for maximum impact. Question 5 in the Start Up Sheet asks: What's my reader's attitude toward the topic? Is my reader responsive? Unresponsive? Neutral?

You need to put yourself in your reader's shoes and understand how she'll respond to your message.

- ✔ For a **responsive or neutral reader,** put the key issue at the beginning of the document—perhaps it can serve as the subject line.

- ✔ For an **unresponsive reader,** cushion the key issue between buffers—a positive opening and friendly closing.

There are many sequencing strategies you can use. Each works well in certain situations. Table 3-1 lists strategies for sequencing a variety of documents you may write.

Table 3-1 Strategic Organization for Different Documents	
Document Type	*Sequencing Strategy*
Instructions, procedures, or processes	Step-by-step
Trip reports, accident reports, test protocols	Chronological
Feasibility studies or research results	Comparative
Proposals, research reports, evaluations, or status reports	Most important to least important
Something controversial	Least important to most important
Problem-solving	Cause and effect

The next two sections take you through sequencing strategies for two different scenarios—being the bearer of good news and sequencing for bad news.

Being the bearer of good news

When the reader is responsive, the message is easy to write—everyone likes to be the bearer of good news. Your message is also easy to write when the reader is neutral, because you're *giving* information the reader may find useful. So, when you sequence a good-news message, focus on the primary piece of information the reader needs to know. Why hide it?

Use the direct approach and good judgment in deciding what to include. Do you need to include background information, or is the reader familiar with the topic?

1. **Deliver the *key issue* in the subject line.**

   The following subject lines are actually main headlines. If your reader doesn't have time to read your entire message, she can look at the subject line and get the piece of information she needs to know.

Subject: Jon Allan, new Vice President of MIS

Subject: Adding one more personal day

2. Include the necessary details in the supporting paragraph(s).

Include facts or details to support the subject line, like who, what, when, where, and how. You can address these questions in whatever order makes sense for your document. Try answering the questions in the priority in which the reader will most likely ask them.

3. End on a friendly, positive note.

Conclude with a sentence or two stressing your appreciation, your willingness to help further, the action you took, and so on. The following are examples of ending on a friendly note:

- We want you to be a satisfied customer.

- Within the next week, you'll receive an assortment of rollie pollies. We want you to enjoy them so thoroughly that you become one of Round and Proud's most satisfied customers.

Sequencing for bad news

There will be times when you have to send distressing information, offer a compromise, or just say "No." You need special planning if you have to disappoint your reader. Your intention is to keep the customer (or client) happy while sending unfavorable information.

Here are a few points to keep in mind:

- ✔ **Remember that most documents are written to persuade:** You're trying to persuade the reader that your news—even though it's contrary to her request—is fair.

- ✔ **Put yourself in the reader's shoes:** Couch your statements tactfully.

   Tactful headline: **Where to find the information**

   "The warranty is good for 30 days. However, on page 2 of the instructions you received, you'll find. . . ."

   Tactless headline: **The warranty has expired**

   "If you had read the instructions that came in your package, you would have noticed that our warranty is good for only 30 days. If you look at the instructions, you'll find. . . ."

- ✔ **Avoid citing company rules:** Company policies won't soothe the reader. Customer-benefit reasons will.

Tactful headline: **Timing is everything**

"Thank you for giving us the chance to consider your application for a loan to finance your proposed home purchase. We regret, however, that we're unable to grant you a loan at this time. Perhaps at a later date. . . ."

Tactless headline: **Company policy**

"It's against company policy to grant loans to people in your income bracket."

✔ **Look for the best in the reader:** Even though a customer may be mistaken, show your confidence in the fact that she was trying to do the right thing. Use phrases like

"We are confident that you . . ."

"You can certainly understand. . . ."

Planning the document

Before you sequence the headlines for a document conveying bad news, try this: Imagine yourself as the recipient of the news you're going to send. How would you react? Now consider how you can sequence the headlines so that the bad news doesn't pack such a wallop. Here are a few suggestions:

1. **Create a buffer.**

   Begin with a headline relevant to the reader.

   - We agree with you.

   - Thank you for bringing this to our attention.

   - You have an excellent record.

   - We're happy to grant part of your request.

2. **Explain the decision.**

   Include honest, convincing reasons why you can't grant the reader's request. Here are some headlines you may consider:

   - This is how we may help you:

   - With your best interests in mind. . . .

   - Won't you accept this as a substitute?

   - May we offer this suggestion?

3. End on a friendly, positive note.

Your intention is to maintain goodwill and keep the reader as a customer. Use sentences like

- You're a valued customer.

- Won't you try. . . (Offer a sales promotion, if you think it's appropriate.)

- We look forward to being of help next time.

In a bad-news document, consider eliminating the subject line or using a neutral one (such as a policy number).

A participant in one of my workshops worked for an insurance company and had to deny benefits to a woman requesting cosmetic surgery. Hitting her between the eyes with a blunt, "No!" wasn't an option, and "You look lovely the way you are" wouldn't work either. Example 3-7 shows how he wound up using headlines. Example 3-7 is an outline—not a finished letter. I take you through writing drafts in the next chapter.

After writing your headlines, revisit them. Ask yourself these questions:

- ✔ Are they sequenced for maximum impact?
- ✔ Do they tell the story without babble?
- ✔ Will they create goodwill?

Your headlines aren't carved in granite. They merely serve as a structure for your draft.

- ✔ If your reader is responsive or neutral, put the key issue at the beginning of the document.
- ✔ If she's unresponsive, cushion the key issue between a positive opening and a friendly, positive closing.

Example 3-7:
An outline using headlines.

> **You're a Valued Customer**
> - Thank her for her business.
> - Mention the strengths of the insurance company.
>
> **Decisions Aren't Always Easy**
> - We'd love to say "Yes." However, . . .
>
> **Keeping Your Premiums Down**
> - Appeal to her pocketbook.
> - Offer to be of help in the future.

Name the headlines

Can you translate the following headlines into the names of commonly known stories or fairy tales? In the book of life, there are no answers; in this book there are: Turn this book upside-down to find them.

1. Youngster Vanishes in Freak Storm

2. Couple Suffering From Dietary Allergies Reaches Agreement

3. Poor Bargain Brings Ultimate Wealth

4. Friends Eager to Assist in Painting Project

5. Unique Individual Mortally Injured in Crash

6. Odd Pair Embarks on Ocean Voyage in Chartreuse Vehicle

7. Remote Country Home Vandalized by Blond

8. Browbeaten Girl Courted by Royal Heir

9. Friendless Waif Adopted by Group of Miners

10. Sherpardess Proves Derelict in Duty

Answers

1. The Wizard of Oz; 2. Jack Sprat; 3. Jack and the Beanstalk; 4. Tom Sawyer; 5. Humpty Dumpty; 6. The Owl and the Pussycat; 7. Goldilocks and the Three Bears; 8. Cinderella; 9. Snow White; 10. Little Bo Peep

Create headlines and sequence them strategically for the document that you need to write.

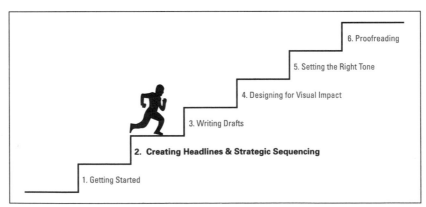

Now you're ready for Step 3: Writing Drafts.

Chapter 4
Step 3: Writing Drafts

● ●

In This Chapter

▶ Preparing to write
▶ Composing the draft
▶ Taking a break
▶ Taking a final peek

● ●

You don't write because you want to say something; you write "because you've got something to say."

—F. Scott Fitzgerald, *The Crack-Up*

You've probably heard the story of the aspiring novelist who kept rewriting the opening sentence. He never got beyond the first sentence because he didn't have structure. You do. You used strategies for getting started and have written headlines to provide that much-needed structure.

You probably expect this chapter to be long and cumbersome because that's how you view drafting a document. However, this is where all the planning that you do in Steps 1 and 2 pays off. You should be able to write your draft by filling in the blanks. Check out Chapters 2 and 3 for more tips on how to prepare to write your draft.

Before You Write a Draft

A draft isn't a finished document. It's a first pass—your initial thoughts. This is your chance to express yourself without being critical of anything you write. You can censor yourself later. Your task right now is to transfer your thoughts from your head to the computer (or paper). Just get all your information down.

When you write a draft, don't wait for inspiration. Treat the draft as you would any on-the-job task. Just do it. Here are some suggestions to help you get started:

1. Create a comfortable environment.

Try to create an environment that encourages concentration. If you try to write between phone calls and walk-in visitors, you'll be too distracted. It takes time to reorganize your thoughts after each interruption.

Each person's idea of a comfortable environment is different. Asking yourself a few questions can help you create a more ideal working environment:

- Do you work best with or without music?
- Is the lighting appropriate?
- Do you think better while snacking on munchies?
- Do you like to kick off your shoes?

It's not always easy to create a comfortable environment in today's cubicle-style office. So you may need to get creative. I once put a "quarantine" sign outside my cubicle. People chuckled as they walked by, but they didn't interrupt me. (Whatever works!)

2. Get your stuff together.

Have all your supplies and reference materials handy. Stopping to look for things often breaks your train of thought. And you don't want to be derailed.

3. Set attainable goals.

Set reasonable and attainable goals for yourself based on the time you have. Your goal can be to write for 15–30 minutes. Or it can be to expand one or two headlines. Write continually until your goal is met, no matter how good or bad your writing seems to be. The point is to keep writing.

Be honest with yourself about what works for you. If you're on a roll, you may not want to stop. So, if you're sure that you'll just procrastinate when you get out of your chair, keep plugging away. On the other hand, if you feel yourself getting worn out, stop, or just take a break. (This may be a good time to pull out those munchies. And they may be carrot sticks!)

4. Stay focused.

After you create a comfortable environment, get your stuff ready, and set goals, you're ready to start drafting.

If you're drafting on a computer, you may want to darken your monitor so you're not distracted by typos. However—as in freewriting, which I discuss in Chapter 2—be sure your fingers are on the right keys!

Writing the Draft

Okay, you're in the comfortable environment you created, and you're confident the goals you set are attainable. Now you're ready to begin drafting.

Look at first two questions on the Start Up Sheet:

> Who's my primary reader? Do I have multiple readers?

> What does my reader *need to know* about the topic?

Use your assessment of the reader's background, knowledge, and preconceptions to include only those facts he needs to know.

Here are some suggestions for tackling the draft:

1. **Work on one headline at a time.**

   Start with the headline that seems easiest. Don't worry about starting at the beginning. (Your reader will never know where you started.) Write one or two paragraphs to support the headline. If subheads are appropriate, add them. After you finish the easiest headline, move to the second easiest, and continue until you meet your goal.

2. **Keep writing.**

   Avoid the temptation to go back over what you wrote. The most important thing is to keep moving forward. If you can't think of the right word, use another and keep going. Or leave a blank space and fill it in later. Keep writing until you meet your goal.

Getting Distance from Your Work

After you finish writing the draft, get some distance. It's hard to be objective about your work when you're too close to it. (In a perfect world, you could put your draft down and revisit it in a day or two—but this isn't a perfect world.)

Following are some tips for getting distance when you're pressed for time. Even a 5–10 minute break can make a difference:

- ✔ Put your feet up and clear your mind.
- ✔ Go for a short walk.
- ✔ Get a cup of coffee.
- ✔ Make a quick telephone call.
- ✔ Pat yourself on the back.

Revisiting or Revising the Draft

After you get some distance, it's time to be more critical. You're not proof-reading yet, just fine tuning. Start with major changes, such as adding, deleting, or amending sections. Ask yourself:

- **Are the headlines action packed?** You can pump up headlines for greater impact.

    Action packed: Confirming tomorrow's staff meeting

    Actionless: Meeting

    Action packed: Rick Smith takes new position as of 12/5

    Actionless: Moving On

- **Did I use paragraphs appropriately?** A *paragraph* is a grouping of sentences that develops a single idea in support of the headline. Each paragraph starts with a *topic sentence* that supplies the direction of the sentences to follow.

- **Did I explain the problem or situation clearly?** Your wording must be clear so that the reader understands the significance of the problem, solution, or conclusion.

    Clear: Ted's supervisor couldn't make the meeting. The airport was closed because of the storm.

    Unclear: Ted's supervisor said he couldn't make the meeting be cause of the weather. (Who couldn't make the meeting? Ted or his supervisor? Why was the weather significant?)

- **Should I change my sequencing?** After you write the draft, you may find that it makes sense to resequence some of your headlines and paragraphs for greater impact. Ask yourself whether your headlines tell the story and deliver your message in the proper sequence. Check out Chapter 3 for more help on strategic sequencing.

For example, the following are headlines from a first draft. They start with what the writer can't do, rather than what he can do.

    No, we can't meet your deadline.

    Here's an alternative.

    Let us know.

The following are the headlines *after* resequencing. They cushion the bad news by starting with what the writer *can* do, rather than what he *can't* do.

    May we offer an alternative.

    We regret we can't meet the deadline.

    Please let us know how we may be of help.

✔ **Does the reader need background information?** Most backgrounds are dull, and people don't read them. Refer to the second question on your Start Up Sheet, "What does the reader *need* to know?" Include only the information the reader needs to know—not information he already knows. Here's how you can determine what to include:

- If the reader isn't familiar with the situation, he needs information to gain a general understanding of your message.

- Perhaps the reader is familiar with the situation but will be resistant to your message. You need him to understand the details that led to your decision.

✔ **Did I provide closure?** Look at Question 6 on your Start Up Sheet, "My purpose is to _____ so my reader will _____." Exactly what do you want the reader to do? The action item may be for the reader to do something specific. It may be to wait for the writer's action. Or it may be to do nothing. Check out these possibilities:

- Write a report

- Attend a meeting

- Mail a check

- Do nothing

Evaluating Your Drafting Process

After you finish sequencing and writing the draft, take a step back:

✔ Did the Start Up Sheet help you identify your audience, purpose, and key issue?

✔ Did the Start Up Sheet point to a new or surprising audience, purpose, or key issue?

✔ Did the Start Up Sheet help you to zero in on what you needed to say?

✔ Did the start up strategies trigger new ideas?

✔ Did the headlines give structure to the writing process?

✔ Was writing the draft easier because of Steps 1, 2, and 3, as opposed to trying to write without a process?

If you didn't save as much time as you expected, the next time you will. As with anything you do, it takes longest the first time and gets quicker each time through.

Write a draft for the document you're working on. Use the headlines as your outline and fill in the blanks.

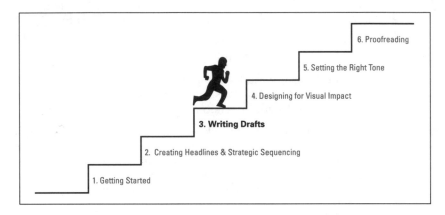

Now you're ready for Step 4: Designing for Visual Impact.

Chapter 5
Step 4: Designing for Visual Impact

● ●

In This Chapter

▶ Using white space

▶ Pumping up your text

▶ Adding boxes and borders

▶ Generating charts, tables, and figures

▶ Applying the finishing touches

● ●

Your first impression lasts. So, don't make your first impression your last.

—My Mother

*U*sing visual elements in your writing grabs your reader's attention and communicates information at a glance. Visual elements like charts, graphs, tables, figures, and borders provide a subtle signal that your message is worth a reader's attention. A message with the visual impact attracts attention, invites readership, and establishes the credibility of the message even before you state your case because:

✔ **Visual impact organizes information.** A good visual design breaks the message into manageable, bite-sized chunks, making it easy for the reader to find the key pieces of information. The reader can concentrate on one idea at a time.

✔ **Visual impact emphasizes what's important.** You can create a hierarchy of information so your readers can separate major points from supporting ones. In today's harried world where people are pulling their hair out because of tight schedules, your reader will appreciate your logical presentation of ideas.

A picture *is* worth a thousand words. This is true of every document you'll ever read or write. People's eyes automatically go to something visual, whether it's a headline, a graph, a table, or anything else that breaks up the text. Yet writers often overlook the importance of including visual elements in their writing, especially in letters and memos.

You don't have to have a degree in graphic design to put together good-looking documents that have impact on the reader. This chapter gives you the nitty-gritty on how to prepare documents so you can look like a pro.

Enjoying White Open Spaces

White space includes all areas of the page where there's neither type nor graphics; it's a key ingredient in visual design. People take for granted that white space is something a document should have, but they don't always know why. Following are a few reasons for using white space:

- ✔ White space makes the document inviting and approachable.
- ✔ It provides contrast and a resting place for the reader's eyes.
- ✔ A document with ample white space creates the impression that it's easy to read.

Here are some tips for using white space effectively:

- ✔ Use 1- to 1½-inch top, bottom, and side margins to create a visual frame around all the text and graphics.
- ✔ Keep paragraphs to between five and seven printed lines. (That's not sentences, but lines on the page.)
- ✔ Double-space between paragraphs to help the reader see each paragraph as a separate unit.
- ✔ Emphasize key pieces of text (words, phrases, or paragraphs) with white space or a different font. For more information about fonts, see "Having Fun with Fonts" later in this chapter.

White space doesn't have to be white. If your paper is ivory, tan, or whatever, the background color is still called *white space*.

Take a look at the document that you're working on and see whether it has enough white space to look inviting to readers.

Toying with Text

You don't have to become a Madison Avenue graphic artist with fancy software to create a pleasing visual design that has impact on your reader. You can do a great job with whatever word-processing software you use. The following are ways to dress up the text you created in Steps 1 through 3.

Using headlines, subheads, and sidelines

In Chapter 3, I discuss how to write the text for headlines, subheads, and sidelines. This section addresses how to make them visually appealing.

Choose one or two font styles and stick to them. For example, you may select **bold** for the all main headlines and *italics* for all the subheads. If you use too many fonts, your document becomes "noisy." For more information about fonts, see "Having Fun with Fonts" later in this chapter.

Using headlines

Each headline serves as a guidepost. The reader should be able to skim the message and be carried along by the headlines. If your message has only one level of headlines, consider using one of the following text treatments:

- ✔ ALL CAPS
- ✔ First Letter Caps
- ✔ **ALL CAPS BOLD**
- ✔ <u>First Letter Caps Underscored</u>

Using subheads

The first level of subheads may be ALL CAPS; the second level may be First Letter Caps, *italicized*, or <u>underscored</u>. Chapter 2 has a detailed discussion of subheads. Check it out.

Using sidelines

Sidelines, which run the headlines down the left column of your document, offer an alternative to headlines and subheads, as shown in Example 5-1. You often see sidelines in resumes, user manuals, data sheets, agendas, fliers, and any document where the reader needs to scan the left column to find the key information at a glance.

Example 5-1:
Sidelines at
a glance.

Meeting:	October 3, XXXX
Purpose:	Determine Plans and Objectives for Next Fiscal Year
Team:	Kerry Dolan, Tony Giannelli, and Tony Martinez.

Take a look at the document you're working on and see whether you're utilizing headlines, subheads, and sidelines to your best advantage.

Optimizing sentence and paragraph length

It's crucial to present your sentences and paragraphs so they're visually appealing. Think of text you've seen that's either too dense or too fragmented.

- ✔ When text is too dense, it's overwhelming and the reader often skips it.
- ✔ When it's too fragmented, the reader misses the connections between thoughts.

Optimizing sentence length

Vary sentence length to make for interesting reading. In general, use long sentences for detailed explanations and short sentences for emphatic statements. Limit sentences to no more than 25 words.

One way to cut the length of a sentence is to look for compound sentences— you know, those separated by "and," "but," or other conjunctions. (For more information about conjunctions, see Appendix A.) Look at the sentence length in the following:

> ***Just right:*** The company was founded in Boston, Massachusetts, in the early 1900s. It now employs more than 5,000 people and has branches in Boston, Marlborough, Salem, Foxboro, and Springfield.

> ***Too long:*** The company was founded in Boston, Massachusetts in the early 1900s, and it now employs more than 5,000 people, with branches in Boston, Marlborough, Salem, Foxboro, and Springfield.

Optimizing paragraph length

Although no hard and fast rules about paragraph length exist, try to limit each paragraph to between five and seven lines. A document full of short paragraphs looks choppy and makes it difficult for the reader to see the logical relationship between ideas. Conversely, long paragraphs are intimidating. They fail to provide manageable subdivisions of thought.

Each paragraph should support the headline it follows. Start each paragraph with a strong topic sentence, and then be certain every sentence that follows explains, expands, illustrates, or contributes to the topic sentence or headline. If a sentence doesn't relate to the topic, move it or remove it.

Take a look at the document you're working on and see whether your sentences and paragraphs are the appropriate length for your reader.

Making a list and checking it twice

Lists help the reader focus on important information by vertically listing key pieces information, breaking them out from the stream of the sentence. Lists draw the reader's attention to key ideas.

Be sure that you don't weaken your impact by making an entire page one long laundry list of bulleted or numbered items—if everything is emphasized, nothing stands out.

Check out these big-picture tips for listing information:

- List only similar items (such as items on a menu, parts in a warehouse, and the like).

- Use parallel structure and a uniform style. (See the full discussion of parallel structure later in this chapter.)

- Use words, phrases, or short sentences.

- Provide adequate transitions before and after a list.

- Consider sidelines if the list contains more than five items.

- Don't overuse lists. Save them for key points.

Using bulleted lists

Use a bulleted list when rank or sequence isn't important. Bullets give everything on the list equal value, as shown in Example 5-2. A key advantage to using lists is that you write less. *Less is more,* and your reader will love you.

Example 5-2:
All bullets
are created
equal.

> Please send us a list of the following estimates:
>
> • Cost
>
> • Tooling
>
> • Weight saved

Using numbered lists

There are four occasions when you may consider numbering a list:

1. To list items in order of *priority,* as shown in Example 5-3.

2. To *describe steps* in a procedure, as shown in Example 5-4.

3. To introduce the list by *quantifying* how many items appear in the list, as shown in Example 5-5.

4. To refer to items in the list easily, as shown in Example 5-6.

Example 5-3:
Putting first
things first.

> At our next meeting we must discuss your
>
> 1. Progress towards sales objectives
>
> 2. Suggestions for the next district meeting

Example 5-4:
Using a
numbered
list to show
steps.

> After the drums are put in the storage area
>
> 1. Separate them by waste code
>
> 2. Put them on skids
>
> 3. Store them in racks

Example 5-5:
A numbered
list showing
quantity, not
quality.

> The following five dates are available for our meeting:
>
> 1. April 22
>
> 2. April 29
>
> 3. May 3
>
> 4. May 14
>
> 5. June 12

Let's plan to address each of these questions at Tuesday's board meeting:

1. Have all participants been contacted?

2. Have presenters been given their assignments?

3. Have presenters been asked for suggestions for topics and subtopics?

4. Have alternate speakers been contacted?

5. Have special exhibits or props been ordered?

6. Has the meeting room been reserved?

7. Have arrangements been made for refreshments?

Example 5-6: A list of items numbered for easy reference.

Punctuating lists

When you create a bulleted list from a sentence, the bullets take the place of the commas, and the word *and* is omitted. But, you still need to put a period at the end of the sentence. Take a look at the following sentence and bulleted list shown in Example 5-7.

Today I'll call Barbara, schedule the June staff meeting, and prepare next month's goals.

Things to do today:

• Call Barabara

• Schedule the June staff meeting

• Prepare next month's goals.

Example 5-7: A bulleted list with no priority.

Using a colon to start a list

Start a list with a colon when the words *the following* or *as follows* are stated or implied.

Example: You must consider the following three factors:

1. Distance from the warehouse
2. Means of transportation
3. Availability of qualified employees.

Of course, there is an exception. Don't use a colon after a verb.

Example: The three factors to consider are

1. Distance from the warehouse
2. Means of transportation
3. Availability of qualified employees.

It isn't necessary to capitalize the first letter of an item on a list. Many writers like to do it because it makes the list visually stronger. The choice is yours.

Using complete sentences in lists

When the list consists of complete sentences, place a period after each sentence as shown in Example 5-8.

Example 5-8:
A bulleted
list of
complete
sentences.

> We suggest that the following issues be considered for reasons of safety:
>
> • Entrances to stations should face the main street.
>
> • Underground tunnels should not include blind turns.
>
> • Stations that have few riders should be closed during off-peak hours.

Using parallel structure

Examples 5-9 and 5-10 show parallel structure. *Parallel structure* means that elements in a sentence that function alike should be treated alike.

Example 5-9:
Parallel
structure
with gerunds
(words that
end in *ing*).

Security actions should include:

- Distributing throughout the system a description of the perpetrator

- Recommending that additional security be assigned to patrol high-risk areas

- Providing security with portable radios

Example 5-10:
Parallel
structure
with infinitive
verb forms.

Security actions should include the following:

- Distribute throughout the system a description of the perpetrator

- Recommend that additional security be assigned to patrol high-risk areas

- Provide security with portable radios

John F. Kennedy wowed the American public with his inaugural address. One dynamic portion shows parallel structure in its finest hour: "We shall pay any price, bear any burden, meet any hardship, support any friend, and oppose any foe to assure the survival and the success of liberty." He was the ultimate communicator.

Take a look at the document that you're working on and see whether adding bulleted or numbered lists can make your message clearer to your reader.

Boxing match

Consider boxing in text you want to stand out. A variety of boxes are available on your word processor. Example 5-11 shows just a few.

Having Fun with Fonts

The *font*, or typeface, displays words, and words convey your message. Yet, fonts can also create visual impressions that act upon your reader. At best, fonts reinforce your message and add impact. At worst, they conflict with your message and distract your reader from it.

This text is surrounded by a box.

This text is surrounded by a double-lined box.

This text is in a shadow box.

Example 5-11: A few of the boxes available on most word processors.

Selecting fonts

Today's word-processing software comes with a large variety of font options. Conventional wisdom says: Don't be like a kid in a candy store and start picking one of each. Consider when to use serif and sans serif.

 ✔ **Serif** is the font with feet—ascenders and decenders. Serif is great for blocks of text because it tends to move your eye along. That's why most books are printed in serif. In word processing, Times New Roman is a popular serif font.

 ✔ **Sans serif** (without feet) is great for adding contrast to headlines. Ariel is a popular sans serif.

Limit your visual display to two fonts or your message will be "noisy." For example, you may choose **BOLD ALL CAPS, 14 pt.** for headlines and 12 pt. for the text.

Using text treatments

After you select a font, you can apply a variety of text treatments to any font. Here are some popular text treatments:

 ✔ ALL CAPS

 ✔ SMALL CAPS

 ✔ Upper and Lower Case

 ✔ **Bold**

✔ **BOLD ALL CAPS**

✔ *Italics*

✔ <u>Underscore</u>

Some of the things to watch out for when using text treatments:

✔ <u>Be careful of underscores: they tend to cut through descenders (small g, j, p, q and y, for example) making the text difficult to read.</u>

✔ DON'T USE ALL CAPS FOR LARGE BLOCKS OF TEXT. PEOPLE TEND TO SEND E-MAIL MESSAGES IN ALL CAPS. IT'S KNOWN AS "FLAMING" AND IS AKIN TO SHOUTING AT SOMEONE. IF YOU WANT TO GET SOMEONE'S ATTENTION, DON'T SHOUT; YOU'LL TURN THEM OFF. ALSO, MESSAGES THAT APPEAR IN ALL CAPS ARE DIFFICULT TO READ.

✔ *Don't use italics for large blocks of text. It's difficult to read. Don't use italics for large blocks of text. It's difficult to read. Don't use italics for large blocks of text. It's difficult to read. Don't use italics for large blocks of text. It's difficult to read. Don't use italics for large blocks of text. It's difficult to read. If you read through this text, you get the idea.*

Following the signs

If you want to look savvy in print, use the special signs and symbols that come with your word processor. If you use (c) for copyright or -- for the em dash, your visual effect will appear amateurish. These "prehistoric" signs date back to the dark ages of typewriters when you were limited to 50 characters. Computers typically have 256 characters. Table 5-1 shows a few of the more popular signs and symbols.

Table 5-1	Popular Signs and Symbols
Sign or Symbol	*Used for*
*	copyright
®	registered trademark
™	trademark
—	em dash (formerly typed as --)
$\frac{1}{2}$	fractions (formerly typed as 1/2)
¶	paragraph marker
~	tilde

Take a look at the document that you're working on and see whether adding another font or text treatment can spice up your writing.

Coloring your world

People use color to interpret the meaning of what they see. Color adds visual impact so you can separate the ripe from the unripe, match your clothes, enjoy flowers, and so on. You can use color to create a mood and give a real-world look to the written word. With today's technology, the ability to invoke certain feelings in the viewer is at your fingertips. Press carefully!

The following mini-table shows a list of colors and the visual impact they may have on the reader:

Color	*Visual Impact*
White	Sanitary, Pure, Clean, Honest
Black	Serious, Heavy, Somber, Elegant
Red	Arresting, Danger, Excitement, Heat
Dark Blue	Calm, Stable, Trustworthy, Mature
Light Blue	Masculine, Youthful, Cool
Green	Growth-oriented, Organic, Action, Positive
Gray	Neutral, Cool, Mature, Honest
Brown	Organic, Wholesome, Unpretentious
Yellow	Positive, Cautious, Emotional
Gold	Elegant, Stable, Rich, Conservative
Orange	Emotional, Organic, Positive
Purple	Contemporary, Youthful
Pink	Feminine, Warm, Youthful, Calming
Pastels	Sensitive, Feminine, Soft
Metallic	Wealthy, Elegant, Lasting

A Pixel is Worth a Thousand Words: Using Charts, Tables, and Figures

If a visual element is well designed, it stands on its own and doesn't need explanation. So don't waste the reader's time (or yours) explaining information that appears visually. Also, too many visual elements can intimidate the reader. Save them for important information.

Charting your course

I worked on a project for a major branch of the U.S. Government. The sponsor gave me a 180-page document and asked me to edit it. The document abounded with repetitive information. I pared it down to a final document of 28 pages by creating a variety of charts and visual elements. I was a hero.

Pie charts

Pie charts (also called circle graphs) show percentages that total 100, as shown in Example 5-12. Some people believe it's important to begin the most important percentage at 12 o'clock and continue clockwise. Others believe that because people read from left to right, the most important information should be to the left of 12 o'clock. Use your own judgment.

Line charts

Line charts show trends, the change of one or more variables over time, or the relationship between two sets of numbers, as shown in Example 5-13. Line charts use points plotted in relation to two axes drawn at right angles. The axes must be descriptive and clearly labeled.

Bar charts

Bar charts show the relationship between two or more variables, as shown in Example 5-14. Bar charts can also rank items in a certain time period or over a period of time. As in a line chart, clearly mark the axes.

Preparing charts

Keep these tips in mind when you prepare charts:

- ✔ Use a descriptive title and place it above the chart.
- ✔ Use an appropriate scale.
- ✔ Use a legend to explain the symbols.
- ✔ Keep the design simple.
- ✔ Prepare a separate chart for each point.
- ✔ Eliminate any information the reader doesn't need.

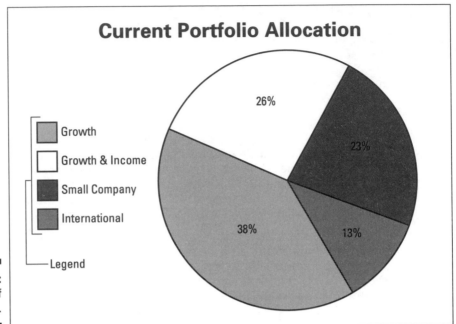

Example 5-12:
A slice of
the pie.

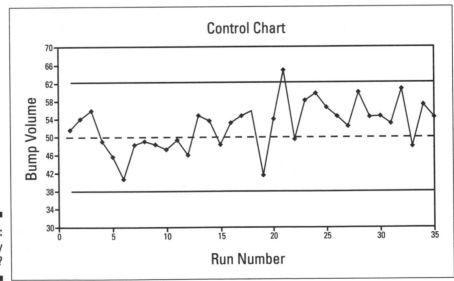

Example 5-13:
What's My
Line?

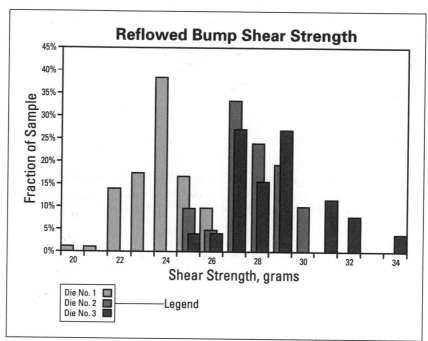

Example 5-14:
A horizontal
bar chart.

Creating tables and figures

Use tables and figures to present a large number of specific, related facts or statistics. Tables and figures carry more information per space than the same amount of text—yet they're often overlooked by business writers.

Creating tables

Create tables to arrange information in tabulated columns and rows. Use tables when

- ✔ You want to include more than three or four items of quantitative data.
- ✔ The reader needs to have all the data available.

Informal tables may be as simple as two or three columns. They don't require a title but do require column headings. If you include a title, place it above the table and describe what the table represents, as shown in Example 5-15.

	Office Products to Order	
Product	*Brand*	*Quantity*
Stapler	Bossko	3
Desk Lamp	Lumiere	2
Blotter Write	EZ	5

Example 5-15:
An informal
table.

Formal tables, in contrast, are generally numbered and require more formatting, as shown in Example 5-16. Formatting may include boxed headings, vertical and horizontal rules (lines) in the table, and a box around the table.

Office Products to Order		
Product	*Brand*	*Quantity*
Stapler	Bossko	3
Desk Lamp	Lumiere	2
Blotter Write	EZ	5

Example 5-16:
A formal
table.

If you're using more than four or five tables in a document, assign each a number—even if they're informal. Center the number and a concise title above the table. Keep tables simple and uncluttered.

Creating figures

What's the difference between a table and a figure? To put it simply: *If a visual element is not a table, it's a figure.* Figures aren't columns and rows. Figures can be anything from a simple graphic to any visual presentation. Even though I call the boxed-off writing samples in this book "examples," these examples are really just figures. Example 5-17 shows a figure that illustrates how different financial systems feed into a Web broswer.

If you're using more than four or five figures in a document, assign each a number. Center the number and a concise title below or next to the figure. Keep figures simple and uncluttered.

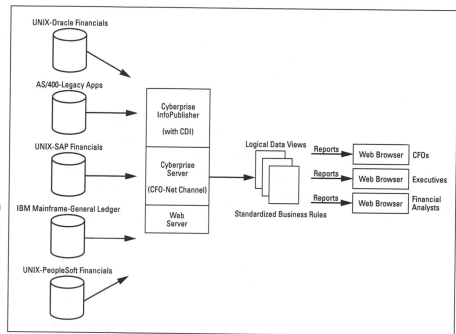

Example 5-17: A figure can explain a complex process quickly and clearly.

Take a look at the document that you're working on and see whether adding charts, tables, or figures can make your message clearer to your reader.

Choosing Your Visual Flavor

The following examples, numbers 18 through 22, show five "flavors" of the same memo. I'm not endorsing one over the other, just showing visual options. What flavor do you like?

Date: March 12, XXXX
To: Arlene Karp
From: Janice Teisch
Re: Welcome to Training at Marlborough Educational Center

Welcome to the Marlborough Education Center. We're delighted to have you here and hope your training experience will be a memorable one. Please don't hesitate to direct any questions or concerns to us. We'll be more than happy to address them immediately. Following is some information that may be helpful as you start your day:

- If you need assistance of any kind, our Educational Coordinator, Lynne Sullivan, is here to assist you. Lynne can be reached at extension 4545.

- Restrooms are located down the main corridor to the right of the main entrance. Follow the corridor to the yellow section and turn right. The restrooms will be on your left.

- In our break area, directly across the hall, you'll find snacks during the morning and afternoon breaks. If you'd like anything else, our cafeteria is located to the left of the main entrance. Cafeteria hours are from 7:30 to 10:30 in the mornings and from 11:30 to 2:30 in the afternoons.

- Public telephones are located directly opposite the entrance to the cafeteria. If at all possible, please wait until break time to make phone calls.

- A message board is located to the right of the entrance to this room. If you're expecting messages, please give callers Lynne's extension and she'll ensure that your messages are posted on the board outside this room.

- Coat closets are located next to the phones.

- You may leave course material in the room during breaks and overnight, but be sure to take your valuables.

Have a wonderful two days!

Example 5-18: Rocky road. This is as basic as you can get. The road's a little rocky because the reader stumbles along without having her attention called to anything.

Date: March 12, XXXX
To: Arlene Karp
From: Janice Teisch
Re: Welcome to Training at Marlborough Educational Center

Welcome to the Marlborough Education Center. We're delighted to have you here and hope your training experience will be a memorable one. Please don't hesitate to direct any questions or concerns to us. We'll be more than happy to address them immediately. Here's some information that may be helpful as you start your day:

- If you **need assistance** of any kind, our Educational Coordinator, Lynne Sullivan, is here to assist you. Lynne can be reached at extension 4545.

- **Restrooms** are located down the main corridor to the right of the main entrance. Follow the corridor to the yellow section and turn right. The restrooms will be on your left.

- In our **break area**, directly across the hall, you'll find snacks during the morning and afternoon breaks. If you'd like anything else, our **cafeteria** is located to the left of the main entrance. Cafeteria hours are from 7:30 to 10:30 in the mornings and from 11:30 to 2:30 in the afternoons.

- **Public telephones** are located directly opposite the entrance to the cafeteria. If at all possible, please wait until break time to make phone calls.

- A **message board** is located to the right of the entrance to this room. If you're expecting messages, please give callers Lynne's extension and she'll ensure that your messages are posted on the board outside this room.

- **Coat closets** are located next to the phones.

- You may leave **course material** in the room during breaks and overnight, but be sure to take your valuables.

Have a wonderful two days!

Example 5-19: Plain vanilla. This is a little better. Some of the key information is in boldface.

Date: March 12, XXXX
To: Arlene Karp
From: Janice Teisch
Re: Welcome to Training at Marlborough Educational Center

Welcome to the Marlborough Education Center. We're delighted to have you here and hope your training experience will be a memorable one. Please don't hesitate to direct any questions or concerns to us. We'll be more than happy to address them immediately. Here's some information that may be helpful as you start your day:

Need Assistance?
Our Educational Coordinator, Lynne Sullivan, is here to assist you. Lynne can be reached at extension 4545.

Restrooms
Restrooms are located down the main corridor to the right of the main entrance. Follow the corridor to the yellow section and turn right. The restrooms will be on your left.

Food and Beverages
In our break area, directly across the hall, you'll find snacks during the morning and afternoon breaks. If you'd like anything else, our cafeteria is located to the left of the main entrance. Cafeteria hours are from 7:30 to 10:30 in the mornings and from 11:30 to 2:30 in the afternoons.

Telephones
Public telephones are located directly opposite the entrance to the cafeteria. If at all possible, please wait until break time to make phone calls.

Messages
A message board is located to the right of the entrance to this room. If you're expecting messages, please give callers Lynne's extension and she'll ensure that your messages are posted on the board outside this room.

Closets
Coat closets are located next to the phones.

Valuables
You may leave course material in the room during breaks and overnight, but be sure to take your valuables.

Have a wonderful two days!

Example 5-20: French vanilla. Here you see the key information broken into headlines.

Date: March 12, XXXX
To: Arlene Karp
From: Janice Teisch
Re: Welcome to Training at Marlborough Educational Center

Welcome to the Marlborough Education Center. We're delighted to have you here and hope your training experience will be a memorable one. Please don't hesitate to direct any questions or concerns to us. We'll be more than happy to address them immediately. Here's some information that may be helpful as you start your day:

Need Assistance?   Our Educational Coordinator, Lynne Sullivan, is here to assist you. Lynne can be reached at extension 4545.

Restrooms   Restrooms are located down the main corridor to the right of the main entrance. Follow the corridor to the yellow section and turn right. The restrooms will be on your left.

Food and Beverages   In our break area, directly across the hall, you'll find snacks during the morning and afternoon breaks. If you'd like anything else, our cafeteria is located to the left of the main entrance. Cafeteria hours are from 7:30 to 10:30 in the mornings and from 11:30 to 2:30 in the afternoons.

Telephones   Public telephones are located directly opposite the entrance to the cafeteria. If at all possible, please wait until break time to make phone calls.

Messages   A message board is located to the right of the entrance to this room. If you're expecting messages, please give callers Lynne's extension and she'll ensure that your messages are posted on the board outside this room.

Closets   Coat closets are located next to the phones.

Valuables   You may leave course material in the room during breaks and overnight, but be sure to take your valuables.

Have a wonderful two days!

Example 5-21: Vanilla fudge. This is a classic example of how sidelines can help the reader find information quickly.

Date: March 12, XXXX
To: Arlene Karp
From: Janice Teisch
Re: Welcome to Training at Marlborough Educational Center

Welcome to the Marlborough Education Center. We're delighted to have you here and hope your training experience will be a memorable one. Please don't hesitate to direct any questions or concerns to us. We'll be more than happy to address them immediately. Here's some information that may be helpful as you start your day:

Need Assistance?	Our Educational Coordinator, Lynne Sullivan, is here to assist you. Lynne can be reached at extension 4545.
Restrooms	Restrooms are located down the main corridor to the right of the main entrance. Follow the corridor to the yellow section and turn right. The restrooms will be on your left.
Food and Beverages	In our break area, directly across the hall, you'll find snacks during the morning and afternoon breaks. If you'd like anything else, our cafeteria is located to the left of the main entrance. Cafeteria hours are from 7:30 to 10:30 in the mornings and from 11:30 to 2:30 in the afternoons.
Telephones	Public telephones are located directly opposite the entrance to the cafeteria. If at all possible, please wait until break time to make phone calls.
Messages	A message board is located to the right of the entrance to this room. If you're expecting messages, please give callers Lynne's extension and she'll ensure that your messages are posted on the board outside this room.
Closets	Coat closets are located next to the phones.
Valuables	You may leave course material in the room during breaks and overnight, but be sure to take your valuables.

Have a wonderful two days!

Example 5-22: Deluxe supreme. The difference between vanilla fudge and deluxe supreme is that horizontal rules separate the key pieces of information.

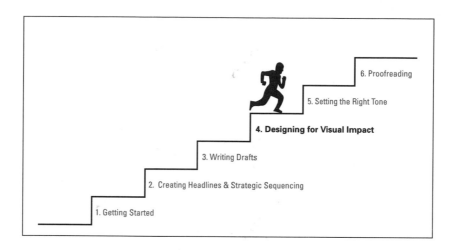

Now you're ready for Step 5: Setting the Right Tone.

Chapter 6
Step 5: Setting the Right Tone

- -

In This Chapter
▶ Keeping your writing short and simple
▶ Being positive
▶ Livening text with the active voices
▶ Avoiding sexist language

- -

> *Our life is frittered away by detail. . . Simplify, simplify.*
>
> —Henry David Thoreau, *Walden*

Some people say that business writing was developed during the Victorian era. Perhaps it was. Think about how styles have changed through the ages. In the 1940s and 1950s women in the workforce held menial jobs and (if they were employed in an office) they showed up to work donned in a hat, white gloves, and nylon stockings with seams. (Yes, stockings were nylon in those days.) Men with professional jobs always dressed in three-piece suits, not in the casual attire you see today.

People today are less formal in all aspects of their lives. Times have changed, and writing has followed suit—pardon the pun. This is apparent in the more relaxed tone people use in business writing.

Tone is a key factor in the written word. It's how you "sound" to the reader. Through your choice of words you can sound personable, enthusiastic, positive, or active. Or you can sound stuffy, skeptical, hostile, or passive. It's all in the words you select.

In this chapter, you polish up the material that you've planned, written, and designed in earlier steps. (Check out Chapters 2 through 5 for more tips on how to prepare, draft, and design your writing.) In this part of the Six Steps, you need to put yourself in your reader's shoes and try to experience his reaction. Remember that the tone of your the message influences your reader as much as the message itself.

Putting Your Personality on Paper

When you speak to someone face to face, much of what you say is interpreted through nonverbal cues (gestures, voice, inflections, eye contact, movements, and so on). This type of "reading between the lines" isn't possible with the written word, so it's critical that you choose your words carefully.

Always remember that a real person reads what you write. The words you choose and use in your writing—your tone—helps readers figure out your attitude toward the topic that you're writing about—as well as what their attitude should be.

Tone is especially important in e-mail, which is often thought of as cold and impersonal. Check out Part III for tips on e-mail issues.

Writing styles generally fall into three categories:

- ✔ **Personable and conversational.** This is the preferred style for business communications—writing as you speak.

- ✔ **Formal.** This is a stuffy and stilted style that may be appropriate for academic journals and such, but not for business writing.

- ✔ **Chatty.** This is a very loose, "talky" style that you should save for writing a two-line message to your close friends.

You can write as though you're talking (without the um's, of course) and still maintain a professional tone. Take a look at the following writing style categories and their matching examples. Each declines an invitation to a speaking engagement but uses a different tone:

- ✔ **Personable and conversational:** Thank you for asking me to speak at the New York chapter of the American Spiritual Association. I would very much like to accept the invitation, but I must be on the West Coast that week. (This style is preferred for business communications.)

- ✔ **Formal:** I am writing with reference to your invitation to address the New York chapter of the American Spiritual Association. I appreciate your regard for my expertise. However, it is with deep regret that I must decline your kind invitation. (This style is so stuffy it borders on taxidermy. But if you write a dissertation or legal brief, you may need to use it.)

- ✔ **Chatty:** Many thanks for the invite to chat with the American Spiritual Association. Sorry—can't make it. Have to be on the West Coast then. (This style is much too casual, even for e-mail.)

A Little KISS Goes a Long Way

Keeping your writing simple is the epitome of honing the tone. Choosing simple yet specific words that convey your message helps you write in a tone appropriate for your reader.

As you work on your tone, remember the acronym *KISS*. Some people say that stands for: "Keep it simple, stupid." I'd rather think it stands for "Keep it short and simple." In either event, the key word is *simple*.

Major publications and well-known authors have learned the value of keeping it simple. *The Wall Street Journal, Time,* and *Newsweek* are written at a high school reading level. Classic novels such as *The Catcher in the Rye* and *Moby Dick* are at an eighth-grade reading level. And Hemingway rarely used words with more than two syllables.

Even sophisticated scientific magazines have become conscious of readability. For many years, my husband has subscribed to two scientific magazines: *Science* and *Scientific American*. Years ago, I wouldn't pick up either magazine. The titles of the articles were riddled with 15-syllable words. Today, even these publications are starting to become more readable. I find myself reading many of the articles—now that I can understand the titles.

Keep it simple, Uncle Sam

Even the U.S. government is taking a stab at simplifying. On October 1, 1998, Bill Clinton took aim at government gobbledygook. He signed a directive requiring bureaucrats to use plain English. Following are a few highlights from the mandate:

> "Clutter and unnecessary technical terms are out. . . Shorter is better than long. . . Active is better than passive. . . Clarity helps advance understanding. By using plain language, we send a clear message about what the government is doing, what it requires, and what services it offers. Plain language saves the government and private sector time, effort, and money."

Too bad this mandate wasn't in effect when Franklin D. Roosevelt issued this blackout order in 1942:

> "Such preparations shall be made as will completely obscure all Federal buildings and non-Federal buildings occupied by the government during an air raid for any period of time from visibility by reason of internal or external illumination." (37 words)

FDR probably would have stated:

> "Tell them to cover the windows in buildings where they have to keep work going." (15 words)

Forget what you learned in school

In school, you're taught how *not* to write for business. Can you recall an instructor saying, "Write a five-page paper on Puritan mores as interpreted in Hawthorne's *The Scarlet Letter*" or whatever? So you do your research, gather your information, and come up with four and a half pages. You know you're not going to get that "A" because your paper isn't long enough. (Some instructors don't read papers; they weigh them.)

So you rehash some of what you already said and eke out another half page of gobbledygook. Voilà! You reached five pages. The instructor tosses the papers down the stairs . . . yours weighs enough to land at the bottom . . . and you get that "A."

Business people don't have time for the gobbledygook you put into your school assignments. The essence of good business writing is to shave everything down to its bare essentials. Get to the point in the shortest possible way. If information doesn't add value, leave it out. Remember, the less you say, the more impact it has.

Simon says, "Simple sentences"

Keep it short and simple by limiting your sentences to no more than 25 words. Many years ago a graduate student at the University of Illinois did his thesis on readability. He found that noted people such as columnist Ann Landers, World War II correspondent Ernie Pyle, and Sir Winston Churchill all share a sentence length of 15 words. Even Churchill's blood-sweat-and-tears radio speeches and his journalism from the Boer War averaged 15 words.

Eliminating gobbledygook

The following sentence was written by a participant at one of my workshops. It's full of gobbledygook that doesn't add value. Just for fun, try reading aloud with one breath.

"Because we have a small shop with limited personnel whose primary purpose in my opinion is to support the reactor operations and experiments, I recommend we send all major projects to outside shops who have better machines and capabilities so as to not tie up our machinists for extended periods of time which can be a problem when an emergency job is required where they are interrupted." (67 words)

This is how it read after the participant pared it down:

"Because of staffing limitations, I suggest we send major projects to outside vendors. This will keep our equipment free for emergencies." (21 words)

Whether a sentence is long or short, make it concise. Concise isn't the opposite of long; it's the opposite of wordy.

Imagine every word you write costs $100—that gives you a motivation to cut to the bare essentials. Every word that doesn't add to the effectiveness of your message wastes the reader's time, reduces his interest, and costs you money.

Puckering up for a KISS

Why use several words when one will do? Check out Table 6-1 for some KISSable examples:

Table 6-1	KISSing Your Prose
Try Writing	*Rather Than*
Agree	Come to an agreement
Apply	Make an application
Consider	Give consideration to
Examine	Make an examination of
Experiment	Conduct experiments
Investigate	Conduct an investigation
Invite	Extend an invitation
Meet	Hold a conference
Refer to	Make reference to
Return	Arrange to return
Save	Realize a savings of
Show	Give an indication of

Garnering advice from the greats

Perhaps the shortest letter ever written that most effectively expressed the writer's intentions was the one received by Victor Hugo from his publisher on February 26, 1802. Mr. Hugo had written to his publisher asking how he liked the manuscript, *Les Miserables*. This is the publisher's entire response:

!

Another punchy letter—one that keeps things short and simple:

Gentlemen:

You have undertaken to cheat me. I won't sue you for the law is too slow. I'll ruin you.

Yours truly,

Cornelius Vanderbilt

The following examples show how to use the preceding list of KISSable phrases to convert wordiness to conciseness. At $100 a word, how much money could you save?

Concise: Please send us your ideas. We will give them our full consideration. (12 words)

Wordy: I would greatly appreciate any ideas or suggestions that you would like to offer and assure you that each of your ideas will be given our strongest consideration and our fullest attention. (32 words)

Concise: We appreciate the views you expressed in your frank message last Monday. (12 words)

Wordy: We have received and read your message of Monday, February 25, and wish to say that there is much truth in each and every statement you made and that we fully understand your position. (34 words)

Concise: We'll let you know as soon as we have an answer. (11 words)

Wordy: We note your request and would state that we will communicate with you further at our earliest convenience. (18 words)

Concise: Please check all heavily used equipment quarterly. (7 words)

Wordy: The crucial factor is to make sure that all the heavily used equipment is checked no fewer than four times a year. (22 words)

Avoid redundancies

Avoid wordy, repetitive, repeated, and repetitious redundancies (kidding, of course) by paying attention to subtleties. Some are illustrated in Table 6-2.

Table 6-2	Repetitious Redundancies
Try Writing	*Rather Than*
As soon as	At the earliest possible date
Breakthrough	New breakthrough
Concluded	Arrived at the conclusion
Consensus	General consensus
Costs	Costs a total of
Developments	New developments
Enclosed is	Enclosed herewith please find
Essential	Absolutely essential
Experience	Actual experience, past experience

Try Writing	Rather Than
Fact	True fact
Factor	Contributing factor
First	First and foremost
Fundamentals	Basic fundamentals
Group	Group together
Have	Are in receipt of
Loan	Temporary loan
Opposite	Completely opposite
Outcome	Final outcome
Result	End result
Status	Current status
Thank you	I wish to take this opportunity to thank you
Truth	Honest truth

SHERYL SAYS

Using clear and simple words

Think of the great master William Shakespeare's famous line from *Hamlet*: "To be or not to be. . ." Notice that not one word is longer than three letters. And, take the opening line from the Bible: "In the beginning God created the heaven and the earth." These lines have such simplicity, an eighth-grader can write them.

Simple writing is profound, memorable, and elegant.

Following are some quotes from some different writings that I've come across. Do you think these writers impressed anyone with their verboseness?

"aircraft with lower noise emission characteristics" (What they mean is *quieter planes*.)

"pollutant emissions under control strategies"(What they mean is *smog filters*.)

"olfactory impact" (What they mean is *odor*.)

"The efficacy of hydrochloric acid is indisputable, but the corrosive residue is incompatible with metallic permanence. We can't assume responsibility for the production of toxic and noxious residue with hydrochloric acid. We suggest you find an alternative procedure." (What that means is: *Don't use hydrochloric acid. It'll eat your pipes*.)

Simplicity now!

Can you simplify the following sentences into commonly known expressions? The answers appear at the bottom of the sidebar.

1. Members of an avian species of identical plumage congregate.

2. The stylus is more potent than the claymore.

3. Eschew the implement of correction and vitiate the scion.

Answers: 1. Birds of a feather flock together; 2. The pen is mightier than the sword; 3. Spare the rod and spoil the child.

It's okay to be redundant when you want to emphasize or strengthen a thought. But use this technique sparingly and strategically. Consider the following example:

Strong: Keep it short. Keep it simple. Keep it flowing.

Weak: Keep it short, simple, and flowing.

KISSing in technical documents

Clear and simple wording is especially important in technical messages because technical information, by its very nature, can be difficult to read. If you surround technical words with simpler ones, your writing is easier to read and has a more personable tone. (In the following examples I underline the technical information, so you see how surrounding it with a KISS makes the sentence so much easier to read.)

Concise: Please let us know whether the <u>HBE exchangers (5%/9%RD)</u> can. . .

Wordy: We wish to request that you notify us if the <u>HBE exchangers (5%/9%RD)</u> can. . .

Using contractions

Years ago contractions belonged only in labor and delivery rooms—they were taboo in business documents. Today, however, contractions are preferable because they add a personal, conversational tone to your writing.

Apply the conversational test to see if a contraction works. Read your document aloud to hear how it sounds. For example, if you read the following sentence aloud, you wouldn't say *I'm* instead of *I am*.

I can't tell you how happy I am that you'll be able to attend the meeting.

Take a look at your document to find where you can make it shorter and simpler. Can you be more conversational? Are there opportunities to make the wording concise? Are your sentences limited to 25 words? Are you using contractions to convey a personal, conversational tone?

Using Positive Words

Presenting yourself as an optimist is a winning strategy. ("The glass is half full, not half empty.") Let the reader know what you *can and will do,* not what you can't and won't do. Using positive words engages the reader's goodwill and enhances your tone—ultimately improving the effectiveness of your writing.

The following sentences are positive and negative ways to send the same message. Notice the difference in tone:

Positive: I'm glad to tell you that your shipment will be sent on January 3.

Negative: Unfortunately, your shipment won't be sent until January 3.

Positive: We're sure you'll be delighted with the test results.

Negative: We hope you won't be disappointed with the test results.

Positive: Thank you for your suggestions about our prices. We do believe, however, that our prices are in line with those of our competitors.

Negative: Your letter complaining about our prices was wrong. We are definitely in line with those of our competitors.

The following words deliver a positive message:

Benefit	Bonus	Congratulations	Convenient
Delighted	Excellent	Friend	Generous
Glad	Guarantee	Health	Honest
Immediately	I will	Of course	Pleasant
Pleasure	Pleasing	Proven	Qualified
Right	Safe	Sale	Satisfactory
Save	Thank you	Vacation	Yes

The following words deliver a negative message:

Apology	Broken	Cannot	Complaint
Impossible	Inconvenient	Loss	Damages
Delay	Difficulty	Disappoint	Discomfort
Failure	Guilty	Mistake	Problem
Regret	Sorry	Suspicion	Trouble
Unable to	You claim	You neglected	Carelessly
Your failure	Your inability	Your insinuation	Your refusal

SHERYL SAYS

Take a look at your document to find where you can fill the glass, rather than empty it.

Invoking the Active Voice

Using the active voice is a major factor in projecting a tone that's alive and interesting. *Voice,* by the way, is the grammatical term that refers to whether the subject of the sentence or clause acts or receives the action.

- ✔ In a sentence written in the *active voice,* the subject is the actor or the doer.
- ✔ In a sentence written in the *passive voice,* the subject is acted upon. Sentences that use a passive voice are often dull and weak.

Imagine this scenario: You're vacationing in the tropics with your loved one. The fiery crimson sun is slowly sinking into the distant horizon and the waves are crashing over the craggy shore. You're sipping a glass of fine wine and affectionately click your glass with your companion's. That special someone leans over and whispers in your ear . . . "I love you." Doesn't that make you feel warm and fuzzy?

"I love you" is probably the most wonderful example of the active voice. It's animated and alive! What if that same special someone leans over and whispers in your ear, "You are loved." (By whom, the dog?) Or worse yet, "You are loved by me." (At that point, I'd probably start checking the personal ads.) The last two attempts at passion are passive. They're dull, weak, and absolutely ineffective.

Livening up your text

Check out these two examples of a similar message:

Active voice: Marc played the piano.

Passive voice: The piano was played by Marc.

Who do you envision when you read the active sentence? Marc—the actor—playing the piano. You can almost see him sitting at the piano totally absorbed in the music with his fingers moving magically across the keys.

The changes in the passive sentence make for a boring read. First, added words rob the sentence of simplicity (see "Using clear and simple words" in this chapter). Second, the emphasis shifts to the piano, and is no longer on Marc. The action and the actor are gone. The focus shifts from an active voice with the subject performing the action, to a passive voice where the subject receives the action. This passive sentence makes it hard to conjure up much of a vision.

Identifying passive voice in your writing

Following are a few tricks to help you tell when a sentence is passive.

- ✓ **Look for sentences that start with the action, rather the actor.** Sentences where the action comes before the actor are often passive.

- ✓ **Look for the various forms of the verb "to be"** (*is, are, was, were, will be, have been, should be,* **and so on**). These verbs don't always mean the sentence is passive, but they can give you a clue.

In the following sentences, forms of the verb "to be" are underlined, showing they are passive.

Active: Jim will train Patricia next Tuesday.

Passive: Patricia <u>will be</u> trained next Tuesday by Jim. (Even though Patricia is mentioned first, she receives the action.)

Active: John Smith will prepare the agenda.

Passive: The agenda <u>will be</u> prepared by John Smith.

In some cases, the actor is some*thing,* rather than some*one.* The following sentences deliver the same message.

Active: Up-to-date equipment means new business. (Up-to-date equipment is the actor.)

Active: New business depends on up-to-date equipment. (New business is the actor.)

Active: Growth depends on up-to-date equipment. (Growth is the actor.)

Passive: Equipment must be up to date or new business will be lost. (Equipment receives the action.)

Knowing when to use a passive sentence

There are times, however, when you may want to use passive voice because it's more appropriate. Check out these examples:

✔ **You want to place the focus on the action, not the actor.**

The shot was heard 'round the world. (The accent is on the shot, not the one who fired it.)

The law firm was established in the early 1900s. (The accent is on the law firm, not those who established it.)

Dennis was cited for his outstanding contribution. (The accent is on Dennis, not the person who cited him.)

✔ **You want to hide something.**

"The tapes were erased." (Perhaps you remember this famous line that came out of the Watergate scandal? The passive voice was used deliberately, so that no one would take the rap for that 18$^{1}/_{2}$-minute gap.)

The check is in the mail. (Sure it is. Who sent it?)

Differentiating between passive voice and past tense

Don't confuse passive voice with past tense. Both active and passive voices can be in any tense, as Table 6-3 shows.

Table 6-3	Active and Passive Tenses	
Tense	**Active**	**Passive**
Present	Jon sends the contracts every Thursday.	The contracts are sent every Thursday.
Past	Jon sent the contracts.	The contracts were sent.
Future	Jon will send the contracts next Thursday.	The contracts will be sent next Thursday.

Take a look at your document to find where you can liven up your text with the active voice.

Hey, I'm Talking to "You"

Notice how often the words "you" and "your" appear in the headlines of advertisements. Advertisers know the importance of using a tone that talks directly to the readers.

In the following sentences, six writer-focused references (<u>designated with underlines</u>) are turned into four reader-focused references.

Reader focused: As one of Mason & Green's valued customers, <u>you</u> will be receiving a convenient credit card. With this card, <u>you</u> can phone <u>your</u> orders and merely give us <u>your</u> charge number.

Writer focused: <u>We</u> want you to know that <u>we</u> appreciate having you as one of Mason & Green's catalog customers. <u>We</u> decided that <u>we</u> can make catalog shopping a lot easier by issuing you one of <u>our</u> credit cards. With this card, <u>we</u> can take your orders by phone.

Here are some you may try:

Reader focused: You'll be happy to hear. . .

Writer focused: I'm happy to tell you. . .

Reader focused: By now you should have received. . .

Writer focused: On May 2 we sent you. . .

Reader focused: This is in answer to your. . .

Writer focused: I'd like to respond to. . .

Be careful, however, that you don't insult the reader with the "you" attitude. Occasionally, keeping the focus on the author is useful, as you can see in the following:

Good taste and writer focused: We're sorry about the delay. We'll have our shipping department look into it and accept responsibility if we're at fault.

Bad taste and reader focused: Your error caused the delay. You will assume the responsibility for the extra charges on your bill.

Take a look at your document to find where you can turn the focus from yourself to the reader.

Avoiding Sexist Language

Language is a living and breathing thing that grows and shrinks with the culture. As people welcome a new vocabulary, it shapes the way we look at the world. Years ago women were practically invisible in professional writing. Now the gender gendarmes are out in full force. The English language, as rich as it is, has no pat solution to sexist language. So without getting into absurdities (such as changing *man*hole cover to *person*hole cover), the key is to be

- Aware of hidden and overt meanings
- Sensitive to your reader

Perhaps we should consider ourselves lucky that English is mercifully gender free. Think of many of the romance languages that assign genders to words like *pen* (*la plume* in Spanish) or *pencil* (*el lapiz* in Spanish). I can ever understand why a pen is female and a pencil is male.

The following are some tips that may help you bridge the gender gap in your writing.

- **Reword the sentence.** Gender neutrality is often a matter of rewording the sentence. The examples that follow show a number of ways to say the same thing:

     Acceptable: Each person did *the* work quietly.

     Acceptable: Each person *worked* quietly.

     Acceptable: Everyone *worked* quietly.

     Unacceptable: Each person did *his* work quietly. (Sexist)

     Unacceptable: Each person did *their* work quietly. (Grammatically incorrect. Check out Appendix B for more information on grammar.)

- **Avoid gender judgments in job titles.** When you're speaking of someone's job title, don't make a gender judgment. Judges aren't necessarily males, and nurses aren't necessarily females. If you can, identify the person by name.

- **Use gender-neutral terms.** A female adult isn't a girl—she's a woman. Someone who's employed in a stockroom isn't a stockboy, but a stockclerk. Table 6-4 shows other gender-neutral terms worth considering.

✔ **Think plural.** In some cases you can make a sentence plural to avoid the clunky he/she or his/her situations.

> *Plural:* Doctors are trained to heal their patients.

> *Singular:* A doctor is trained to heal his/her patients.

> *Plural:* All candidates for the human resources position must file their applications no later than June 5. They should include their educational backgrounds. . .

> *Singular:* Each candidate for the human resources position must file his/her application no later than June 5. He/she should include his/her educational background. . .

✔ **Apologize in advance.** When all else fails consider using *he* (or *she*) to refer to both sexes. State your intentions (and apologies) at the outset of your writing.

Notice how I address this delicate issue in *Business Writing For Dummies*. I use the male gender in the even chapters; the female gender in the odd chapters. (I didn't determine that women are odd. I flipped a coin.)

Be sure to take a look at your document to find where you can change a sexist term to a gender-neutral term.

Table 6-4	Gender Neutral Terms
Try Saying	*Rather Than*
Ancestor	Forefather
Cinematographer	Cameraman
Chair, moderator	Chairman, chairperson
Firefighter	Fireman
Flight attendant	Steward, stewardess
Humanity, human race	Mankind
Insurance agent	Insurance man
Letter carrier	Postman
Member of the clergy	Clergyman
Messenger	Delivery boy, delivery person
Meteorologist	Weatherman
Nonprofessional	Layman
Police officer	Policeman, policewoman
Reporter, journalist	Newsman

(continued)

Table 6-4 *(continued)*

Try Saying	Rather Than
Sales representative	Salesman, salesperson
Service technician	Repairman, repairwoman
Spokesperson	Spokesman
Synthetic	Man made
Worker	Workman

Honing Other Tonal Tidbits

There are a few other areas where you may need to hone your tone: word associations, humor, slang and idioms, and clichés.

Using word associations (euphemisms)

Imagine this scenario: The CEO at a major corporation drives to work in his spiffy new car. A young, fledgling executive parks next to him and comments, "I like the color of your car, Mr. Jones—bottle green." "Thank you," Mr. Jones smirks rather pompously. "However, the dealer calls it 'British racing green.'"

Tone plays a part in the unspoken meanings that words and expressions invoke. For example, years ago stores had "complaint departments." The name gave the impression that the people who worked there dealt with one thing—complaints. Realizing the implication, those departments are now called "customer service departments." The focus is on *customer service,* not on *complaints*. Table 6-5 gives *euphemisms* that make other words or phrases less objectionable:

Table 6-5	Useful Euphemisms
Use the Euphemism	Rather Than Saying
Customer service department	Customer complaint department
Deposit, initial investment	Down payment
Direct report	Subordinate
Economical	Cheap
Opportunity	Problem
Previously owned	Used

Use the Euphemism	Rather Than Saying
Supervisor, manager	Boss
Talk	Speech
Unsophisticated	Ignorant

Euphemisms can be overdone, so don't take things to an extreme. I worked with a young man at a federal facility. One of his assignments required that he find the name of a garbage collector in the area. This man had become so accustomed to the government's gobbledygook that he started checking the Yellow Pages looking for *Refuse collectors, Sanitary engineers,* and so on. He finally found what he needed listed under—what else—*Garbage collectors.*

Thinking seriously about being funny

Will Rogers once said, "Humor is funny as long as it is happening to somebody else." Humor *is* a sensitive area. It's wise to avoid attempts at humor unless you know your reader very well.

Even among friends, humor can be cutting.

George Bernard Shaw once sent tickets for his latest play to his good friend Winston Churchill. Mr. Shaw included this note:

> Here are two tickets to the opening of my new play—One for you and one for a friend—if any.

Mr. Churchill returned the tickets with this note:

> Sorry, I'm unable to attend opening night. Please send me tickets for another performance—if any.

If there's the slightest chance that your humor may be mistaken for a tone of sarcasm, avoid it. Also, be careful of using humor when writing to people of other nationalities or ethnic backgrounds. What's humorous to you may be insulting to them.

Take a look at your document to find where you may have used humor inappropriately.

Throwing the book at idioms

Idiomatic expressions have meaning only in certain areas of the world. For example, if you tell someone to "eat their words," you're not going to get a knife and fork. So, it's best to avoid idiomatic expressions.

The global marketplace has opened opportunities to communicate with people all over the world. Foreigners, even those who live in an English-speaking nation and have studied our language, are sometimes puzzled by idiomatic expressions.

Avoid clichés like the plague

What meaning do clichés have anyway? In most cases, the literal meaning of a cliché bears no relevance to the topic at hand and bogs down the text. Face it: Clichés are nothing more than figures of speech and strong comparisons that have caught on. To illustrate, have you heard the cliché "happy as a clam"? Are clams really happy? These hapless bivalves are pried open, minced, steamed, stuffed, casinoed, and lampooned by Odgen Nash:

> The clam, esteemed by gourmets highly
> Is said to live the life of Riley.
> When you are lolling on a piazza,
> It's what you are as happy as-a.

> —Ogden Nash

For the jargon-impaired

Jargon (sometimes referred to as slang) is specialized "shop talk" that's unique to people in an industry. Technical jargon—used properly—can be a hallmark of a good document to readers with a vast knowledge of the subject and the terminology. In these cases, it makes no sense to water down the language. Doing so may damage the integrity of the document and insult the reader.

When you're writing to people outside the industry, avoid jargon. The tone may become tangled in abstract words that the reader may view as exclusionary. Table 6-6 offers some terms for the layperson:

Table 6-6	Jargon Fixes
Try Using	*Rather Than*
Daily	Per diem
Date of final payment	Maturity date
History of the property	Abstract
Increase the balance of your loan	Charged to your principal
Reserve account for taxes and insurance	Escrow account
Value of property for tax purposes	Assessed valuation
Yearly payment	Annual premium

Use the Audience section of your Start Up Sheet to help determine what level of knowledge you can expect from your readers. Remember that managers in high tech industries aren't always familiar with the technical language of their engineers.

Take a look at your document to find where you can shore up word associations, humor, jargon, idioms, and clichés.

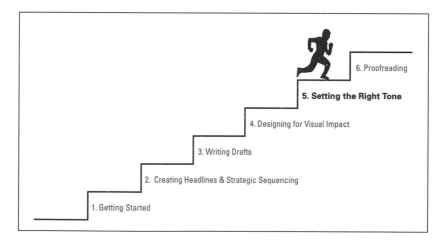

Now you're ready for Step 6: Proofreading

Chapter 7
Step 6: Proofreading

In This Chapter
▶ Guidelines for proficient proofreading
▶ Avoiding embarrassing simple mistakes
▶ Using the Editing Checklist

How would you like a job where, if you made a mistake, a big red light goes on and 18,000 people boo?

—Jacques Plante, former National Hockey League goalie

Imagine this scenario: The new CEO of a major corporation walks into his first Board of Directors meeting. He really wants to dazzle the board. He's wearing a $2,500 pin-striped suit, silk shirt, red power tie, and $200 black leather shoes. He sits down, crosses his leg, and (Oops!) you notice that he's wearing one black sock and one blue sock.

What do the mismatched socks do to his dazzling image? They blow it, right? Every time you think of Mr. CEO, you're going to snicker and think of his mismatched socks.

Well, imagine yourself spending hours or days preparing a document you're proud of. If you send it with even one error. . . that's your mismatched socks. The error is what your reader remembers.

You already put a great deal of work into Steps 1 through 5, but don't overlook this step. You experience a real sense of pride and accomplishment by sending something that's as good as it can get.

Proofread Before "Ewe" Send

Proofreading is akin to quality control. In a manufacturing environment, quality control is making sure the merchandise is free from defects so the customer doesn't wind up with a lemon. In the world of writing, it means making sure that the document is free from errors so it reflects well on you, the writer. Here are some of the things to look for:

- ✔ **Check all names, including middle initials, titles, and company distinctions.** Are you spelling *Glenn* with two n's instead of one? Are you writing *Corp.* instead of *Co.*?

  Most names generally identify the sex of the person. However, you can't make assumptions. For example, there's Stevie Nicks (female), Carroll O'Connor (male), and Michael Learned (female). Who'da thought?

- ✔ **Double-check all numbers.** Are you telling the reader she should send $2,115.00 instead of $2,515.00?

- ✔ **Keep an eye out for misused or misspelled homophones (words that sound the same but are spelled differently).** Do you write *principal* where you want *principle?*

- ✔ **Look for repeated words. (Some word-processing and e-mail packages check for this, but not all.)** Perhaps you wrote, "I'll call her her back in a week."

- ✔ **Be on the alert for small words that you repeat or misspell.** You can easily type *of* instead of *if* and not notice the error. (You tend to read what you expect to be there.)

- ✔ **Check dates against the calendar.** If you write *Tuesday, April 10,* be certain April 10 is a Tuesday.

I received an invitation to attend a meeting of a local organization on Monday, June 16. When I went to mark it on my calendar, I realized that June 16 was a Tuesday. The organization was bombarded with calls. And some people who didn't catch the error showed up on Monday: No one was there.

- ✔ **Check for omissions.** Are you leaving off an area code, parcel number, or other critical piece of information?

Following are a few tips to make the proofreading process easier:

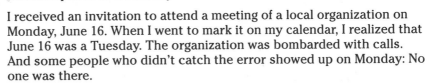

- ✔ **Check spelling, grammar, and punctuation.** Use your eyes as well your computer tools. For more information about spelling, grammar, and punctuation, see the appendixes in the book.

- ✔ **Print out the message and read the hard copy.** Face it, despite the hours you spend in front of your computer, you're still more used to reading the printed word. Therefore, you tend to see errors on a hard copy that you may miss on a computer screen. Also, on a hard copy, you can see how your document flows from paragraph to paragraph and page to page.

✔ **Read the message aloud.** Can you read the document just once and thoroughly understand it? If *you* have to scratch your head, wrinkle your brow, back up, and reread something you wrote, so will your reader. Rewrite it.

✔ **Get a second opinion.** Ask an office buddy to take a look at your document, especially if it's something critical.

✔ **Read from bottom to top and/or from right to left.** Doing so lets you view each word as a separate entity and helps you find errors.

✔ **Scan the document to see that it looks right.** Is the text aligned properly? Did you allow at least 1 inch margins on the top, bottom, and sides? Are the paragraphs or sentences too long to be readable?

✔ **If time allows, reread the message after you get some distance.** If you just let off steam by writing a heated e-mail message, wait. Save the message to a file and reread it after you cool off.

✔ **Look for parallel structure.** Remember, elements in a sentence that are alike in function should be alike in construction. Check out Chapter 5 for more on parallel structure.

> *Correct:* Peter is honest, capable, and worthy of a promotion.

> *Incorrect:* Peter is honest, capable, and ought to be promoted.

Using Your Electronic Tools

Although the spelling and grammar checkers available on most word-processing programs today can be invaluable, *don't turn your computer on and your brain off.* Look at the difference between these sentences. Although they're both correct, they deliver very different meanings, and your spell checker wouldn't detect an error.

> I will no*w* go to the meeting.

> I will no*t* go to the meeting.

With one incorrect letter (*w* instead of *t*), you deliver the opposite message. Even the smallest typo can radically change your meaning. Take the time to proofread carefully.

Although your electronic dictionary abounds with words, some you typically use may not be there. Consider adding those unique words to your electronic dictionary. Either check your software's user manual or follow the prompts.

Using Proofreader's Marks

Generally, you use proofreader's marks to convey changes when you're reviewing other people's text, not your own. Therefore, your edits must be neat and understandable so anyone reading the document can understand your intentions. Table 7-1 lists some commonly used proofreader's marks.

Table 7-1	Commonly Used Proofreader's Marks		
Instruction	**Mark in Margin**	**Mark on Proof**	**Corrected Type**
Delete	ℐ	the good word	the word
Delete and close up space	ℐ	the wor̂d	the word
Insert indicated material	good	the‸word	the good word
Let it stand	stet	the good word	the good word
Transpose	tr	the word good	the good word
Insert space	#	the‸word	the word
Close up	◠	the woȓd	the good word
period	⊙	This is the word‸	This is the word.
comma	∧	words‸words, words	words, words, words
apostrophe	∨	Johns words	John's words
double quotation marks	∨/∨	the word word	the word "word"
uppercase	uc	the word	The Word
lowercase	lc	The Word	the word

Avoiding real-life faux pas

The following are real-life blunders that could have been avoided if the writer had proofread carefully.

Faux pas 1

A friend of mine is the Vice President of Public Relations at a prestigious international corporation. Last year she sent an important, quickly composed e-mail message to hundreds of coworkers worldwide. In her haste, this Vice President of Public Relations inadvertently left out the *l* in *Public*. Think about that for a moment!

Faux pas 2

A writer colleague of mine was out of work and applied for a proofreading position at a publishing company. He wanted to emphasize his writing, editing, and proofreading skills. Despite his wonderful qualifications, he didn't get any response. Why? He called the company and learned that his electronically transmitted résumé was quite memorable. Instead of typing *proofreading*, he typed *poofreading*. That little *r* cost him a job. (He was memorable all right, but for the wrong reason.)

Faux pas 3

I received in the mail a beautiful brochure from a company selling software that can prepare brochures electronically. There was one major element missing from the brochure—how to get in touch with the company. The sender had spent a lot of money preparing the brochure and mailing it out. Had she proofread, she would have known that some very important things were missing: an address and phone number.

Faux pas 4

These notes are from parents explaining why their children missed school:

- ✔ Please excuse Pat on February 27, 28, 29, and 30.
- ✔ Donna couldn't come to school yesterday; she was in bed with gramps.
- ✔ Jack had loose vowels.
- ✔ Please excuse Grace for being. It's her father's fault.
- ✔ Mary Ann was absent Dec. 11-15 because she had a fever, sore throat, headache, and upset stomach. Her sister was also sick, fever, and sore throat; her brother had a low grade fever and ached all over. I wasn't the best either, sore throat and fever. There must be the flu going around—her father even got hot last night.

Faux pas 5

And I, too, have embarrassing moments. I sent an e-mail message to a business associate who was helping me with research for one of my books. I asked him to send me information from his publication *The Anals of Improbable Research*. Was my face red when I received his answer! "Sheryl, I've changed the spelling of Annals (two n's) and raised the price."

Using the Editing Checklist

The following Editing Checklist appears as the flip side of the Cheat Sheet in the front of this book. Keep the Cheat Sheet handy and go through this checklist before you send out any document. This can save you many embarrassing moments!

- ❑ My subject line and/or headlines are informative and spark my reader's interest.
- ❑ My document includes a key word(s).
- ❑ My document tells a story.

❑ My message has visual impact, including

    ❑ Ample white space

    ❑ Bulleted and numbered lists, and charts and tables, where appropriate

    ❑ Sentences limited to 25 words

    ❑ Paragraphs limited to 5–7 lines

❑ My message is clear, well-organized and properly formatted.

❑ The message is sequenced to keep the reader interested and moving forward. The action I want the reader to take is clearly spelled out.

❑ The tone reflects my personality on paper, including the active voice and *you* approach.

❑ The spelling, grammar, and punctuation are correct.

Use the Editing Checklist to ensure that your document is one you're proud to send.

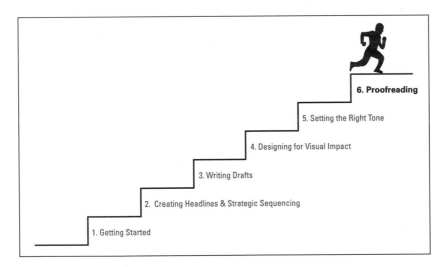

Now you're ready to dazzle your reader with your document!

Part II:
Business Writing In Action

In this part. . .

Combine the *yin* of Parts I and II with the *yang* of the business skills you already have, and you can write any document. This part features the four most common areas of business writing today: letters and memos, reports, proposals, and presentations.

And don't forget the Cheat Sheet featured in the front of this book. It has the Start Up Sheet on one side and the Editing Checklist on the other. Tear it out and keep it handy to energize all your business writing.

Chapter 8

Enlightening Letters

- -

In This Chapter

▶ Dissecting a letter

▶ Writing in style

▶ Letting your personality shine

▶ Managing longer letters

▶ Writing memorable memos

- -

I have made this letter longer than usual, only because I have not had the time to make it shorter.

—Blaise Pascal, French philosopher

*B*usiness letters account for about 90 percent of all written business communications—proving that letters are a powerful medium by any standard. A well-written letter can mean

✔ Advancement for your career

✔ Profit for your company

✔ Sterling relationships with clients or customers

In order for your letter to stand out from the myriad of others competing for readers' attention each day, you must unite the mechanics of writing with the human factor—the reader. Check out Chapter 15 for reasons letters fail.

Before you begin writing a letter, go through the the Six Steps of effective business writing that I introduce in Part I. The Six Steps guide you through everything from getting started to proofreading.

Don't let your dynamic ideas be overshadowed by mediocre writing. Fill out the Start Up Sheet on the Cheat Sheet in the front of this book so you can write letters with confidence and competence.

This chapter starts with all you ever wanted to know about letter formats and styles and ends with letters you may actually adapt for your own use. Jump around the chapter to find what you need.

The Anatomy of a Letter

Just as doctors must know and understand all the parts of the body, business writers must know and understand all the parts of a letter. The following is a listing and description of all the letter parts from head to toe. Of course, you won't use them all in your letters at any one time. Take a look at Example 8-1, which shows where each part goes.

Date

Write the date using Arabic numerals with no abbreviations.

October 12, XXXX

12 October, XXXX (military or European usage)

Mailing or in-house notations

When you use a special method of delivery, place the mailing notation (special delivery, certified mail, registered mail, air mail, by messenger) or in-house notations (personal, confidential) two lines below the date—in all caps.

CONFIDENTIAL

CERTIFIED MAIL, RETURN RECEIPT REQUESTED

Inside address

Start the inside address four lines below the date. It includes any or all of the following: addressee; addressee's title; company name; street address; and city, state, and zip code. Following are two alternatives:

Either:

Ms. Lynne Schwartz, President
Michael & Associates
203 Monsey Avenue
Spring Valley, NY 10977

Or:

Ms. Lynne Schwartz
President
Michael & Associates
203 Monsey Avenue
Spring Valley, NY 10977

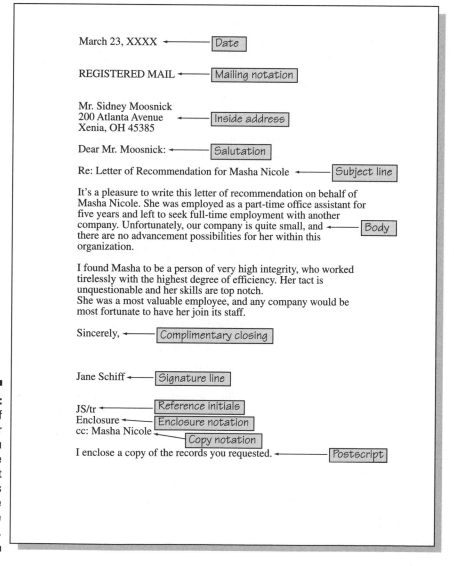

March 23, XXXX ← Date

REGISTERED MAIL ← Mailing notation

Mr. Sidney Moosnick
200 Atlanta Avenue ← Inside address
Xenia, OH 45385

Dear Mr. Moosnick: ← Salutation

Re: Letter of Recommendation for Masha Nicole ← Subject line

It's a pleasure to write this letter of recommendation on behalf of
Masha Nicole. She was employed as a part-time office assistant for
five years and left to seek full-time employment with another
company. Unfortunately, our company is quite small, and ← Body
there are no advancement possibilities for her within this
organization.

I found Masha to be a person of very high integrity, who worked
tirelessly with the highest degree of efficiency. Her tact is
unquestionable and her skills are top notch.
She was a most valuable employee, and any company would be
most fortunate to have her join its staff.

Sincerely, ← Complimentary closing

Jane Schiff ← Signature line

JS/tr ← Reference initials
Enclosure ← Enclosure notation
cc: Masha Nicole ← Copy notation
I enclose a copy of the records you requested. ← Postscript

Example 8-1:
A sample of
all the letter
parts. You
rarely use
them all, but
this shows
you the
whole
enchilada.

When should you type the addressee's title on the same line as the name or on the following line? It depends on the length of the line. Try to square the address as much as possible. If the title appears on the same line, place a comma between the name and title. If it appears on the next line, dispense with the comma—as in the preceding example.

When you mail a letter outside the United States, be sure to include the name of the country on a separate line below the city. I generally use capital letters to make it stand out.

Mail is delivered to the address element on the line above the city, state, and zip. If you want the letter delivered to a post office box, place the P.O. number underneath (or instead of) the street address.

> 607 Codger Lane
> P.O. Box 7344
> Austin, TX 78959-7344

The United States Postal Service requests that you use the two-letter state abbreviation. Check out Appendix C.

Attention line

Use an attention line on the rare occasion when you're writing to a company and want the letter directed to a specific person and/or department. For example, the letter is company business and needs to be handled by someone at the company if the intended reader isn't available. The following are a few styles to consider:

ATTENTION BETH BERREAN (using all caps)

Attention Human Relations Manager (using initial caps)

Attention: Training Department (using colon)

Following are two ways to deal with the attention line:

Either:

Marric Brothers
Attention: Alan Laurence
4 Thom Court
Monsey, NY 10952

Or:

Marric Brothers
4 Thom Court
Monsey, NY 10952

ATTENTION ALAN LAURENCE

Salutation

The salutation is a greeting—a way of saying "hello" to the reader. Place it two lines below the address. The salutation should correspond directly to the first line of the inside address, as Table 8-1 shows you.

Use someone's first name *only* if you're on a first-name basis, and follow the salutation with a comma. Otherwise use a colon.

Table 8-1	Matching the Salutation with the Address	
Inside Address	*Formal Salutation*	*Informal Salutation*
Mr. Joel Kingsley	Dear Mr. Kingsley:	Dear Joel,
Ms. Phyllis Kingsley	Dear Ms. Kingsley:	Dear Phyllis,
Mr. and Mrs. Joel Kingsley	Dear Mr. and Mrs. Kingsley:	Dear Phyllis and Joel,
Messrs. Max and Harry Lorenz	Dear Messrs. Lorenz:	Dear Max and Harry,
Mmes. Ethel and Marilyn Lorenz	Dear Mmes. Lorenz:	Dear Ethel and Marilyn,
Messrs. James Taylor and Bob Grant	Dear Messrs. Taylor and Grant:	Dear James and Bob,
Mmes. Sally Jones and Jan Fox	Dear Mmes. Jones and Fox:	Dear Sally and Jan,

Never write "To Whom This May Concern." It's cold and impersonal. Instead, try to find the name of the person you're writing to. You can often do it by calling the company and talking to the receptionist. (That's when you don't have to punch through the maze of "press 1 then press 2.")

Figuring out inside addresses and salutations for members of the armed services and government organizations can be tricky. When writing to anyone in the U.S. Armed Services, refer to Table 8-2 or Table 8-3. When writing to U.S. Government officials, refer to Table 8-4.

Table 8-2 Addresses and Salutations for the U.S. Armed Services*

Rank	Inside Address	Salutation
General	General Tammy Brassi	Dear General Brassi:
Major General	Major General Otto Gordon	Dear General Gordon:
Colonel	Colonel Asa Danforth	Dear Colonel Danforth:
Lieutenant Colonel	Lieutenant Colonel Sam Adams	Dear Colonel Adams:
Captain	Captain Grace Gilly	Dear Captain Gilly:
Second Lieutenant	Second Lieutenant Buck Rogers	Dear Lieutenant Rogers:
Warrant Officer	Warrant Officer Kenneth Riley	Dear Mr. Riley:
Sergeant Major	Sergeant Major Alan Ansel	Dear Sergeant Major Ansel:
Master Sergeant	Master Sergeant Pat Sykes	Dear Sergeant Sykes:
Corporal	Corporal Leslie Matthews	Dear Corporal Matthews:
Private First Class (or Private)	Private First Class Gerry Taylor	Dear PrivateTaylor: (or Private)
Airman First Class (or Airman)	Airman First Class Dick Tucker	Dear Airman Tucker:

* Excludes the Navy (See Table 8-3.)

Table 8-3   Addresses and Salutations for the U.S. Navy

Rank	Inside Address	Salutation
Admiral	Admiral Gene Babson	Dear Admiral Babson:
Rear Admiral	Dear Admiral Elliel Jones	Dear Admiral Jones:
Captain	Captain Sally Wilde	Dear Captain Wilde:
Lieutenant Commander	Lieutenant Commander Rob Roy	Dear Commander Roy:
Lieutenant	Lieutenant Paul Hersch	Dear Mr. Hersch:

Rank	Inside Address	Salutation
Ensign	Ensign James Taynet	Dear Mr. Taynet:
Warrant Officer (all grades)	Warrant Officer Pam Levine	Dear Ms. Levine:
Enlisted Personnel (all grades)	(Rank) Erik Strassman	Dear Mr. Strassman:

Note: Address all retired military personnel by the rank they reached at retirement.

Table 8-4 Addresses and Salutations for U.S. Government Officials

Official	Inside Address	Salutation
President	The President, The White House	Dear Mr. President: or Dear President (surame):
Vice President	The Vice President, United States Senate	Dear Mr. (Madam) Vice President (surname):
Chief Justice	The Chief Justice of the United States, Supreme Court	Dear Mr. (Madam) Chief Justice:
Senator	Honorable (full name)	Dear Senator (surname):
Representative	Honorable (full name)	Dear Mr. (Ms.) (surname):
Cabinet Member	Honorable (full name)	Dear Mr. (Madam) Secretary:
Ambassador	Honorable (full name)	Dear Mr. (Madam) Ambassador:
Governor	Honorable (full name)	Dear Governor (surname):
Mayor	Honorable (full name)	Dear Mayor (surname):
Judge	Honorable (full name)	Dear Judge (surname):

Subject line

Place the subject line two lines below the salutation. Its purpose is to direct the reader to the theme of the letter. For more information about crafting dynamic subject lines, check out Chapter 3. You can use any of the following styles.

Instead of the word *subject,* many writers prefer *Re:* which stands for regarding. It's pronounced *"ree"* (as in green).

SUBJECT: Agenda for Monday's meeting

Re: Special Rebate, Act Before 12/5/XX

Subject: Year-End Sales Results—15% increase

The subject line used to be placed between the inside address and salutation. Who changed it and why? Beats me.

Body (message)

Single space the body of the letter. Double space between paragraphs, and use headlines. For more information about writing paragraphs, check out Chapter 5. Here are some suggestions for breaking down the body:

- **Make the *opening paragraph* relatively short and include a headline.** Its purpose is to introduce the reason for the letter.

  We apologize for the error
  Thank you for your letter of July 16 calling our attention to our mistake in filling your order.

- **Support the *opening paragraph* with one or more paragraphs.**

  Your valuables are safer than your neighbors'
  In its annual report, the XYZ Fire Insurance Company stated that our community has suffered the least fire damage of any district in the state. Of course, this means that your valuables are safer than those of your neighbors. But more important is the fact that your family is well protected from the dangers of ravaging fire.

- **Make the *final paragraph* short.** It serves as a summation, request, suggestion, or look to the future.

  We're delighted to help you
  If you'd like to take advantage of this order, please sign the enclosed form and return it to me in the enclosed envelope.

Complimentary closing

Place the complimentary closing two lines below the last line of the body. Capitalize only the first letter of the first word and end with a comma.

Formal: Yours truly, Very truly yours, Yours very truly, Respectfully, Respectfully yours,

Informal: Sincerely, Sincerely yours, Cordially, Cordially yours,

Personal: Best wishes, As always, Regards, Kindest regards,

Signature line

You can prepare the personal signature in any of the following ways. Leave four to five line spaces for your signature, and don't forget to sign it.

Very truly yours,

Jon Dough

Jon Dough

Very truly yours,

Jon Dough

Jon Dough, Process Manager

Very truly yours,

JON, INC.

Jon Dough

Jon Dough, Process Manager

Very truly yours,

Jon Dough

Jon Dough
Process Manager

Reference initials

Use reference initials to identify the typist if someone other than the writer prepares the letter. Place the initials at the left margin, two lines below the signature line. You can use any of the following styles (where LZ is the typist).

ASmith/lz

AS:lz

AS/LZ

lz

If you're writing your own letter, forget initials.

Enclosure notation

When you're enclosing anything in the envelope, include an enclosure notation. Place the enclosure notation on the line directly below the reference initials. Consider any of the following styles:

Enclosure
Attachments: 3
Encls.
Enclosure:

1 Enc.
Enc. (2)
  1. Purchase Order No. 452
  2. Check No. 1671

When you're stapling or clipping something rather than enclosing it, consider using the word *Attachment* instead of *Enclosure*.

Copy notation

When sending a copy of the letter to a third person, make a notation directly below the enclosure notation (or reference initials). The *cc* notation is a holdover from the olden days when people made carbon copies. Another option is *pc* for photocopy. If you don't want the addressee to know you're sending a copy to a third party, use *bc* for blind copy.

Use the bc notation sparingly because it's a clear indication that you're going behind someone's back. (The stock market won't crash. Governments won't fall. And the world won't shake. But it may be pretty embarrassing.) Place the bc notation on the *office copy* and the *third-party copy only,* otherwise it's no secret from the addressee. You can use any of these styles.

pc: Ira Sharfin   bc: Ira Sharfin
CC Ira Sharfin   Copy to: Ira Sharfin

Postscript

It's appropriate (and sometimes advisable) to use a postscript for emphasis. Place it two lines below your last notation. Use postscripts sparingly because you don't want the words to appear as an afterthought, indicating a lack of organization.

New style guides are saying you shouldn't include the *P.S.* notation. However, I still see the notation used. I use it.

What's Hot and What's Not in Letter Styles

Choosing a letter style is a big step in delivering your message because it may be an indication of how "fashionable" your company is. Regardless of the style you use, center the letter vertically and horizontally so that the margins form an imaginary frame around the text. Table 8-5 gives examples of the popular styles.

Table 8-5	Letter Styles	
Letter Style	*Characteristics and Comments*	*Fashion Trend*
Full block (Example 8-2)	Everything starts at the left margin. Efficient, businesslike, and very popular. Critics feel it looks somewhat crowded.	Chic. Right off the fashion runway.
Block or Modified Block (Example 8-3)	The date and complimentary closing are slightly to the right of center. Everything else starts at the left margin. Involves setting one tab. Very traditional and very popular.	Sophisticated and always in good taste.
Semiblock (Example 8-4)	Identical to block, except the first line of each paragraph is indented. Involves setting two tabs. Somewhat of an old-fashioned look.	Slightly dated but still functional.
Simplified (Example 8-5)	Salutation and complimentary closing are omitted. Everything else is in full block. Triple space above and below the body of the letter. Critics say it lacks warmth and is too unconventional.	Futuristic.

The style you choose for a letter may be dictated by your company or may be your choice. If the decision is yours, here are some guidelines to consider:

- ✔ **Pay close attention to the letterhead.** Some companies have letterhead that complements one style over another.

- ✔ **Know the image your company is trying to project.** A traditional letter style (full block, block, or semiblock) projects the image of a solid, well-established company. An informal style (simplified) may work well for younger people but may appear unconventional to the mature set.

- ✔ **If you want to keep up with the latest fashion, follow the trends.** This applies to letter writing as well as clothing. Pay attention to what others are doing. With the steady stream of letters you get each day, that should be easy.

Date

Addressee
Street Address
City, State Zip

Salutation:

Subject: Full Block Letter Style

Characteristics

The full block letter is quickly becoming the style of choice in
the modern office. It's a very efficient style and is the easiest to
prepare. Why? _Everything starts at the left margin._ There's no
need to set tabs or wonder where to put the date and
complimentary closing.

Benefits

We live in a fast-paced society and people are constantly trying
to simplify their cluttered lives. This style will—over
time—increase the flow of paperwork and save time.

Complimentary closing,

Name of Sender

> Everything starts
> at the left margin.

Example 8-2:
Full block is
a dapper
look.

Date

Addressee
Street Address
City, State Zip

Salutation:

Subject: Block or Modified Block

The date and complimentary closing are to the right of the middle.

Characteristics

The block or modified block style is quite similar to the full block style. The key differences are that the date and complimentary closing are slightly to the right of center. Everything else is flush with the left margin.

Benefits

This letter style has traditionally been the most commonly used of all letter styles. Therefore, it's the one most people are comfortable with.

Complimentary closing,

Name of Sender

Example 8-3:
Block is a
refined look.

Date

Addressee
Street Address
City, State Zip

Salutation: Parargraphs are indented.

Subject: Semiblock Style

Characteristics

    The semiblock style is quite similar to the block or modified
block style. The key difference is that the first line of each
paragraph is indented one tab stop. Therefore, you need to set
two tabs: one for the paragraph indent and one for the date and
complimentary closing.

Recognition

    This familiar-looking style is one people are comfortable
with. However, it is currently playing second fiddle to the full
block or modified block styles.

Complimentary closing,

Name of Sender

Example 8-4:
Seimblock is
a dated look.

Date

Addressee
Street Address
City, State Zip

> No salutation. Subject line in all caps.

SIMPLIFIED STYLE

> Three lines of space above and below the subject line.

Characteristics

The simplified letter is quite streamlined. Here are some characteristics to remember if you use this letter style:

- Eliminate the salutation and complimentary closing.
- Eliminate the *Subject:* or *Re:* notation. Just type the subject.
- Type the SUBJECT LINE and NAME OF SENDER in all caps.

Recognition

This letter style isn't commonly used. It is, however, expected to become more popular because it's the least time-consuming of all the letter styles.

> No complimentary closing.

NAME OF SENDER

Example 8-5:
Simplified is
a radical
look.

Question: Example 8-6 is a thank you letter following an interview. Can you see what's wrong with this format?

Answer: The date is in the full block position. The complimentary closing and signature line are in the block or modified block position. Don't mix metaphors and *don't mix letter styles*.

August 15, XXXX

Ms. Debra Hahn
Bailey & Kenneth Associates
11 Colorado Street
El Dorado, AR 71730

> The date is in the full block postion.

Dear Ms. Hahn:

Subject: **I'm eager to join your team**

I very much enjoyed meeting with you this afternoon to discuss the possibility of my becoming your new Manager of Desktop Publishing. I'm sure that the combination of my experience and your needs would give me the chance to make an immediate contribution.

Next step

I look forward to returning for my next interview with the hope of sharing my enthusiasm and talents with Bailey & Kenneth Associates.

Sincerely yours,

> The closing is in the block or semiblock position.

Dale Phelps

Example 8-6:
Mixed styles
are taboo.

Your Letter Spilleth Over

Some people feel compelled to get all the information on one page. Don't try to cram everything on to one page if it means narrowing the margins, decreasing the font size, or compromising the visual impact of your letter in any way. There's nothing wrong with an occasional two-, three-, or four-page letter or memo when it's absolutely necessary. *Absolutely necessary* means your letter addresses only one topic and is streamlined as much as possible. For more information about streamlining text, check out Chapter 6.

Here are some tips for multipage letters.

- ✔ When a letter is longer than one page, use letterhead for the first page and *matching plain paper* for the ensuing pages.

- ✔ When you divide a paragraph between pages, leave at least two lines on the current page and carry at least two lines to the next page. If you can't do that, don't divide the paragraph.

- ✔ Never divide a three-line paragraph. And never carry a complimentary closing over to a second page without having at least two lines above it.

Following are examples of how to head the second page of a two-page letter.

Example: Full Block Second Page

> Ms. Leah Zimmerman
> Page 2
> October 2, XXXX

Example: Modified Block or Semiblock Block Second Page

> Ms. Leah Zimmerman   Page 2   October 2, XXXX

Magical merging

Mail merge is one of the nifty things about word processing. It lets you create a letter once and send as many personalized copies as you want. Each copy can have an original name, address, salutation, and whatever variables you designate. You can also create personalized envelopes. Whether you're running a large-scale sales campaign, inviting people to a seminar, or doing a massive job search, mail merge can save you hours. Check the user manual of your word processing program to get the scoop or consult the ...*For Dummies* book that covers your program.

Letters That Sizzle

After you know the *mechanics* of letter writing, you can dive into the *art* of letter writing. You'll be called upon to write a variety of letters in the course of your career. This section highlights some special letter-writing situations like giving recommendations, responding to a request to be a guest speaker, notifying an also-ran, extending and denying credit, and soothing an irate customer.

You'll also be called upon to write *application letters* and *sales letters*. I explore each of these topics in Part IV. Check out Chapter 16 for application letters and Chapter 17 for sales letters.

Getting personal

The most appreciated letters are those that extend a personal wish. Look for occasions to preserve your humanity in this dog-eat-dog world—whether you're offering congratulations (see Example 8-7), sending an apology (see Example 8-8), expressing get well wishes (see Example 8-9), or expressing sympathy (see Example 8-10).

These tips help you walk the fine line between being too "touchy-feely" and too businesslike.

- ✔ Generate the letter on your computer, hand-write it, or a use combination of the two (perhaps a computer-generated letter with a handwritten postscript). You may also use e-mail for some situations. Use your judgment based on the situation and how well you know the reader.

- ✔ Don't use letterhead; it's too businesslike. Instead, use plain white paper or your personal note paper.

- ✔ Write promptly and sincerely.

- ✔ Be brief. Even a one liner is a personal touch: "Pat, I'm very proud of you."

Congratulations Bill! I can't think of anyone more qualified to assume the position of district manager.

You've been a wonderfull mentor, I'll certainly miss working with you on a day-to-day basis. But I know we will continue to stay in close touch.

Best wishes,
Rowena

Example 8-7:
Offering congratulations.

From the Desk of Pete Moss

Arthur,

This is one of the most difficult letters I've ever had to write because I know that I've hurt you.

My remark this morning was unforgivable, and I'm truly sorry. I hope you will show me the mercy I seem to be lacking. Never again will I think, much less make, a remark like that.

I hope that you can find it in your heart to forgive me.

Pete

Example 8-8:
Handwritten note of apology.

Dear Stan,

On behalf of everyone at Tandem Access Systems, I'd like to wish you a speedy recovery from your emergency surgery. We are all relieved to hear that the surgery was a success and that you're resting comfortably.

As far as work is concerned, please don't give it a second thought. Concentrate on getting well. Janice and Raoul will pitch in to handle some of your responsibilities.

We miss your friendly smile and look forward to your return. Please let us know when you're feeling up to having visitors.

Best wishes,

Jane

Example 8-9:
Expressing
get well
wishes to a
colleague.

From the Desk of Donna Randall

Dear Nel,

Those we love never leave us; they live forever in our hearts.
I hope that the wonderful memories of your mother will be of
comfort to you during this very difficult time.

I'll call you in a few days to see how I can be of help.

Sincerely,

Donna

Example 8-10:
Letter of
sympathy to
a colleague.

Giving recommendations

If you're asked to give a written recommendation for someone who's left your company, be very careful. In today's litigious society, people bring suits at the drop of a hat. Some companies have strict policies about this and don't allow employees to give out more than start and end dates of employment.

When you're asked to write a letter of recommendation for a friend or colleague, here are some guidelines:

✔ If the recommendation is positive, talk enthusiastically about the person's qualifications. Example 8-11 is a strong recommendation for membership to a club.

✔ If the recommendation isn't positive, consider being noncommittal, rather than negative. Example 8-12 is a lukewarm response. It speaks for itself.

Dear Mr. Haskill:

Susan Warren would be a welcome addition to the club

It is my pleasure to recommend Susan Warren for membership in Bergstein's Executives Club. It's my privilege to have known Susan for 15 years and to have watched her career flourish. The attached biography details Susan's numerous accomplishments, as well as her membership and contributions to several non-profit institutions.

Susan has made an outstanding contribution to the field of nursing and has a reputation for being a person who cares about her community and *does something about it*.

Susan is a wife and mother of two. She has managed to juggle caring for her family and a distinguished nursing career with an expert sense of balance. I know of no one who would make a more suitable member of Bergstein's Executives Club. I hope the membership will look kindly on this proposal.

Let's facilitate this

Please feel free to contact me if I can add anything to facilitate Susan's membership.

Cordially,

Bob Nawrocki

Enthusiasm shines in the headlines.

Example 8-11:
Herculean
recommend-
ation

Dear Mr. Haskill:

I'm acquainted with Susan Warren

In response to your request, I am addressing this letter to the Membership Committee of Bergstein's Executives Club on behalf of my colleague, Susan Warren, who is very anxious to join. I have known Susan professionally for 15 years and have enclosed a copy of her biography for your review.

Next step

If any members of your committee would like to discuss Ms. Warren's qualifications and her suitability for membership, they should feel free to contact me.

Sincerely,

Bob Nawrocki

Noncommittal headlines show a lukewarm response.

Example 8-12:
Indifferent
response.

Responding to a request to be a guest speaker

When you're invited to speak before a group (either at your company or outside), it's a great honor and an indication of the respect the requester has for you. Chapter 19 has some great tips on preparing a speech, and Chapter 11 has pointers for preparing various types of presentations.

✔ If you're accepting the invitation, express your delight immediately. Notice that Example 8-13 restates the date, place, time, and topic. If the topic isn't yet determined, the tips in Chapter 19 can help you decide your subject matter.

✔ If you're declining the invitation, sequence your writing for bad news. Example 8-14 shows an example of handling a rejection tactfully. Take a look at Chapter 3 for ways to let the reader down gently.

April 20, XXXX

Mr. Frank Thompson
Barnegat Marina
103 Constitution Avenue
Cambridge, MA 02139

> Acceptance is obvious from the headlines.

Dear Mr. Thompson:

Subject: Your kind invitation to speak at the Barnegat's Marina

It's our pleasure to accept
It's our pleasure to accept your invitation to speak at the dinner meeting of Barnegat's Marina on July 8, XXXX, at eight o'clock to tell about our experiences diving off the coast of Italy. After all those harrowing weeks, there were times we thought it was unlikely that we'd ever have the opportunity to relate our experiences to anyone. So we're especially grateful to you for providing such a sympathetic audience.

The hotel sounds perfect
Yes, the Constitution Hotel would be a wonderful place for you to arrange our lodging. We'll plan to arrive at the hotel about five, which will give us ample time to freshen up.

Next step
Please send directions telling us how to get to the hotel at least a month in advance because we'll be out of town most of June. We look forward to seeing you there.

Sincerely,

Phyllis and Ted Bially

Example 8-13:
Yes we can!

April 20, XXXX

Mr. Frank Thompson
Barnegat Marina
103 Constitution Avenue
Cambridge, MA 02139

Dear Mr. Thompson:

Subject: Your kind invitation to speak at the Barnegat's Marina

Thank you for the invitation
Your invitation to speak at the dinner meeting of the Barnegat's
Marina on July 8, XXXX, at eight o'clock is quite an honor.
We're very proud to have been asked.

Our sincere regrets
Unfortunately, we're committed to teaching diving classes in
Turkey during the entire month of July. After all those harrowing
weeks diving off the coast of Italy, there were times we thought it
was unlikely that we'd ever have the chance to relate our
experiences to anyone, and we certainly would welcome the
opportunity.

Please ask again
Would it be possible for us visit with your group later this year or
next year? We'd enjoy it.

Sincerely,

Phyllis and Ted Bially

Example 8-14:
May we have
a rain check?

Notifying an also-ran

Letting someone know he didn't get a job or assignment is never easy. No one
likes to be the bearer of bad news. Notice how tactfully Mr. McCusker handles
this in Example 8-15. Take a peek at Chapter 3; it offers great tips for sequencing for bad news. Here are some tips specific to this type of situation:

✔ Stress the candidate's strengths.

✔ Give a palatable reason why he wasn't selected.

✔ End with hope for future possibilities.

Don't send the also-ran the disappointing news until your No. 1 choice has accepted. If your No. 1 choice doesn't accept, the also-ran may become No. 1.

August 20, XXXX

Ms. Valerie Taylor
Nashua & Associates
One Darth Parkway
Ludlow, CO 80304

> Cushioning bad news between a positive opening and closing.

Dear Ms. Taylor:

You were very impressive
Our entire team was most impressed with the professionalism of your group during both of your presentations.

It was a difficult decision
As I mentioned to you on the phone yesterday, the Vice President has selected SSK, Inc. to handle the account. This was a very difficult decision to make because you are all highly qualified candidates. The decision finally came down to the fact that SSK, Inc. has had a lot more experience in the telecommunications marketplace. We all know what an outstanding job you would have done and appreciate all the time and creativity that went into your presentation.

We look forward to other opportunities
Please thank your entire team and commend them on a job well done. When we have another project that matches your expertise more closely, we will certainly call you in. I offer my personal best wishes for your continued success.

Sincerely,

Richard McCusker
Director of Public Relations

Example 8-15:
Notifying an
also-ran.

Extending or denying credit

Credit has become a way of life. It's estimated that nearly 90 percent of all the buying and selling in the United States is done on a credit basis. Charge accounts flourish; businesses burgeon; and letter carriers collapses under weight of the end-of-the-month billings that greet customers each month.

✔ If you're honoring someone's credit application, that's a good news letter and easy to write. Example 8-16 is a sample of a letter extending credit.

March 20, XXXX

Ms. Dawne Roberts
103 Green Bread Way
Staten Island, NY 10305

Dear Ms. Roberts:

Welcome!
We're pleased to present your new Jill & Brian's Credit Card—your entree to a world of special privileges reserved exclusively for you. You can be sure that our sales associates will do everything possible to make shopping at Jill & Brian's a pleasant and satisfying experience. If you have any special needs—just ask!

Please attend our private showing
Starting now, you'll be invited to attend private sales and enjoy savings not advertised to the general public. And you'll be notified by mail in advance of selected sales at all of your favorite Jill & Brian's locations.

We look forward to seeing you at Jill & Brian's, where the exciting world of shopping awaits you!

You Can Count on Me,

Arthur N. Roy
Credit Manager

P.S. If you have any questions about your account or would like to apply for a higher credit limit, please call me at Ext. 440.

Example 8-16:
Welcome
aboard.

✔ If you're denying credit, do it in such a way that you retain the customer's goodwill. Example 8-17 handles that tactfully. Take a look at Chapter 3 for tactful ways to let the reader down gently and keep him coming back for more. Here are a few hints specific to credit applications:

- Thank the customer for his loyalty.

- State the reason for denying the credit.

- Express your desire to revisit the credit issue when the reason for the denial no longer exists.

August 12, XXXX

> Notice that the only headline is a positive one.

Mr. Otto Mann
7 Inland Road
Suffern, NY 10901

Dear Mr. Mann:

Thank you for your credit request with Bronx Brothers; it is a compliment to us. Your references all agreed that you've been cooperative and are always willing to discuss the details of your account.

Our experience has taught us that next to credit references, the most important aspect affecting business success is cash on hand. This is especially true for new businesses such as yours. We always encourage our customers to maintain a cash balance that allows them to cover salaries and expenses for at least six months. We are certain that within the next few months you'll be able to increase your average cash balance.

We look forward to serving your needs
We will be more than happy to review your credit request in the near future and look forward to having you join our family of satisfied customers.

Sincerely,

Kathy Wertalik
Credit Manager

Example 8-17:
Sorry,
perhaps at
another time.

Soothing an irate customer

Satisfied and loyal customers are the backbone of any business. A study by Bain & Company, a Boston-based consulting firm, found that: "If a small to midsize company were to increase its customer retention by 5 percent, its profits would double in 10 years." Do everything you can to keep your customers happy and coming back for more. Example 8-18 shows a formal letter of apology.

The customer is always right!

October 12, XXXX

Ms. Cyn Hawkins
Jackson & Associates
443 Sudbury Street
Kadesh, LA 71454

Dear Ms. Hawkins:

My sincere apology
I'm very sorry to learn of the problem you've had with our salesman, Frank N. Stein. All our salespeople attend a one-week training program because we expect them to be honest with and courteous to all our customers. Please accept my apology.

We've taken corrective action
You can be assured that Mr. Stein will not call on you again. Ms. Hawkins, your business is important to us. We're anxious to continue the productive relationship we've enjoyed for so many years.

Next step
I'll call you personally next week to see how we can continue to offer you the fine service you've received over the last several years.

Sincerely,

Jurgen Lehnert
Manager of Customer Service

Example 8-18:
We're so
sorry.

Memorable Memos

Although e-mail has replaced many of the memos that were once the mainstay of the business community, memos are still alive and kicking and living in the business world. What's the difference between letters and memos? Primarily form and methods of delivery.

Even though memos may appear more casual than letters, they still require you to answer the questions on the Start Up Sheet. Check out the Start Up Sheet on the Cheat Sheet in the front of the book.

Sensible styles

Memos are frequently used to transmit information, ideas, decisions, and suggestions among people in the same organization. If your company uses memos frequently, it probably has printed forms for you to use. If not, consider the following:

Date:

To:

From:

Subject:

Anyone can send a memo and use someone else's name. Although this doesn't happen often, you may want to safeguard yourself by writing your initials or signing your name next to your name on the From: line or on the bottom of the memo. After you get people used to seeing your "mark" on the memos you send, an unsigned memo from you will give people pause and may raise an eyebrow or two.

Following protocol

On the To: line, type the names of all the people to whom you're sending the memo. Each organization has its own protocol for the order in which to list the recipients. If you have an employee handbook, you may find protocol there. If not, here are a few tips:

- ✔ List people in order of ranking, from high to low. For example, the President's name would appear before the VP's.

- ✔ Who should receive a copy? Err on the side of copying everyone who may be offended if they don't receive a copy.

Memo madness

From an actual memo written by a VIP at a major corporation (both shall remain anonymous):

"As of tomorrow, employees will only be able to access the building using individual security cards. Pictures will be taken next Wednesday and employees will receive their cards in two weeks."

Limit each memo to one subject only. If you need to cover two or more subjects, send two or more memos. Here are a few examples of memos in action: Example 8-19 squelches a rumor, and Example 8-20 details a sexual harassment policy.

Before you send any letter or memo, be sure to go through the Editing Checklist featured on the Cheat Sheet in the front of this book. You don't want to be the patron saint of bunglers.

Date: October 31, XXXX
To: All Staff Members
From: Bob Littlehale, President
Re: Company Merger

Yes, we're merging

If rumors are the "information virus," here's the antidote. I'd like to set the record straight. Perhaps you have heard rumors to the effect that the company is going out of business, is being sold, or is merging. Well, I am pleased to tell you that the latter is true. We are merging.

Effective date: November 1

Effective January 1, we will become a wholly owned subsidiary of ACME, Inc., of Dallas, Texas. Principals at ACME have asked me to let you know of their sincere intentions to continue operating this division on a autonomous basis and to **retain all the employees** who are currently on the payroll.

Come and hear the details

Several people from ACME will be on hand to personally answer any questions. I'm sure that you'll approve of the merger wholeheartedly once you understand what we all have to gain.

Where: **Auditorium**
Date: **Monday, November 8, XXXX**
Time: **12:00 through 1:30 (Lunch will be served.)**

Example 8-19:
Squelching a
rumor.

Date: December 20, XXXX
To: All Employees
From: Moe Lester, Director of Human Resources
Re: Continental's Sexual Harassment Policy

Continental has provided workplace guidelines for preventing and addressing sexual harassment. It has come to our attention recently that these guidelines need additional clarification.

What Is Sexual Harassment?

Sexual harassment at work occurs whenever unwelcome conduct—on the basis of gender—affects an employee's job. Harassment includes when anyone in authority threatens the employee with termination, demotion, or intimidation for refusing sexual advances or when anyone creates an abusive or hostile work environment or interferes with the employee's job performance through words or actions.

Sexual harassment is illegal and will not be tolerated at Continental. Further, any employee found to have committed sexual harassment will be subject to severe disciplinary action, which can include termination.

What Is a Hostile Work Environment?

A hostile work environment is created by unwelcome conduct, either verbal or physical.

- **Verbal** harassment includes: commenting on physical attributes, telling off-color jokes, using demeaning or inappropriate terms and nicknames, discussing sexual activities, ostracizing employees because of gender, and using crude or offensive language.
- **Physical** harassment includes: unnecessary touching, using suggestive gestures, and displaying sexually aggressive pictures, calendars, or photos.

Example 8-20:
Memo reiterating sexual harassment policy.

(continued)

Page 2

Complaint Procedures and Responsibilities

Supervisors are responsible for assisting in preventing sexual harassment by maintaining a productive work environment. Should a report of harassment occur in their work areas, supervisors are responsible for assisting in the investigation and resolution of the complaint.

If You've Been Victimized

An employee who feels victimized by an act of harassment should immediately report the incident to his/her immediate supervisor. If the immediate supervisor is the source of the harassment, discuss the incident(s) with the supervisor's manager or with someone in the Human Resources Department.

Strictly Confidential

All complaints will be treated with respect and confidentiality. Further, no employee will be subject to any form of retaliation or discipline for pursuing a sexual harassment complaint.

Chapter 9

Rousing Reports

This report, by its very length, defends itself against the risk of being read.

—Sir Winston Churchill

What constitutes a report? An impartial, objective, planned presentation of facts. A report should be skillfully planned and organized, logically sequenced, objective, accurate, reliable, and easy to read. Business reports fall into two categories:

✔ An *informal report* can range from a few paragraphs to several pages. Whether an informal report is written as a letter, memo, or e-mail message, it generally includes an introduction, body, and conclusion recommendations.

✔ A *formal report* is generally lengthy. It may include: title page, executive summary, table of contents, list of figures and tables, list of abbreviations and symbols, body, conclusions or recommendations, appendixes, index, and more.

Before you write a report—informal or formal—be certain you fill out the Start Up Sheet. Chapter 2 gives you the nitty-gritty on how to use the Start Up Sheet. A copy is also included on the Cheat Sheet in the front of this book.

When you're the writer of a report, the buck stops with you. While you have the responsibility of writing an accurate and thorough document, you also have a great opportunity to make your writing as effective and useful as possible.

Making Your Reports Measure Up

Participants in my workshops often ask: "How long is a typical report?" I generally answer: "How big is the typical person?" There's no such thing as typical. People range from inches (infants) to many, many feet (basketball players). And reports range from less than one page to thousands of pages.

A report should be long enough to be *thorough* and short enough to be *concise*. To ensure that your report is thorough, cover all the key issues. To ensure sure that it's concise, KISS it (keep it short and simple). To make sure your report is sealed with a KISS, check out Chapter 6.

Sequencing to Meet the Needs of Your Audience

Most books tell you to put the most important information first in a report. While that may often be a good strategy, you must be sensitive to how your reader may react. Pay close attention to Question 5 on your Start Up Sheet, "What's my reader's attitude toward the topic?"

With sensitivity to your reader's reaction, sequence the report for maximum impact. For everything you ever wanted know about sequencing, I recommend that you check out Chapter 3. Here are some highlights:

- ✔ **For a responsive or neutral reader,** put the key issue at the beginning of the report.
- ✔ **For an unresponsive reader,** cushion the key issue between *buffers*—a positive opening and closing.

Bearing good news

When you're reporting good news, use the direct approach and put the key issue at the beginning. Why hide it? For example, say you're writing a report on improving inventory control methods and you find affordable software that will expedite your processes. Why not begin your report with that good news and make your case in the following order:

- ✔ Recommendation(s)
- ✔ Findings

- ✔ Purpose
- ✔ Background (if necessary)
- ✔ Conclusion

Don't shoot the messenger

When you're dealing with unresponsive readers who are resistant to your views, cushion the blow by presenting your case first. For example, if you just investigated a problem your company is having and your findings lead you to conclude that the company must purchase a half-million-dollar piece of equipment to solve the problem, try presenting the bad news in this order:

- ✔ Purpose
- ✔ Background
- ✔ Findings (cushioned)
- ✔ Recommendation
- ✔ Conclusion

Notice that the information in both versions is the same; however, the sequencing meets the needs of the reader.

No Jacket Required: Writing Informal Reports

An *informal report* is generally intended for a single reader or small group of readers. It can range in length from a few paragraphs to a few pages. Because of their brevity, informal reports are customarily written in the form of letters, memos, or e-mail messages. Feasibility studies, investigative reports, progress reports, trip reports, seminar reports, and trouble reports all lend themselves to a casual format.

Example 9-1 is an informal report written in the form of a memo. It offers good news and starts with a Recommendations section. (Check out Chapter 8 for more on preparing memos.)

SHERYL SAYS You probably notice that Example 9-1 doesn't have a problem statement or background information. That's because the readers are familiar with both. The report would be accompanied by a transmittal letter giving a problem statement and necessary background.

Date: June 30, XXXX
To: Walter James, COO
From: Committee to Address Parking Problems
Subject: Three Possible Solutions to the Problem of Overcrowding in the Parking Lots

> Good news that starts with the solution.

Recommendation
The committee recommends the following solutions in the order in which they're presented. We strongly feel that Solution 1: *Flexing morning and evening hours is the best choice.*

Solution 1: Flexing morning and evening hours
The 450 non-management employees can be divided into three groups. Each group would begin and end its shift at different times. For example:

- Group 1 may work from 7:30 through 4:30
- Group 2 may work from 8:00 through 5:00
- Group 3 may work from 8:30 through 5:30

Advantages	Disadvantages
Greatly reduces congestion during standard hours: 8:50 to 5:30.	Doesn't solve the problem of limited parking spaces.
Increases employee morale due to more flexible work hours.	May interfere with existing carpools.

Solution 2: Hire parking attendants
Hire one or two parking attendants to work—not only during morning and evening hours—but all day.

Advantages	Disadvantages
Keeps traffic flowing in and out of the lots.	Doesn't solve the problem of limited parking spaces.
Eliminates illegal parking and blocked cars.	The cost factor.
Attendants can recommend alternative parking places when the lots are full.	

> Tables are a great way to display advantages and disadvantages.

Solution 3: Encourage carpools
A final alternative is to encourage employees to form carpools.

Advantages	Disadvantages
Solves the problem of limited parking spaces.	Cuts down on number of people willing to work overtime.
Eliminates congestion during rush hours.	
Saves on energy consumption.	Arranging carpools requires much time and effort.

Example 9-1: Informal report to a responsive reader in the form of a memo.

Example 9-2 demonstrates an informal report. This is going to cost the company a lot of money so the reader may be unresponsive. The author needs to make a strong case and starts with "Background."

Subject: Bring the *Successful Money Management* seminar in-house.

Background
I was selected to attend the *Successful Money Management* seminar on April 17, XXXX from 9 to 5 at the Gateway Hotel in order to evaluate whether this seminar is suitable to bring in-house.

The Seminar's Structure
The seminar was divided into two sections:

> *Section 1:*
> Foundation for Financial Independence
> Making Your Dollars Work for You
> Money Markets, Stocks & Bonds, Balanced Funds, and
> Limited Partnerships
> College Funding

For an unresponsive reader, the writer "sells" the seminar and doesn't mention money.

> *Section 2:*
> Tangible Assets
> Retirement Planning
> Risk Management

Why I Recommend It
I found the seminar extremely valuable. The seminar leader provided us with real-world examples that even the novice investor can relate to. The atmosphere was relaxed with a lot of interaction, and we were given plenty of opportunity to discuss individual situations.

Next Step
Alex Stark, the company president, would be happy to tailor the seminar for our needs, and she looks forward to hearing from you. I put a seminar brochure and one of Ms. Stark's business cards in your mailbox. Please give her a call.

Example 9-2:
Informal report to an unresponsive reader.

Example 9-3 is an actual informal report that describes a business trip. This type of humor is probably most appropriate when you plan to share the report only with your immediate coworkers.

Presentation 1

There was one memorable "first" at this trade show. We actually had someone bleed during one of my presentations. It's a little bit of a long story, but here goes:

When Lorene and I first entered the demo room, I noticed a brass chandelier hanging in the middle of the room. It seemed to be about $5^1/2$ feet above the floor. I noticed that it had brass spikes protruding from all sides and commented to Lorene that it presented quite a hazard. I thought someone might walk into it. (Lorene, who's under 5 feet tall, walked under it and didn't think it was a problem.)

Toward the end of the first presentation, a guy at the back of the room got up suddenly and bonked his head against the chandelier. As he staggered, I asked if he was all right. He said "I think so . . ." and went over to the mirror to examine himself. Next thing I know, this guy's coming back to his seat with a bloody tissue pressed to his forehead. I asked if he needed a bandage (or a lawyer). Once again he replied in the negative and took his seat.

Presentation 2

Ten minutes later I started my second presentation. Suddenly, into the room burst three men: 1 hotel employee; 1 law enforcement-type; and 1 guy who looked like Dr. Quincy, complete with elbow-length rubber gloves, white lab coat, and medical bag.

I had no idea why they were there, but "the show must go on," so I continued my presentation. The three guys look around the room, didn't see what they were looking for and held a mini-conference in our doorway while I continued talking about quote generation or some other nonsense.

Suddenly, the police officer-like guy says, "Have you checked the bathroom?" and off to the can rushes the Quincy-like guy. Two minutes later, Dr. Quincy emerges from the necessarium and announces, "There is no BODY in the bathroom."

I think this is where my presentation started to falter slightly. I mean, I don't mind people sleeping during my talks, and even a little blood-letting is okay, but I definitely draw the line at having corpses during my demo.

Example 9-3:
Informal
report of a
business
trip.

Top Hat and Tails: Writing Formal Reports

A *formal report* is often the culmination of a project that may have taken a team of people weeks, months, or even years to complete. (For more information on collaborative writing, check out Chapter 20.) Formal reports can address a wide range of issues such as new developments in a field, new product feasibility studies, service expansions, periodic reviews, and the like.

The term *formal* doesn't imply that the tone should be stuffy. It merely means that the report includes supplemental parts, as the following section explains. You find details on tone in Chapter 6.

You generally divide formal reports into three main parts that can include any or all of the following subitems in each part:

1. **Front Matter.** You can precede the front matter with a letter of transmittal (see the "Letter of transmittal" section). Number the pages in the front matter with lowercase Roman numerals. Front matter may include:

    - Title page
    - Abstract
    - Table of Contents
    - List of Figures
    - List of Tables
    - Preface (or Foreword)
    - List of Abbreviations and Symbols

2. **Body.** This is the meat and potatoes of the report—the substance. Number the pages in the body with Arabic numerals.

    - Executive Summary
    - Introduction
    - Text (including headings)
    - Conclusions
    - Recommendations
    - References

3. Back Matter. The back matter is everything that comes after the body. Continue numbering the body in Arabic numerals.

- Bibliography
- Appendixes
- Glossary
- Index

I present the parts of a formal report in the order in which a report is presented, not the order in which it's written. You most often write the body first, then the back matter, then the front matter. The very last thing you write is the table of contents.

It's what up front that counts

In some cases, the front matter is all the reader looks at. For example, a manager (who wants the big picture) will read the executive summary. She may refer to the table of contents to find a few details.

Letter of transmittal

A letter of transmittal isn't mandatory; it's basically a cover letter. I recommend including one because it gives your report a professional look. A letter of transmittal identifies what you're sending and why you're sending it. Use letterhead and follow all the guidelines of effective letter writing. (Check out Chapter 10 for a sample letter of transmittal.)

You often transmit reports as e-mail attachments. A short e-mail message can work as a transmittal message. In the e-mail message, be sure to mention what you're sending the reader and whom they should contact with questions.

Title page

The *title page,* shown in Example 9-4, identifies the report, the completion date, the author, and the recipient. Although this page is not numbered, it's considered page i (small Roman numeral 1). The back of the title page, also unnumbered, is page ii.

Procedures for Preparing an Environmental Impact Study

Prepared by:
The Environmental Impact Committee

Presented to:
Norman Conquest
Champion Associates
November 12, XXXX

Some folks put the "Presented to" information at the bottom of the page.

Example 9-4: Title page.

Abstract

An *abstract* is a condensed version of a report, generally between 200 and 300 words long. Some companies distribute copies of the abstract to readers who can then decide if they want to read the entire report. The following table mentions some of the things you should and shouldn't include in an abstract.

Include	Don't Include
Subject of the report	Background of the study
Scope of the study	Details of the methods
Purpose of the study	Administrative details such as funding, those who participated in the study, and so on
Methods used	Figures or tables (don't even make reference to them)
Results	Anything that doesn't appear in the original report
Recommendations	

An abstract is similar to an executive summary. The main difference is that an abstract is front matter and may stand alone. An executive summary is part of the body and can't stand alone; it must always be part of the report. It's not likely that you'd ever use an abstract and executive summary in the same report (more about exective summaries later in this chapter).

Table of contents

Example 9-5 is a table of contents that lists all the headings, subheads, and corresponding page numbers. It helps the reader find sections of information quickly.

Use your word-processing software to create a table of contents with multiple levels of entries. Check your user manual or online help to find out how.

List of figures and list of tables

The *list of figures* and *list of tables* are (surprise!) separate listings of all the figures and tables in the document. If the lists are short, they may appear on one page. If not, two or more. The numbering continues with lowercase Roman numerals following the table of contents. Take a look at Example 9-6 for the List of Figures and Tables.

Preface

Including a *preface* in your report is optional. The decision is generally dictated by corporate style. You may use a preface to

✔ Announce the purpose, background, or scope of the report.

✔ Acknowledge the people who participated in the project or helped prepare the report.

If you don't use a preface, put descriptions of your purpose, background, and scope—as well as acknowledgements—in the introduction.

Table of Contents

Leaders help to connect the sections with the page numbers.

Example 9-5:
Table of
Contents.

Example 9-6:
Lists
of Figures
and Tables.

List of abbreviations and symbols

A *list of abbreviations and symbols* helps the reader who may not be familiar with those included in the report. If the lists are short, they may appear on one page. If not, use separate pages. Example 9-7 shows a List of Abbreviations, and you structure a List of Symbols the same way.

List of Abbreviations

ADP: Automatic Data Processing

AIS: Automated Information Systems

ANSI: American National Standards Institution

Example 9-7:
List of
Abbreviations.

Body beautiful

In the body you discuss your methods and procedures, tell how you arrived at your results, and offer conclusions and recommendations.

Executive summary

The *executive summary* is the first section of the body of a report and perhaps the most important. It's a one- or two-page summary of the key issues: purpose, findings, and recommendations. It's for people who want a very condensed version of the report and don't have the time or interest to read the details. Example 9-8 shows a sample executive summary that condenses a 28-page report. The table in the executive summary was boiled down from 13 pages.

Participants in my workshop are often shocked when I mention putting a table or other visual in an executive summary. Why not in an executive summary? Put a table or visual wherever it makes sense.

You can't write an executive summary until you've written the entire report—so don't even try. Think about it. Can you write a book report before you read the book? (I'm not talking about cheating and copying the flyleaf as I did for my junior high school book reports.)

Body text

You expect the *body text* to be long because it's the "meat and potatoes" of the report. It's where you state all the information to support its purpose.

The body text is where following the Six Steps really pay off.

In Step 1, you fill out the Start Up Sheet and understand your audience, purpose, and key issue(s).

In Step 2, you write headlines and sequence them for maximum impact. Be sure to pump up the headlines. Why limit a headline to "Conclusion" when you can give the reader a snapshot of the conclusion: "Conclusion: Sales will rise 25% in Q3."

Now, writing the draft in Step 3 should be a snap—much like filling in the blanks. Create more headings or subheads if you need to and fill in those blanks.

Executive Summary

Introduction: A Changing Economic Picture

In the days of single-purpose software, it was perceived that a product wouldn't be around for very long, so people didn't worry about incremental costs. The economic picture has changed dramatically over the last several years as software has become more complex. Companies can't risk infrastructure instability, so they are now looking at long-term software investments. Companies now seek out enterprise-wide software solutions to integrate all customer-centric activities. This realization has spawned one of the most flourishing markets in all of commerce—the service provider. And with it has grown the total cost of ownership (TCO).

Cost Is Not Just the Sticker Price

When you think of the cost of a product, you rarely consider the incremental costs. For example, if you purchase a car, you typically

Example 9-8: Executive summary.

Cost Component	What the Component Involves	Can the TCO be Reduced?
Implementation	Three factors that affect this component are: out-of-the-box functionality, degree of enterprise—component integration (native vs. API), and ability to perform incremental implementations.	Yes
Deployment	The cost of distributing the application tousers in a diverse hardware environment. Some of the challenges companies face are: having different types of computing platforms; encountering slow response time; and not all users having state-of-the-art equipment on their desktops.	Yes

Holding up the rear

The *back matter* is the final section of the report that includes additional information the reader finds useful.

Bibliography

A *bibliography* is an alphabetical listing of the all written sources you consulted to prepare the report. Example 9-9 shows a bibliography, which is part of the back matter section of a report.

 Bibliographies are tricky to write. Many wonderful bibliographic resources are available—check out your local bookstore for the most up-to-date guides. One of my favorites is (written in bibliographic style):

Brusaw, Charles T., Gerald J. Alred, Oliu, Walter E. *Handbook of Technical Writing*, Fourth Edition. New York: St. Martin's Press, 1993.

Appendixes

A report can have several *appendixes* (or appendices), which supplement the material in the body of the text. Each appendix begins on a right-hand (or recto) page. An appendix may include any or all of these:

> ✔ Long charts that would take up too much room in the body of the report
>
> ✔ Supplementary graphs, tables, or figures
>
> ✔ Text of interviews
>
> ✔ Relevant correspondence
>
> ✔ Questionnaires
>
> ✔ Any other data that adds to the depth of information for the reader

Glossary

Include a glossary—list of defined terms—only if your report contains many words and expressions the reader won't understand. Arrange the terms alphabetically and start each entry on a new line, as shown in Example 9-10.

Bibliography

"Aristotle." *Webster's New Biographical Dictionary*. Springfield, Mass: Merriam-Webster, Inc., 1995.

Boone, Louis E. *Quotable Business*. New York: Random House, 1992.

Covey, Stephen R. *The 7 Habits of Highly Effective People*. New York: Fireside, 1990.

Lindsell-Roberts, Sheryl. *Loony Laws & Silly Statutes* New York: Sterling Publishing 1994.

Lindsell-Roberts, Sheryl. "What's in a Name?" *Northeast Sailing Life* Jan/Feb 1997, page 15.

Williams, Bard. *Web Publishing for Teachers*. Foster City, Calif: IDG Books Worldwide, Inc. 1997.

Example 9-9:
Bibliography.

Glossary

Color separation
A process of separating full-color originals into four primary color printing groups.

Drilling
Punching holes in paper so that the paper can be inserted into a binder.

Greeking
Simulating the document using Latin or nonsense text where the actual text will appear. Greeking is used to suggest a layout.

Indicia
Mailing information required by the post office as a substitute for a stamp.

Perfect binding
The process of gluing the spine of printed material, such as in a book.

Saddle stitching
Binding that places staples through the middle of folded sheets.

Example 9-10:
Glossary.

Index

Last, but not least, is the index—an alphabetical listing of all the subjects in the report. Use your judgment as to whether your report needs an index. Put yourself in the reader's shoes and ask: "If I were reading this report, would I need more detailed information than I get from the table of contents?" If the answer is "yes," include an index. Be guided by content, not length. Use your word-processing software to create an index with multiple levels of entries. Check your user manual or online help to find out the details.

SHERYL SAYS

I wrote a report for a company in the chemical industry. Although the report was only 23 pages long, I included an index. When I put myself in the reader's shoes, I knew that I'd want to find references for specific chemicals. A table of contents doesn't get down to that level of detail.

A little-known factoid: In 1247 Hugh de St. Caro, with the help of 500 monks, compiled the first index. It was for the Bible.

The route more traveled

There are several routes reports may travel:

- ✔ **Downward from managers to support staff.** This can be a vehicle to inform the "troops" of decisions being implemented.

- ✔ **From peer to peer.** Peers prepare reports to coordinate activities or keep the lines of communications flowing.

- ✔ **From one person or committee up the management ranks.** Managers can't participate in all department activities. Reports provide them with information to make informed decisions.

- ✔ **From inside the organization to outside the organization.** This can take many forms, including reports to customers or stockholders.

As you write a report, take into account how the report will be routed. The routing your report takes affects your tone, visual design, and the technology you use to communicate your message.

Creating Reports with Visual Impact

Take a look at Examples 9-11 through 9-14 to see different ways to format the same report. You may have great visual presentation ideas of your own.

Introduction: How Attitudes Have Changed

Old Attitudes: Single-Purpose Software

Try it. Use it. If it doesn't work, throw it out. That may have been the case 10 to 12 years ago when inexpensive, single-purpose software flooded the market. When this old way of thinking was prevalent, TCO wasn't an important issue. It was perceived that a product wouldn't be around for very long, so there was no need to worry about incremental costs.

New Attitudes: Complex Software

The economic picture has changed dramatically over the last several years as software has become more complex. Gone is the do-it-yourself mentality which dictated that a company could implement a software product simply by slipping a purchased disk into a drive.

Software no longer stands alone. When a company adds or changes a software application, all of the integrated software is affected, not just the application itself. Companies are looking at long-term investments. They can't risk the instability that comes with replacing software applications frequently.

These realizations invalidated the "old attitudes" and created the need for companies to analyze the TCO of software, and to consider *all* the costs incurred during the lifetime of an application.

TCO Applied to Enterprise-Wide Software Solutions

Enterprise-wide software solutions integrate all customer-centric activities (from lead creation through customer service request processing) in an effort to improve customer acquisition, retention, and loyalty. This includes a diverse segment of application vendors, from accounting, logistics, and human resource vendors.

Example 9-11:
Plain and
simple.

Introduction: How Attitudes Have Changed

Old Attitudes: Single-Purpose Software

Try it. Use it. If it doesn't work, throw it out. That may have been the case 10 to 12 years ago when inexpensive, single-purpose software flooded the market. When this old way of thinking was prevalent, TCO wasn't an important issue. It was perceived that a product wouldn't be around for very long, so there was no need to worry about incremental costs.

New Attitudes: Complex Software

The economic picture has changed dramatically over the last several years as software has become more complex. Gone is the do-it-yourself mentality which dictated that a company could implement a software product simply by slipping a purchased disk into a drive.

Software no longer stands alone. When a company adds or changes a software application, all of the integrated software is affected, not just the application itself. Companies are looking at long-term investments. They can't risk the instability that comes with replacing software applications frequently.

These realizations invalidated the "old attitudes" and created the need for companies to analyze the TCO of software, and to consider *all* the costs incurred during the lifetime of an application.

TCO Applied to Enterprise-Wide Software Solutions

Enterprise-wide software solutions integrate all customer-centric activities (from lead creation through customer service request processing) in an effort to improve customer acquisition, retention, and loyalty. This includes a diverse segment of application vendors, from accounting, logistics, and human resource vendors.

Example 9-12:
Hanging indents.

Introduction: How Attitudes Have Changed

Old Attitudes: Single-Purpose Software

Try it. Use it. If it doesn't work, throw it out. That may have been the case 10 to 12 years ago when inexpensive, single-purpose software flooded the market. When this old way of thinking was prevalent, TCO wasn't an important issue. It was perceived that a product wouldn't be around for very long, so there was no need to worry about incremental costs.

New Attitudes: Complex Software

The economic picture has changed dramatically over the last several years as software has become more complex. Gone is the do-it-yourself mentality which dictated that a company could implement a software product simply by slipping a purchased disk into a drive.

Software no longer stands alone. When a company adds or changes a software application, all of the integrated software is affected, not just the application itself. Companies are looking at long-term investments. They can't risk the instability that comes with replacing software applications frequently.

These realizations invalidated the "old attitudes" and created the need for companies to analyze the TCO of software, and to consider *all* the costs incurred during the lifetime of an application.

TCO Applied to Enterprise-Wide Software Solutions

Enterprise-wide software solutions integrate all customer-centric activities (from lead creation through customer service request processing) in an effort to improve customer acquisition, retention, and loyalty. This includes a diverse segment of application vendors, from accounting, logistics, and human resource vendors.

Example 9-13:
Rules
separating
headings.

Introduction: How Attitudes Have Changed

Old Attitudes: Single-Purpose Software

Try it. Use it. If it doesn't work, throw it out. That may have been the case 10 to 12 years ago when inexpensive, single-purpose software flooded the market. When this old way of thinking was prevalent, TCO wasn't an important issue. It was perceived that a product wouldn't be around for very long, so there was no need to worry about incremental costs.

New Attitudes: Complex Software

The economic picture has changed dramatically over the last several years as software has become more complex. Gone is the do-it-yourself mentality that once a company purchased a software product it could be implemented by simply slipping in a disk.

Software no longer stands alone. When a company adds or changes a software application, all of the integrated software is affected, not just the application itself. Companies are looking at long-term investments. They can't risk the instability that comes with frequently replacing software applications.

These realizations invalidated the "old attitudes" and created the need for companies to analyze the TCO, considering *all* the costs they will incur

TCO Applied to Enterprise-Wide Software Solutions

Enterprise-wide software solutions integrate all customer-centric activities (from lead creation through customer service request processing) in an effort to improve customer acquisition, retention, and loyalty. This includes a diverse segment of application vendors, from accounting, logistics, and human resource vendors.

Example 9-14:
Using sidelines.

After writing a report—informal or formal—be certain to go through the Editing Checklist that I describe in Chapter 7. A copy of the Checklist is also included on the back of the Cheat Sheet of this book. If you're the one responsible for the project, the buck stops with you.

Chapter 10
Profitable Proposals

> *So we went to Atari and said, "Hey, we've got this amazing thing, even built with some of your parts, and what do you think about funding us? Or we'll give it to you. We just want to do it. Pay our salary, we'll come to work for you." And they said, "No." So then we went to Hewlett-Packard, and they said, "Hey, we don't need you. You haven't gotten through college yet."*
>
> —Steve Jobs, co-founder of Apple Computer, Inc. (1976)

The business world is full of opportunities as well as risks. A winning proposal can maximize your opportunities and minimize your risks. This chapter is chock full of ways to make your proposals winners. For starters, here are a few things your proposal must show:

✔ Evidence that you clearly understand the prospect's problem and situation.

✔ A clear strategy to solve the prospect's problem. (This is the heart of the proposal and must be tailored to meet the prospect's needs.)

✔ Sufficient documentation to convince the prospect that you have the qualifications and abilities to implement and carry out the strategy.

✔ Reasons why the prospect should select you over the other candidates.

✔ Your competence and professionalism.

In this chapter I refer to the reader of a proposal as the *prospect*. Please don't be confused by the shift in terminology.

No matter which category a proposal falls into, don't forget to fill out the Start Up Sheet featured on the Cheat Sheet in the front of this book. It's critical that you understand your audience, purpose, and key issue.

All proposals aren't created equal. They can be internal or external and span anything from a request for capital appropriation to a change in a procedure. Proposals generally fall into one of three categories:

✔ **Sales proposals** are high-level sales pieces you use to persuade a potential customer to purchase your product or service.

✔ **Internal proposals** try to win approval for something within your organization. (I discuss internal proposals briefly in the sidebar "Strictly for insiders" later in this chapter.)

✔ **Funding proposals** try to procure funding for a project.

Regardless of the type of proposal you need to write, here's the long and the short of it: Proposals vary in length and sophistication. They can range from a ten-pound technical presentation written by a team, to a one-page it-was-great-meeting-you-and-here's-how-I can-help-you letter written by one person. (For more information about collaborative writing, check out Chapter 20.)

Seductive Sales Proposals

The *sales proposal* is one of the ultimate business tools. Its primary purpose is to convince a prospective customer that your product or service

✔ Solves a problem

✔ Offers needed benefits

✔ Is a wise investment

What's in it for me?

Prospects want to know what they're going to get from you. Companies purchase products or services to solve business problems; therefore, your proposal should stress benefits *(solutions),* not products or services *(features).* You generally send a sales proposal after meeting with members of the prospective company, so you already have insights into their needs.

For example, say you met with chefs at a major culinary institute to show them your new line of industrial cookware. They tell you their problem of pots with single handles that are unstable and sometimes tip. The key *feature* for your product is that your pots have two handles. The *benefit* is: "A chef can balance each pot when he takes it off the stove without ever worrying about tipping or spilling."

Scoping out prospects

Find out all you can about a prospect and his agenda. Some prospects are very open about their situations, including budgets. Other prospects are not forthcoming with much information. The more open a prospect is, the more focused you can make your proposal. Do whatever you scrupulously and reasonably can to get the inside scoop. Some ways to get additional information include:

- ✔ **Reviewing the request for proposal (RFP) carefully.** For more information on how to use the RFP to your advantage, check out "YOU and RFP."

- ✔ **Surfing the Internet.** Most companies have Web sites that offer a wealth of information. Sometimes they list business partners, customers or clients, or other information that may just pop out as useful.

- ✔ **Scouting around your company.** Speak to people in your company who may have done business with the prospect or know others who have.

- ✔ **Contacting associations or groups specializing in marketing research and analysis.** They have all sorts of information on market trends and who's doing what. Also, find out who the industry analysts are and check out their Web sites.

- ✔ **Determining who your competitors are.** Get literature from competitors to see what benefits and features they stress.

YOU and RFP

When you answer a *request for proposal (RFP),* your job is somewhat simplified because the RFP gives you some of the inside scoop. The prospect has outlined his requirements. Sometimes they're specific; sometimes you have to read between the lines. Read the RFP as many times as it takes to absorb every nuance. Restate each point and elaborate on it in excruciating detail. In addition to reiterating what the RFP says, read between the lines and expand on what it doesn't say.

Example 10-1 shows excerpts from an RFP I answered. The RFP was very specific. I underlined the issues I parroted back in my response, which you see in Example 10-2.

Example 10-1: Excerpts from an RFP dealing with specific needs.

> . . . Your primary job during this phase is to arrange as many meetings as possible.
>
> You will also <u>attend all meetings, provide coaching regarding how to make the meetings more effective, and suggest how to improve ABC Videos, Inc., sales materials.</u> . .

PROCESS

1. Identify three levels of prospect's needs that require solutions.

2. Stimulate interest by generating a dynamite sales letter that discusses how AccountTech can meet those needs.

3. <u>Suggest how to improve ABC Videos Inc.'s sales materials.</u>

4. Follow up with phone calls to <u>arrange as many meetings as possible.</u>

Example 10-2: Proposal sent in response to RFP in Example 10-1.

MEETINGS

- <u>Attend all meetings.</u>

Notice how the response mimics the RFP.

- <u>Provide coaching regarding how to make the meetings more effective.</u>

Understanding the evaluation process

Find out how the prospect plans to evaluate your proposal. The bid doesn't necessarily go to the lowest bidder; it goes to the one who can solve the business problem. Here are some questions to ask the prospect:

✔ Is there a formal scoring mechanism?

✔ What qualities are scored?

✔ How much weight is given to each quality?

✔ How many people are reviewing the proposal?

✔ What level of knowledge do the evaluators have about what you're proposing?

Asking the prospect the preceding questions is always a good idea. Often, a prospect is ready and willing to share additional information—at least that's been my experience.

Demonstrating what makes you better than the competition

Make it crystal clear to the prospect that you stand tall above the competition.

- ✔ If the proposal is for a product, stress what benefits the product offers that the competition's doesn't.
- ✔ If this proposal is for a service rather than a product, stress any applicable credentials and talents your team has.
- ✔ Highlight previous, similar projects that you brought in under budget or ahead of schedule.

Don't babble on with the same boring lines everyone uses: "We have an experienced team of people and highly qualified management." What company's going to say, "We have an inexperienced team of people and unqualified management"?

After you get all the information you can muster up, you're ready to put your pencil to paper, or fingers to keyboard. Before you start to write, make sure you review the Six Steps.

Parts of a simple sales proposal

Although every sales proposal is unique, sales proposals contain similar sections and information. Even a one- or two-page it-was-great-meeting-you-and-here's-how-I can-help-you proposal should have an introduction, a body, and conclusion.

- ✔ **Introduction.** State the purpose and scope of the project, when the project will begin and end, any special benefits, and all costs.
- ✔ **Body.** Itemize the products or services, procedures, materials, time schedule, and a breakdown of the costs. Be specific about what's covered in the costs and what isn't. Check out Example 10-3, a simple one-page proposal.
- ✔ **Conclusion.** Express your appreciation for the opportunity to submit the proposal and your confidence in your ability to do the job. Highlight the advantages of working with your company.

Date: July 10, XXXX
To: Eileen Kenneally
From: Jamie Collins
Proposal: Capabilities Brochure

Thank you for considering me to write your long-awaited capabilities brochure.

Project Description:	Writing text for 6 page (3 panel) brochure Page size: $8^{1}/_{2}$ by 11 inches
Process:	Initial 1 to $1^{1}/_{2}$ hour meeting with key people to brainstorm and fill out Start Up Sheet. (We need to clearly identify the audience, purpose, key issue, and key customer benefits.) Will schedule a second meeting if needed. • Prepare first draft and send for review. • Make appropriate changes and meet if necessary. • Submit second draft and send for review. • Make final changes.
Deliverable:	Hard copy and floppy disk with text layout in MS Word.
Assumptions:	• XYZ, Inc. will supply all the capabilities to be included. • XYZ, Inc. will supply visuals and prepare copy. • There will be two rounds of moderate revisions.
Cost:	Not to exceed $2,450. (Added scope or changes thereafter will be billed at the hourly rate of $60 and will be discussed prior to proceeding.) Payment will be divided into thirds: • 1/3 when we agree to proceed. • 1/3 when the first draft is submitted. • 1/3 when the disk is delivered.
Schedule:	To meet a Labor Day deadline, we need to schedule our first meeting early in the week of June 20. (Bottlenecks generally happen during the revision process, and we're getting into vacation season.)
Next Step:	I look forward to working with you to produce a brochure that will help increase XYZ, Inc.'s bottom line. I'll give you a call next Wednesday to take the next step.

Example 10-3:
A simple one-page proposal in memo format.

Example 10-4 is an RFP I (successfully) responded to. There wasn't a lot of information in the RFP so I called the city that issued it with the hopes of learning more. It turned out to be a WYSIWYG (what-you-see-is-what-you-get) situation. The RFP shared all the information the city was giving out. "Oh well," I thought, "at least I know as much as my competition. I'll have to wing it." Example 10-5 shows my response.

Example 10-4: Sketchy RFP without specific details.

The City of Hollingworth seeks proposal, RFP # 34343, for Editorial and Reporting Services for its Annual Report. The selected firm shall utilize information derived from individual Department Activity Summaries, editorialize and layout in a suitable format for a professional publication, as well as publication in the local newspaper. . . All responses shall include proposed methodology for implementation and culmination of project, references from previous accounts, and three samples of work from past similar projects. All fees must be submitted in a separate envelope, and not be part of the formal proposal.

Pay special attention to the headlines you use to organize and give structure to your proposal: They're crucial. Use strategic headlines and subheads that address the prospect's problems. Sometimes you don't have enough information to make your headlines as descriptive as you'd like, but get as specific as you can. For more information about crafting and sequencing headlines, check out Chapter 3.

Strategic headline: Completion date: April 12, XXXX

Weak headline: Project Schedule

Strategic: Problem: Federal deregulation has increased competition

Weak: Problem Statement

Strategic: Solution: Implement a Full-Scale Training Program

Weak: Solution

Parts of a not-so-simple sales proposal

Long proposals have a more rigid format than their shorter counterparts. If you think it will strengthen your case, consider including advertising literature, annual reports, and testimonial letters from satisfied customers. Here are some inclusions for a long proposal, presented in the order in which you should bind or include them. Your proposals may not include all of the following. Use what makes sense for each situation.

Purpose: Prepare Hollingworth's Annual Report & Public Relations Article

To supply editorial and publishing services to the City of Hollingworth to produce its Annual Report. The team shall

- Use information from individual Departmental Activity Summaries
- Editorialize and create layout in a suitable format for a professional publication
- Create publicity in the local newspaper

About Our Award-Winning Team

My editorial team will consist of an award-winning writer, a photographer whose photos have appeared in leading magazines, and a graphic artist who's worked for major corporations. For more information, please refer to the enclosed resumes.

Process: Getting Started

Everyone involved in the project will meet to determine the scope of the project in the following areas:

Resources Available
- What articles, brochures, and other information are available to help the writer gather information for the text?
- What graphics and photographs are available? What needs to be produced?
- What internal and external resource people will be involved in the production of the annual report?

Approval Cycle
- Who are the people involved in the approval cycle?
- Who has direct responsibility for signing off?

Understand the Audience
- What is the demographics of the audience?
- What do they need to know? What do they already know?

Key Points to Be Conveyed
- What's the key point to be conveyed?
- What are the supporting points?

Example 10-5:
My winning proposal.

Letter of transmittal (also known as a cover letter)

Prepare a one-page letter of transmittal on your letterhead and bind it into the proposal itself. This is your chance to "schmooze" in writing. Express your appreciation for the chance to submit the proposal. And if you've had a positive experience with the prospect in the past, make sure to mention some specifics. Take a look at Example 10-6.

Lester Summers

Dear Ms. Constantine:
| Here's a subject line with impact! |

Subject: Surpassing your goal of 25% growth

We're very excited about the prospect of helping BioNet
Engineering surpass its aggressive business goal of 25% growth
in revenues over the next two years. We're convinced that the
implementation of our open architecture data system will be a
major factor in yielding that growth.

Here's our solution

The attached proposal addresses the specific technical,
implementation, and investment requirements you provided at
our last meeting.

Let's move forward

We've successfully helped companies such as yours meet
ambitious goals, and we're anxious to help you meet yours.
Thanks for this opportunity. I'll call you next Tuesday to
discuss the next step.

Sincerely,

Lester Summers
Lester Summers

Example 10-6:
Letter of
transmittal.

Title page

Make the title page appealing. Err on the side of being conservative. (Check out the title pages in Chapter 9, Example 9-4, for a sample layout.) A title page typically includes

- ✔ The prospect's name and address.

- ✔ The name of the person who signed the RFP and the RFP number, if applicable.

- ✔ The words *Submitted by* followed by your name. Include your address if you're submitting this outside the company.

- ✔ The date on which the proposal *is due*, not the date on which you're submitting it.

Executive summary

Prepare an executive summary for any proposal that is longer than five or six pages. The audience for the executive summary is the person who has the power to accept or reject the proposal. This section should be nontechnical and should summarize your plan for approaching the project. To see an example of an executive summary, check out Chapter 9, Example 9-8.

The order of presentation depends on whether you're delivering good or bad news. For example, if the prospect will think the cost is high, first dazzle him with how effectively you can solve his problem, and put the cost at the end. Whatever the order, the executive summary addresses:

- ✔ Your solution to the problem

- ✔ The details of the solution and why it will work

- ✔ How the project will be managed and by whom

- ✔ The time required to complete the project

- ✔ The total cost

- ✔ Who you are and why you should be selected

- ✔ An obvious *return on investment* (ROI), if there is one

Table of contents

The table of contents lists all major sections, subsections, tables, and figures in the proposal. To see an example of an table of contents, check out Chapter 9, Example 9-5.

Cost breakdown

The cost breakdown outlines *all* anticipated costs. Take a peek at Example 10-7. Here are some of the costs to include in a proposal to purchase software.

✔ Initial purchase

✔ Licensing

✔ Implementation

✔ Maintenance

✔ Options

✔ Anything else

COST BREAKDOWN

Description	Quantity	Unit Cost	Total Quantity Cost
NetWorking Team Pro 4.0	1	**$39,995.00**	**$39,995.00**
This package includes:			
Application Server			
(additional server provided			
at no cost)			
5 C++ Thin Client			
1 Escalation Server License			
1 Notification Server License			
1 Documentation Set			
Full Work Center Licenses	72	**$1,125.00**	**$80,900.00**

Example 10-7:
Where the
money goes.

Schedule

The schedule lists everything from lust to dust. If you know when the project will start and end, give exact dates. If not, list ranges of time in hours, days, weeks, months, or whatever's appropriate. If the project will be implemented in phases, list all the tasks for each phase.

Summary of benefits

Summarize the benefits to the customer. Quantify as many as possible. For example, illustrate the customer benefits in terms of dollars generated, time saved, customers satisfied, and so on. Check out Example 10-8.

Educating the prospect

Sometimes a prospect requests a proposal in an area he knows nothing about. If you have a fire in your belly for the job, educating the prospect is a winning strategy.

I once wrote a proposal in response to a RFP to prepare a video. The RFP was sketchy, at best, so I extended the few guidelines it provided.

I then called the agency and asked for more details; they weren't giving out any additional information. I did find out, however, that the people who would be evaluating the proposals didn't know squat about preparing a video — *and that was a very valuable piece of information.*

From my past experience, I knew that people don't appreciate how much time and work goes into preparing a video. I had to educate the people who would be evaluating the proposal to justify the cost. I, therefore, started the proposal with the "Basics of a Video Production" that explained what happens during each stage of video production.

I was the only submitter who took the time to explain the process. Although my bid was slightly higher than some of the others, I was awarded the contract.

Example 10-8: What the prospect gets for his money.

SUMMARY OF BENEFITS

LaserDat Printer provides the following benefits:

Benefit	*Savings*
Improved productivity	25% (time savings) per week
Perform in-house printing functions	$3,000 per week
Acquire instruments through rental agreements	$20,000 per month

Statement of responsibilities

List all the responsibilities both you and the companies will incur. Name specific people, when appropriate. The format can be similar to the summary of benefits.

Making a formal sales presentation

After you successfully make the short list (your proposal whetted the appetite of the prospects), you may be asked to make a formal presentation. This is actually a "sales talk" during which you have a chance to reiterate and expand on the key points of your proposal. The presentation is your chance to pump up your

- ✔ Thorough understanding of the prospect's problem
- ✔ Ability to solve the problem(s)

A sales presentation is somewhat like a job interview; you're called in because your résumé made the first cut. The prospect obviously liked your proposal and thinks you may be "it." This is your chance to shine and see whether you and the prospect have chemistry. For more information on making a persuasive presentation, check out Chapter 11.

In order to further your chances of being the one chosen

- ✔ Highlight the key points from your proposal. They obviously liked them; that's why they called you in.
- ✔ Use visual aids. For more information on preparing jazzy visual aids, check out Chapter 11.
- ✔ Allow time for a question-and-answer session either during the presentation or afterward.
- ✔ Review your main selling points during your wrap-up.

Strictly for insiders

An *internal proposal* is presented by a person, group, or department to persuade senior management to support an idea, project, or expenditure. The format is much the same as a short sales proposal. Internal proposals may recommend

- ✔ Changing a procedure
- ✔ Creating a new procedure or project
- ✔ Appropriating money for a large purchase

Internal proposals are simple to prepare. You already know the players, the budget, and are armed with the inside scoop. An internal proposal is often presented in the form of a memo. For more information about energized memos, check out Chapter 8.

Getting creative

"To be [creative] or not to be [creative]? That is the question." Sometimes creativity can earn you the brass ring. Other times it can earn you a fall flat on your face.

Jerry, an architect, had the chance to bid on a multimiilion dollar project, and he was determined to win the contract. In response to the RFP, Jerry decided to go out on a limb. Instead of preparing a traditional proposal, Jerry prepared a professional-quality video showing why the prospect should use Jerry's firm.

He selected the projects he was most proud of. He videotaped his architectural drawings and finished buildings. Jerry "morphed" between before and after renovations. He also scrolled (to music) résumés of those who would be involved in the project. Jerry then purchased a brand new VCR and inserted the video into the slot. He wrapped the package and hired a messenger to deliver it to the prospective client.

As you probably guessed, Jerry was awarded the project. After the contract was signed, the prospect admitted that his company was so impressed with Jerry's creativity (and credentials), they didn't even consider anyone else.

So. . . "To be or not to be?" That's a question only you can answer!

Of course, Jerry's method isn't appropriate (or financially feasible) for everyone. I use the story here because I want to encourage you to think of creative ways to "push the envelope" in your own field.

Even after all that hard work, you may not get the nod. If you don't, ask for an appointment and find out why. What did the winner do or have that you didn't? This can be a great learning experience. Great proposals and presentations build bridges. Sometimes these bridges aren't crossed immediately. You may have lost to someone with more experience, but next time the experience a client needs may be yours!

Buddy, Can You Spare a Dime?

The process of successfully soliciting funds is based on the premise of forming a *partnership* between the soliciting organization and a donor. Together, they can create a dynamic collaboration, building on each other's strength and sharing in successes. Example 10-9 shows a portion of a funding proposal that did just that!

Base your request on the idea that you can solve a specific problem but don't have the funding to implement the program.

Proposal for Funding To Develop a Vocational Work Experience

Hancock Centers: Student Treatment Center
Hancock Centers of Los Angeles, California, is a non-profit, residential treatment center. Established in 1974, we currently provide a therapeutic environment for 72 severely disturbed children, ranging in ages from 8 through 21 years. We also have a day program for 15 additional students.

Description of Students and Their Needs
The core of our students have experienced a breakdown in family, school, and community relationships. Most have been unresponsive to previous therapeutic efforts. Hancock Centers accepts only those children with serious learning and adjustment difficulties who can be maintained in an "open" setting. This population can't be served by another facility in the community other than an intensive treatment setting or a hospital. Our students have a variety of special needs:

- Intensive treatment
- Group living
- A special education program.

Our Philosophy and Mission
Our philosophy is based upon supporting and extending each child's identification with the healthy egos of staff and peers. This is done by building positive relationships through appropriate responsive care and setting limits.

Our mission is to return students to family and community after a period of residential treatment so they can adapt more successfully. We implement an Individualized Treatment-Educational Program (ITEP) based upon diagnostic findings to include psychometric, psychological, and social data. The program stresses the development of those ego functions that permit the students to perform optimally in society.

To effect this, individual psychotherapy, educational remediation, vocation training, and guidance are planned to maximize each student's potential. Descriptive programming stems from detailed sociological, psychometric, and cognitive evaluations for each student, which will be reviewed and/or revised at scheduled intervals.

Example 10-9:
A proposal for funding used successfully for five consecutive years.

(continued)

(continued)

Developing a Vocational Work Experience

Throughout our short history, Hancock Centers has attempted to meet the educational, psychological, and vocational needs of our students. With special education, therapeutic recreation, and psychotherapy, we have already met many of these needs. However, we're constantly faced with the difficulty of providing ongoing, meaningful, supervised work experiences.

Program to Begin: November 1, XXXX
Program to End: October 31, XXXX

Gathering background information

In order to prepare a winning funding proposal, you need the following background information:

- ✔ **Concept.** Have a good idea of how the project fits into your philosophy and mission. Articulate the concepts well and make the case compelling.

- ✔ **Program.** Here's some of the information you'll need to round up:

    - The nature of the project and how it will be conducted

    - The timetable

    - The anticipated outcomes and how best to evaluate the results

    - Staffing needs (existing staff and new hires)

- ✔ **Financials.** You probably can't pin down all the expenses until you work out the details and timing. At this stage, sketch out the broad outlines of the budget. Be sure that the costs are in proportion to the outcomes you anticipate. If the costs look to be prohibitive, scale back your plans or adjust them to remove the least cost-effective expenses.

Putting it all together

The extent of the information is relative to how monumental the project is and how much money you're requesting. You can use a variety of sections, including an executive summary, statement of need, project description, budget, organizational information, and conclusion.

Executive summary

Provide the reader with a one- or two-page snapshot of your entire proposal. Check out Chapter 9, Example 9-8, to see an executive summary. You should include:

- ✔ Brief statement of the problem or need
- ✔ Short description of the project
- ✔ Total funding requirements

Statement of need

After you successfully pique your reader's interest with the executive summary, your next step is to give more information. The *statement of need* presents the facts and establishes that you understand the problems and can reasonably address them. If possible, include testimonials from authorities in the field as well as from your agency's own experience.

Be succinct, yet persuasive—like a good debater. Assemble all your arguments and present them in a way that convinces the reader of their importance. As you marshal your arguments, consider the following:

- ✔ **Highlight the facts or statistics that best support the project.** Always be sure that your data is accurate.

- ✔ **Be optimistic and enthusiastic.** For example, if you're looking for funding for a breast cancer prevention education project, you may say: "We know that breast cancer kills. But statistics prove that regular checkups catch most breast cancer in the early stages, thereby saving lives. Therefore, a program to encourage checkups will reduce the risk of death with women diagnosed with the disease."

- ✔ **Propose your program as a model by explaining how your solution can be a solution for others.** Presenting your program as a model can expand the base of potential funding. Of course, make this argument only if it fits.

- ✔ **Toot your own horn.** Does your program address the need differently or better than other projects that preceded it? If it does, then say so!

It's often difficult to promote yourself without being critical of the competition, but be careful not to denigrate competing projects. The potential funder may be invested in those very projects.

- ✔ **Keep in mind that today's funders are interested in collaboration.** Funders may even ask you why you're not collaborating with those you may view as key competitors. So, at the very least, describe how your work complements the work of others without duplicating it.

Project Description

When you describe the project, you need to mention your objectives, methods, staffing and administration resources, and evaluation methods.

- ✔ **Objectives:** Clearly state your *objectives* or what you want to accomplish. An objective must be measurable, tangible, specific, concrete, and achievable in a specified time period. Don't confuse objectives with goals.

  Goal: Our after-school program will help children to read better in a short time.

  Objective: Our after-school remedial education program will help 100 children improve their reading scores by one grade level. This will be measured in standardized reading tests administered after the children participate in the program for six months.

✔ **Methods:** Describe the specific activities you'll use to achieve the objectives. It may be helpful to divide the methods into how, when, and why.

> *How:* Give a detailed description of how the project will run from beginning to end. Your methods should match the objectives.

> *When:* Present a timetable that tells the reader all the pertinent timing details.

> *Why:* Present your methods, especially if they are new or unorthodox. Why will the planned work lead to the outcomes you anticipate?

✔ **Staffing and administrative resources:** Include the details here or in an appendix, depending on its length and importance. Describe how you plan to staff and administer the project—including volunteers, consultants, and permanent staff members—and the salaries involved. Devote a few sentences to discussing the number of staff members, their qualifications, and specific assignments.

✔ **Evaluation method.** An evaluation is often the best way for you and others to learn from your experience. There are two ways to proceed with a formal evaluation:

> • Measure the product.

> • Analyze the process.

Either or both forms of evaluation may be appropriate to your project. For any type of evaluation, you need to collect and analyze data. The approach you choose depends on the nature of the project and its objectives.

Budget

The budget may be as simple as a one-page statement of projected expenses, or it may require a more extensive presentation. You may divide the expenses into personnel and nonpersonnel, travel, equipment, printing, and anything you can foresee. Make sure the budget is as complete as you can get it so there won't be surprises later on.

Organizational Information

In two pages or less, let the prospect know when your company came into being; your mission statement; your organizational structure; and areas of special expertise. Feel free to attach brochures, testimonial letters, or anything else that strengthens your proposal.

The waiting game

Waiting is perhaps the most tedious part of submitting a funding proposal because the ball is no longer in your court.

If your hard work results in a grant, acknowledge the funder's support with a letter of thanks. If not, there's always next year. If you're unsure why your proposal was rejected, ask: Did the funder need additional information? Would they be interested in considering the proposal at a future date?

Put them on your mailing list (if you have a newsletter or something you send out) so that they can become further acquainted with your organization.

Maybe next time you'll have better luck.

Conclusion

Conclude every proposal with a paragraph or two that covers the following points:

- ✔ Show how the project may be self-sustaining without further grant support.
- ✔ If appropriate, outline some of the follow-up activities that you have undertaken to prepare your funders for your next request.

Don't forget to use the Editing Checklist featured on the Cheat Sheet in the front of this book. If you send out a proposal with typos, that may be construed as a sign of the way you do your work, and your grant can be a large goose egg.

And if all else fails, remember the words of the great W.C. Fields: "If at first you don't succeed, try again. Then quit. There's no use being a damned fool about it."

Chapter 11
Persuasive Presentations

● ●

In This Chapter

▶ Divining the right medium

▶ Presenting slide shows and transparencies

▶ Preparing a video on a shoestring

▶ Presenting yourself with confidence and competence

▶ Enjoying your 15 minutes in the spotlight

● ●

The most important parts of any talk are the beginning and the end. And they should be as close together as possible.

—George Burns

As a business professional, you've probably been called upon to make presentations to peers, upper management, customers, or a mixed group. Any time you speak to a group (whether it's to a few people or a large audience) you're a presenter. The image you present will reflect upon you and your company.

This chapter offers tips for presenters at all levels—from the novice to the seasoned pro.

✔ If this is your maiden run, this chapter offers the tools to go through the presentation process from start to finish. Consider reading this chapter from start to finish so you get a full understanding of the process.

✔ If you're a pro, you can enhance your presentation by jumping around to find what you need.

In this chapter, I discuss writing for the most commonly used presentation media: flip charts, white boards (also known as *dry erase boards*), transparencies (also known as *overheads, overhead transparencies,* or *viewgraphs*), slides, and video presentations.

To build a rapport with your audience, you must understand who they are, what they know about the topic, what they need to know about the topic, and what your expectations are. If your audience is diverse, pinpoint common threads: shared interests, ages, related professions, socioeconomic characteristics. The Start Up Sheet featured on the Cheat Sheet in the front of this book can help you identify your audience.

Choosing the Right Medium

Selecting the medium to use for your presentation is often a matter of common sense. For example, if you're trying to convince your manager that she should approve your budget, you don't need to set up a projector. You most likely will submit a report. (For more about killer reports, see Chapter 9.) However, you may choose to enhance your report by holding a brief meeting in which you use a flip chart or white board to illustrate your proposed budget. If you're trying to convince a high-level committee to approve your budget, you probably want to opt for something even more extensive: slides or perhaps a short video.

The medium you use for your presentation is influenced by

- ✔ Your company
- ✔ The industry
- ✔ Your audience
- ✔ Your budget
- ✔ The complexity of data
- ✔ The available resources

Another consideration is whether you'll reuse the presentation. For example, you may not be able to justify outside production costs for a one-time presentation, but you may be able to justify it for a presentation that will be used two times or more.

You have many different ways of getting your message across. Table 11-1 lists some pros and woes of today's popular media.

Table 11-1	Comparing Various Media	
Medium	*Pros*	*Woes*
Marker or white board	Easy to find and use. Inexpensive. Informal. Low visual impact.	Boring. Limits audience size. Hard to face audience and write.
Flip chart	Good for fewer than 20 people. Easy to find and use. Inexpensive. Informal. Good for audience interaction. Pages can be pasted up around room for reference.	Low visual impact. Flipping back and forth can be distracting. Hard to face audience and write.

Medium	Pros	Woes
Transparencies	Good for audiences up to 75–100 people. Preparation is quick. Inexpensive. Can be informal or formal. Easy to change. Flexible for tailoring presentation. Good interaction with audience. Used with lights on so audience can take notes.	Switching visuals may be distracting. Projectors can block audience's view. Photographs don't copy well.
Slides	Good for several hundred people. Higher-quality image than transparencies. Formal. Projectors are easy generally accessible. High visual impact. Long shelf life. Good for copying photographs.	Expensive. Darkened room inhibits interaction with audience. Can't be redone easily. Inflexible.
Video	Audience size limited only by the number and size of your televisions. Very high visual impact. Very formal. High interest level.	Audiences focus on video, not speaker. Most costly medium. Takes time to produce.

Using Flip Charts and White Boards

I clump flip charts and white boards together because you use a similar delivery style with these media. A flip chart is basically a white board on paper. One advantage to using a flip chart is that you can save the pages and have a record of what you write. However, there are high-tech white boards that print out your text and graphics so you can save and distribute your pearls of wisdom at the end of a presentation. You don't need much preparation for these methods because you basically write as you go along.

When you write on a flip chart or white board, write so your back isn't to your audience. Turn to the side.

Using Transparencies and Slides

Today's most popular presentation design software lets you create 35-mm slides, transparencies, and hard copy handouts. Most presentation software has built-in drawing tools and automatic design features—so you can be as creative as you dare.

Understanding the power of color

As you work your presentation, keep in mind the power of color. Here are some tips to make slides and transparencies easy to read:

- ✔ **For Slides:** Use a dark background with light color text. White or light yellow text on a dark royal blue background is popular.

- ✔ **For Transparencies:** Use a neutral or light-tinted background with dark color text. Dark gray, dark blue, or black text on a white, ivory, or light yellow background is popular.

You can try a little variety. After all, why does a musical composition—although it has a basic theme—use high and low notes, fast and slow tempos? To keep people interested. You can create that same level of interest with color. For more information about the psychological effects of color, check out Chapter 5.

Guidelines for text

Designing visuals is an art you can master; it can be done simply and creatively. For example, if you use a large font for headings and a smaller font for the text, you capture the audience's attention. Following are a few simple guidelines that can spare you a lot of grief when preparing the text for slide and transparency presentations:

- ✔ **Use bullets to convey one issue per slide or transparency.** The issue that relates to your topic may be a short list of what, where, when, what, or how much.

- ✔ **Use upper case and lower case, rather than all caps.** Uppercase words (even for titles) are more difficult to read.

- ✔ **Limit each visual to between five and seven double-spaced lines of text.** Otherwise, your visual will be crowded and unreadable.

✔ **Use bulleted or numbered lists rather than sentence structure.** Doing so helps clarify your points. (Check out Chapter 5 for the difference between bulleted and numbered lists.)

✔ **Use 24-point font for headlines and 18-point font for text.** Visuals must be easy to read, even from the worst seat.

Don't put every word of your presentation on your visual. Concentrate on the highlights only. (We've all suffered through sleepers, where the presenter reads her visuals.)

Guidelines for graphics

A picture *is* worth a thousand words. Studies continue to show that people assimilate ideas presented visually more quickly than those presented textually. So, if a pie chart makes the information you're sharing more understandable, use it. For more information about charts and tables (and graphics in general), check out Chapter 5.

The following are a few tips for using presentation graphics like a pro:

✔ **Limit data to what's absolutely necessary and stick to one key issue per visual.** Never put two graphs or two focal points on one slide or transparency.

✔ **Label axes, data lines, and charts for easy understanding.** For example, the vertical data line may be sales in increments of a thousand, and the horizontal data line may be calendar months or years.

✔ **Keep chart lines thinner and lighter than data lines.** The chart lines should create structure, not overpower your visual.

✔ **Use color to punctuate your message.** For example, if you're using a bar graph to emphasize a certain value, a strategically placed red bar makes the value stand out if all the other values are in gray.

✔ **Create a legend, when you need to explain a part of your graphic.** Check out the graphics in Chapter 5.

Most presentation software lets you to develop a *template* or set of styles that you can use to give all your slides and transparencies a consistent look. Check out *PowerPoint 97 For Windows For Dummies* by Doug Lowe and *Macromedia Director 6 For Dummies* by Lauren Steinhauer (both published by IDG Books Worldwide) for the lowdown on how to create and use templates for all your presentations.

The power of persuasion

Your persuasiveness comes through in the way you organize your material. Your ability to analyze, organize, and motivate should be evident in the way you present your material. And, the clearer your message, the more persuasive you are. Here are a few pointers for making your message persuasive.

1. **Start with a summary—a brief overview.** Doing so gives your audience a clear idea of what your presentation covers.

2. **Clearly state the problem or need.** Go back to your Start Up Sheet and answer the question: "What does my audience *need to know* about the topic?"

3. **Solve the audience's problem or need by making recommendations.** Clearly state how you, your company, or product can solve the problem.

4. **Back up your recommendations.** Second-guess your audience and answer questions or objections they may have before they ask them. A lead-in may be: "You may be asking why . . .," then tell them why.

5. **Gently push for action.** Let your audience know what you want them to do. (Don't underestimate your power of persuasion.)

6. **Summarize your main points.** Repeat the conclusions you've drawn.

For the ultimate persuasion, structure your presentation based on the content. For example, if you're presenting growth statistics, procedures, or protocols, structure your presentation in chronological order. If you're presenting feasibility studies or research findings, structure your presentation in columns to show the comparisons. Figure out what structures work best for your personal style and for what you're trying to accomplish.

Supporting materials (handouts)

Bring to the presentation any handouts that strengthen your purpose. Here are a few pieces worth checking out.

✔ Brochures

✔ White papers

✔ Catalogs

✔ Annual reports

✔ Spec sheets

✔ Newsletters

Some presenters distribute the handouts before the presentation and make reference to them early. A disadvantage may be that the audience reads the handouts rather than listens to you. Other presenters save the handouts for after the presentation. The disadvantage here is that there isn't a chance for the audience to ask questions. Many people take the handouts at the end, stuff them in their briefcases, and never read them. Each presenter must decide for herself which is more appropriate.

Giving your presentation

Slide or transparency presentations have several unique challenges. The following tips can help you sail through your presentation:

- **Prepare a glossary.** If there's the slightest chance your audience may not understand your terminology, include a glossary of terms in your handout and make reference to the glossary as you go along. (Of course, you have to distribute the glossary before the presentation.)

- **Use cardboard frames on transparencies.** Consider putting cardboard frames (available at most office supply stores) around your transparencies or separating them with paper. Otherwise, static electricity can cause them to stick together, which is worse than wool socks coming out of the clothes dryer.

- **Switch the projector on and off.** Turn the projector off when going from one transparency to the next. Otherwise, your audience will struggle with a glaring light.

- **Check out all your equipment beforehand to make sure it's in good working order.**

- **Use your presentation as a leave-piece.** It's always a good idea to give the audience a *leave-piece,* something to remember you by. This may include a hard copy of your presentation and/or any supporting materials. If you're distributing a copy of your transparency presentation at the beginning of your talk, you can leave a "Notes" section blank so participants can jot down their own notes.

Never apologize for the quality of your transparencies, slides, or handouts. If you're not proud of them, leave them at the office! What you don't want to leave is a bad impression.

Before you give a new presentation (one you haven't delivered before), practice in front of a mirror so you can pick up any weak points. After you've given it a few times, practice in front of a mirror to make sure you haven't developed any "lazy" habits such as reading, rather than talking.

Making Shoestring Videos

Have you ever aspired to be a screenwriter? If so, here's your chance. Perhaps this is how Gene Roddenberry got started. Maybe the compulsion to make a video dates back to all those Andy Hardy movies old-timers used to watch: "Hey kids, let's put on a show in the barn!" Once you get the urge, it's hard to shake.

But then conventional wisdom rears its ugly head. It tells you that a video can cost between $500 and $2,000 per finished minute if you hire a professional. So you're discouraged. Buck up, Andy. Videos don't have to cost that much. If you write the script and use local seasoned amateurs—*seasoned* is the key word here—you can prepare a video on a shoestring.

Rather than hiring a professional writer, many companies want the script written in-house. After all, that's where the subject matter experts (SMEs) are.

Check out the latest scriptwriting software that makes it easy to format, paginate, shuffle scenes, and other good stuff.

Become a "video potato"

To find out more about how to make a video, take a course at your local cable station. Many stations offer *free* courses. And watch as many videos as you can. Here's where the library can be helpful. The Association for Educational Communication and Technology publishes a four-volume catalog that lists programs from the National Information Center for Educational Media. Through the National Video Clearinghouse, Inc., you can get the names of more than 40,000 videos. And the Video Source Book contains about 40,000 titles. Visit your local library for additional information.

Additionally, there are off-the-shelf programs available through the American Management Association, Eastman Kodak Company, IBM, media centers, local companies, and colleges. Many companies and clearinghouses let you view their videos at no charge.

Call some companies and colleges. Ask the receptionist to put you in touch with the person responsible for training and/or video productions. These folks are generally quite proud of their videos and are happy to share their experiences and finished products. Offer to take them out for lunch. They can be a plethora of information.

On with the show

Regardless of the type of video you want to prepare—marketing or sales, instructional or training, or problem-solving—you can use the same methods. A video production involves three stages:

✔ **Preproduction:** This is the most critical part of the process—the work of the scriptwriter that goes on behind the scenes. Approximately 75 percent of the total effort goes into preproduction. If every step of this stage is handled diligently and everyone does her homework, you should have a minimum number of changes *after* the video has been produced. Reshoots are time consuming and costly. During pre-production, you

- Prepare a writing and shooting schedule
- Round up the information
- Gather, plan, and create visuals
- Create a storyboard
- Get the storyboard approved
- Locate a narrator and actors (as appropriate)
- Rehearse (if possible)
- Finalize the script

✔ **Production:** This is where your production crew makes the difference between a home-quality production and a professional-quality production. During this stage, you assemble all the equipment (lights, cameras, recorders, microphones, monitors, and so on) and technicians you need. You record video and additional audio (if necessary) and edit your video in a studio.

✔ **Postproduction:** On with the show! Remember, reshoots at this late stage are time-consuming and costly. During this stage, you preview the video, make any necessary corrections, review edits (if applicable), and prepare and distribute copies.

Before you plunge into writing the script, fill out your Start Up Sheet. And, for scriptwriting, it's important to answer these additional questions before you forge ahead:

✔ Is the video a stand-alone presentation, or do you need support materials? Do you have support materials available or do you need to prepare them?

✔ Should you break your video into segments? If it's longer than 15 minutes, consider breaking it into segments and engaging in other activities between the segments.

Attention spans

Keep your video (or video segments) short—no more than 10 to 15 minutes. And don't use just a talking head (the head of a person babbling on and on). You can be more creative than that. Remember how bored you were in school as the instructor droned on forever? A poorly planned video can be even worse because it doesn't have the dynamics of interacting with the speaker.

If you're preparing a training video, for example, you can keep the audience's interest by segmenting the video. Have the audience participate with workbook or group assignments, quizzes, role playing, brainstorming, or other activities between segments. Check out Chapter 3 for some brainstorming techniques to consider using during your presentation.

Scripting and storyboarding

The script is the key ingredient in a successful video, not the visuals. You have two ways to draft the text for a video presentation.

- ✔ Most experts tell you to prepare a script, which is similar to most writing you normally do.
- ✔ If you're a visual person, however, you may go right into the storyboard format as you envision the visual that correspond to the words.

The choice is yours. Example 11-1 shows the format for a script, and Example 11-2 shows the format for a storyboard.

Example 11-1:
A typical script format of running text.

Since its inception as the partnership of three gifted scientists, Alberto Santanta, Marissa Klien, and Erick Lloyd, Creative Force, Inc. has generated superior solutions for critical national programs and served commercial markets throughout the world. It manages and supports some of the country's most important defense programs and facilities.

Creative Force manages all base operations at Howard Military Base. The company is responsible for facility operations, security, safety, utilities, and administration for a complex facility. This requires massive levels of technical skill and coordination in support of the United States space program.

Visual	Narration
Creative Force, Inc.	(Music only)
	Since its inception as the partnership of three gifted scientists: Alberto Santanta, Marissa Klien, and Erick Lloyd
	Creative Force, Inc. has generated superior solutions for critical national programs and served commercial markets throughout the world.
	It manages and supports some of the country's most important defense programs and facilities.
Technical Support	(Music only)
	Creative Force manages all base operations at Howard Military Base. The company is responsible for facility operations, security, safety, utilities,
	and administration for a complex facility. This requires massive levels of
	technical skill and coordination in support of the United States space program.

Example 11-2: This is the same text shown in Example 11-1, presented in storyboard format.

Figure that 10 to 15 pages of storyboard text equals 10 minutes of video.

What looks great in print may not sound so great when it's spoken. Give the people reviewing your script an audio tape along with the hardcopy. Suggest that they listen to the tape before they read the script or storyboard. Why? The finished product will be heard, not read.

Remember that a little courtesy goes a long way. Be sure to give on-screen credit to all who participated in the production. Send each person a copy of the video and a personal thank you note. For more about how to craft professional, personal letters, check out Chapter 8.

Lights! Camera! Action!

Use the following tips to keep your video production on a shoestring budget.

✔ Your shooting location influences your entire production. Be certain there's ample electricity for all the equipment. Check that you're not filming near an airport or train station, where you may pick up conflicting background noise.

✔ Finding aspiring stars for your video can be a challenge. (If you go through professional channels, you can expect to pay about $500 per day per person for unknown on-camera talent.) Your video production may simply require a narrator or a few people to interact.

To get free talent and give some welcome experience to aspiring stars, get in touch with a local theater group or nearby school that offers acting classes. Or, place a notice on your company's bulletin board or newsletter. You'll be surprised at the talent that lurks among your coworkers.

Wherever your actors come from, always hold an audition so you can assess their "star quality." Give the actors a preview of the script and have them read for you.

✔ Use a computer as a Teleprompter. Prepare the script on the computer (double-spaced in a large font). The words can scroll down the screen at a controlled pace so scripts don't have to be memorized.

✔ When you shoot the video, your talent should dress conservatively. Stripes and herringbone patterns tend to look distorted on camera. Pure white can cause lighting problems and make a person's face look washed out. Also, heavy jewelry can cause reflections and distractions.

✔ The lights, the camera, and the action can all be donated. You can save about $1,000 per day by using borrowed equipment. Call your local cable company or a school. Elicit the services of an advanced video student. She'll have access to the latest equipment, and the project can be overseen by her instructor—a professional. You may even arrange an internship for an aspiring senior-level video student. She'll have a wonderful portfolio piece, and you'll have free services. It's a win-win situation.

Assuring a Dynamic Presentation

Audiences remember what you say first and what you say last. Don't waste either of these moments. Create a written outline that walks through the entire presentation. Even if you've delivered the same presentation countless times and know it cold, you may get sidetracked and need to refer to your outline. Chapter 19 offers a plethora of tips for preparing the "talking" portion of a presentation. Check it out!

Be very careful when you deliver the same presentation or talk more than once. Your presentation must always seem crisp and current. If you have any time-sensitive material in your visuals, be sure to update them.

Opening do's

Audiences make a judgment about you within the first few minutes of your presentation. If you bore them with opening remarks, you've lost them. Here are a few things to consider:

- ✔ If you aren't introduced, introduce yourself. You may say something as simple as, "Good morning, I'm Terry Talker."

- ✔ Make a brief statement about your qualifications. This is to establish credibility, not to dazzle them with your résumé.

- ✔ Make a strong statement that speaks directly to your audience's needs. Why is this presentation worth their time? What can they leave with that will help them do their jobs better?

- ✔ Address any concerns your audience may have. If you expect opposition, build rapport.

Opening taboos

I always get a kick out of speakers who start with: *"For those of you who don't know me, my name is. . . ."* I often wonder what their names are for "those of you who *do* know me." Following are some openers to steer clear of. (For tips on savvy openings, check out Chapter 19.)

- ✔ Avoid weak statements, such as "Today I'll attempt to. . .," "I'll be speaking on. . .," or "Today you'll be listening to. . ."

- ✔ Avoid forecasts of doom and gloom. They're instant turnoffs.

- ✔ Don't share personal experiences unless they relate to the topic.

- ✔ Avoid overworked quotations or trite phrases.

- ✔ Avoid dictionary definitions. They're condescending and boring.

Appearing natural

If you're more comfortable working with a script, that's fine. But be certain that you don't appear to be reading. To seem natural

- ✔ Practice before peers or a mirror to learn to maintain eye contact with the audience.
- ✔ Tape your talk and listen to it. If you stumble over any parts, rephrase them so you can say them more easily.
- ✔ Use a marker (or other method) to highlight the key statements.

Heart of the presentation

A famous proverb states, "What I hear, I forget. What I see, I remember. What I do, I understand." Make your presentation interactive; get the audience involved.

- ✔ Let your personality show.
- ✔ Identify with the audience.
- ✔ Ask thought-provoking questions.
- ✔ Address people by name, if possible.

For small groups of 10-15, have name tents (inverted V-shaped cardboard place cards) in front of each person so you can call them by name.

Ending the presentation

The ending of your presentation is your last chance to persuade your audience of your purpose for calling them together. Make use of these suggestions for a strong closing:

- ✔ Repeat your recommendations or conclusions.
- ✔ Reiterate the call to action.
- ✔ Recap the major points you want the audience to walk away with.

Having a Good Time

Have you ever felt as if you spend your day-to-day life in the office working in isolation and people aren't aware of your wonderful contributions? If so, giving a presentation is your chance to take center stage and make a sterling impression on your colleagues and customers.

Whatever media you use, think of some of the presentations you've slept through and don't repeat the style of those presenters.

- ✔ Deliver your presentation with panache, enthusiasm, and a mission.
- ✔ Find a common ground with your audience.
- ✔ Be confident, believable, and responsive.

Regardless of the media you choose for your presentation, use the Editing Checklist on the Cheat Sheet in the front of this book. Pay special attention to proofreading. Nothing can blow a dynamite visual presentation more than an error that's larger than life! It can be as conspicuous as a tarantula on a slice of angel food cake. The following is an additional checklist you can use specifically for presentations.

Checklist for Presentations

- ❏ Is my purpose crystal clear? (Look at Question 6 on your Start Up Sheet.)
- ❏ Did I learn everything I can about my audience? (Focus on the Audience section on your Start Up Sheet.)
- ❏ Are my visuals informative and pleasing to look at? (Review Chapter 5.)
- ❏ Have I organized my presentation into topics and subtopics? (Find helpful hints in Chapter 3.)
- ❏ Have I prepared an outline or script?
- ❏ Have I practiced my presentation in front of a mirror or before peers?
- ❏ Have I anticipated some difficult questions? Am I prepared to answer them?
- ❏ Have I confirmed the date, time, and place of the presentation?

Check out the facilities as soon as you arrive. A friend of mine did a training session at a motel, and the conference room had no phone jacks. He needed to hook up computers and ended up stringing a phone line across the lobby, hanging from the grids in the suspended ceiling. He can never show his face in that hotel again.

Part III:
Energizing Your E-Mail

The 5th Wave   By Rich Tennant

"I like getting complaint letters by e-mail.
It's easier to delete than to shred."

In this part. . .

Have you ever aspired to be a screenwriter? You probably do more writing on-screen (the computer screen, that is) than you ever dreamed of. Of course, your professional endeavors may not be as lucrative as Stephen Spielberg's, but you can produce dynamite e-mail messages that shout, "Read me!"

E-mail is as simple as telling your computer you want to send a message, addressing the message, crafting the subject line, composing the message, and telling your computer to send. However, many good writers forget everything they've ever learned about good communication when they need to compose an e-mail message.

Well, this part comes to the rescue, covering the ins and outs of using e-mail as well as tips for minding your manners when you're writing in cyberspace.

Chapter 12
The Ins and Outs of Using E-Mail

> *Technology is a weird thing; it brings you great gifts with one hand, and it stabs you in the back with the other.*
>
> —C.P. Snow, English novelist and physicist

When Alexander Graham Bell invented the telephone in 1876, he never predicted how profoundly it would change the way people think and communicate. It was a remarkable invention that soon became the centerpiece of the workplace. And electronic mail (e-mail)—since its inception in the mid-1970s—has continued to revolutionize the way people communicate. Although e-mail is in its infancy, it's here to stay and continues to mature.

For high-flying business people, e-mail is the greatest thing since frequent flyer miles. As of this writing, more than 80 million people—representing legions of small and large businesses, universities, and government agencies—rely on e-mail as their primary means of communicating. The Electronic Messaging Association estimates that by the year 2000, more than 100 million users will be connected to e-mail services.

This chapter deals with how to use e-mail and e-mail technology as a communication tool, not how to write the text that goes into e-mail messages. See Chapter 13 for more information on how to write e-mail messages.

Choosing E-Mail

In the world of business communications, e-mail is like the un-Cola. It's something like mail, but not quite. E-mail adheres to the guidelines of business communications but has a unique flavor. If you're armed with a computer, a modem, and e-mail software, you can send e-mail messages to one person at a time or to gazillions simultaneously—whether they're across the room or across the world.

The foundation of today's business is "the quicker you get information, the quicker you can use it." E-mail gives us that instant edge. E-mail is the most thriving and fastest-growing community in the vast digital wilderness of cyberspace. It's the main stop on the Information Superhighway.

Improving the way you do business

Sometimes e-mail is used for informal chats, combining the immediacy of a phone call with the measured thought of a letter. Other times it's a serious and powerful business communications tool. E-mail is changing the way people do business and communicate with each other. More and more people are choosing to use e-mail because

- ✔ **E-mail breaks down barriers.** Because e-mail messages are usually delivered in a matter of minutes, or even seconds, you can send and receive messages anytime—no matter where you are. Even road warriors can reach the "mothership" through remote access from anyplace, anywhere. E-mail eliminates "telephone tag" and the charges associated with phone calls. People often respond more quickly to e-mail messages than to traditional media.

- ✔ **E-mail accelerates teamwork.** Using e-mail, you and your coworkers easily can work together and collaborate. You can send files with text and graphics, even video and sound. Project management is vastly improved because you can keep people in different departments, states, or countries in the loop. For example, an engineer may be dedicating his time to solving a specific problem on a piece of machinery. He can receive constant updates (from anywhere) on the progress others are making in related areas, which may shed light on his problem.

- ✔ **E-mail keeps businesses in touch with customers.** Companies are using this exciting medium for more than just day-to-day communications. They use it to send electronic newsletters, price changes, product updates, and the like to customers. This eliminates the cost of postage, presentation, and printing. It's a wonderful way to keep in touch with customers, especially on timely issues such as price changes.

E-mail is as easy as 1, 2, 3

In addition to sending and receiving simple messages, you can send and receive electronic files that contain text, graphics, sound, and video. In essence, e-mail gives you a virtual office—one that's anywhere your computer is.

- ✔ For information on your specific e-mail software, call your technical support group or buy a chocolate bar and bribe a technically savvy office buddy. He'll wait for your pleas for help.

- ✔ For information on general technical issues, check out *E-Mail For Dummies*, 2nd Edition, by John R. Levine, Carol Baroudi, Margaret Levine Young, and Arnold Reinhold (IDG Books Worldwide, Inc.).

This is all you need to do to send an e-mail message:

1. **Let your computer know you want to send a message.**

   Usually, you use your mouse to click a button that says something like New or New Message.

2. **Type in the mailing address, subject line, and message.**

3. **Press a button to send.**

Messages from other folks to you are held in a *mail server,* which is a special computer that sends and receives e-mail messages. It's sort of like the post office, only you don't have to wait for the carrier. You retrieve messages when you want to. Here's how:

1. **Let your mail server know you want to retrieve your messages.**

   Starting up your e-mail programs often takes care of telling your mail server that you want to receive your messages. You can also use a special command to tell your mail server that you're ready to receive your messages. Of course, I can't list all the special commands in this chapter so you may need to do some investigative work or chat with an office buddy.

2. **Review the list of messages in your inbox.**

   Then select (usually by clicking) the message you want to read. Other messages remain in your inbox. You can read them whenever you wish.

3. **Read the message.**

4. **Print the message, save it to a file, forward it, or discard it.**

Weighing the Pros and Woes of E-Mail

E-mail messages are delivered faster than a speeding bullet, but they do have inherent dangers. People have a tendency to compose messages on the fly and not proofread. They press the Send button and copy long lists of people. Some folks pop out angry responses before thinking about what they're doing. (Hopefully, *you* don't fall into this category.)

✔ Think carefully about what you're writing, and never write when you're angry or frustrated. If in doubt, don't send it. Check out Chapter 14.

✔ Proofread carefully. For proofreading tips, check out Chapter 7.

Involved in a love-hate relationship

E-mail makes my professional life a lot easier and enables me to keep in touch with people regularly. The technology certainly has its pros and woes, and I've developed a love-hate relationship with it.

On the love side:

I enjoy the speed and efficiency with which I can send files back and forth to clients and publishers. I prepare drafts in my word processor and attach the files to e-mail messages. (More about "attaching fiies" later in this chapter.)

The reader looks at the draft, modifies it, and e-mails it back to me. No photocopying. No faxing. No retyping.

I no longer worry about whether I have enough paper, envelopes, or stamps, I don't use my printer constantly, and I don't have to wait for snail mail to be delivered by (human) letter carriers.

E-mail is a great way to communicate with people in other time zones. I once worked on a project with a gentleman in Tokyo, Japan.

Boston and Tokyo have (I think) a 17-hour time difference, which leaves virtually no overlap in working hours. But my colleague and I gave each other valuable input through e-mail. Any other type of communication would have been impossible, and we wouldn't have met our deadline.

P.S. And I love the ease with which I can keep in regular contact with family, friends, and business associates.

On the hate side

I'm sometimes overwhelmed by the onslaught of messages and junk mail (known as *spam*) that I receive from family, friends, business associates, and the e-mail provider itself. It's bad enough that my mailbox (the one in front of my house) is choking on junk mail and my meals are constantly interrupted by junk calls.

Now my most efficient means of communication is glutted with digital debris. And for folks who pay for e-mail access by the hour, this costs money. Oh yes: There are also the tasteless jokes and chain letters I can live without.

Although e-mail may be "the greatest thing since sliced bread," it does have some drawbacks. Here's a list of the pros and woes.

Pros	Woes
Fast delivery.	Recipient needs a computer, a modem, and e-mail software.
Inexpensive compared to other forms of mail.	Not secure or confidential. (I discuss security later in this chapter.)
Nonintrusive—you send and receive when you're ready.	Not private.
Helps you reach people who may not take your phone call.	Special formatting may be lost at recipient's end.
You can attach files with text, graphics, sound, and video to your messages.	Some e-mail providers don't have the equipment to handle demand during peak hours.
Recipients can print the message, forward it to someone else, or save it to a file.	Occasionally unreliable. (Computer glitches may cause problems.)
Reach multiple readers at one time.	Junk mail prevails.

Spamming it up

Unsolicited "e-junk mail," known as *spam,* accounts for up to 30 percent of all e-mail messages. Spam can be anything from annoying messages to get-rich-quick schemes to pornography. Often the spammers use false return addresses to avoid being traced.

Unlike snail mail, however, as an online recipient you pay the delivery cost (especially if you pay a per-hour rate for online access and e-mail services). If you're barraged with spam, spam, and more spam, here are a few things you can try:

- ✔ **Never open the message.** Even if the message says something like, "If you'd like to be removed from this list. . ." ignore it. Spammers recognize this as a live address and continue to pester you.

- ✔ **Contact your e-mail provider.** Give the sender's address to your e-mail provider with the strong message that you don't want unsolicited mail from that sender. In many cases, the spamming stops.

> ✔ **Use two addresses.** Give one to your friends, relatives, and business associates. Save the other for public messaging such as chat rooms, registering software, and e-commerce.

As of this writing, there's a movement afoot to require senders of unsolicited e-mail to identify themselves, provide a valid return e-mail address, and inform recipients that they can stop future mailings by replying with the word "remove." The Federal Trade Commission (FTC) intends to enforce this system with fines.

Exploring security concerns

Once in a while your e-mail messages fall into the wrong hands. If you're a law-abiding citizen with nothing to hide, this doesn't matter. If you're unscrupulous, however, here's when it matters:

> ✔ Employers feel they have the right to know if you're using their e-mail system for personal messages. And "big brother" sometimes watches.
>
> ✔ The U.S. Government often monitors its messages to protect against e-mail being used for illegal stuff.
>
> ✔ Corporations that want to keep up with (or exceed) the competition have been known hire former intelligence agents (from the Cold War era) to break into e-mail of competitors.

Teenagers have broken into Pentagon files on several occasions. So you really have to wonder how secure any system is. There are a few things you can do, however, to try to safeguard your system. (The key word here is *try*.)

> ✔ Configure your system to remember your user name and password so you don't have to type them in each time.
>
> ✔ Never, never, never give your password out to anyone—even if you're tortured and deprived of your morning coffee.
>
> ✔ If you're in a high-security position, get a program that can encrypt e-mail when it's sent and decrypt it when it's read. (*Encryption* means messages are coded so no one but the intended reader can read them.)

Exploring privacy concerns

You also need to remember that *e-mail* and *privacy* are mutually exclusive. *E-mail is not private.* Here's why:

> ✔ You don't know what system your message is passing through or what system other people's messages are passing through.

✔ System administrators can read your mail at any point as your message is sent from one place to another. Although most system administrators are ethical, there's nothing to stop them from snooping through your mail.

E-mail has raised a lot of issues about privacy, and many cases have been brought before the courts. In 1986, the Electronic Communication Privacy Act (ECPA) upheld a company's right to monitor its e-mail. The premise is: The company provides it and pays for it. Therefore, the company owns it! So, it's prudent not to send anything that you wouldn't want posted on the company's bulletin board.

SHERYL SAYS

E-mail horror stories

Hit the wrong button and any Machiavellian scheming behind your back may throw your e-mail in your face. There are thousands of horror stories that demonstrate this. You must think of e-mail as a post card; not a sealed letter. Here are a few of those horror stories:

In order to protect the guilty, I changed the names of people and omitted the names of companies.

Big Brother IS Watching

Jennifer was the new office manager of a large company. Her first day on the job, James sent an e-mail message to Sam saying that he thinks Jennifer is "pretty hot." Over the next several weeks James and Sam exchanged messages about Jennifer. The messages got more and more descriptive. The gents in question weren't aware that "big brother was watching." Both were called in for disciplinary action under the company's sexual harassment policy. Even though neither one ever said a word directly to Jennifer, both were reprimanded and their employment records blemished.

You're Under Arrest

In a small New Jersey town, the police seized the e-mail of a murder suspect in order to further the investigation of the homicide case.

On the strength of the evidence—which included incriminating e-mail messages—the man was charged with the murder.

Misusing Company Facilities

Two employees of a large corporation were using their voice mail to communicate risqué jokes and malicious references about their supervisor. They were warned to discontinue this behavior. They stopped using voice mail for these messages, and started relaying them via the company's e-mail system. One man was called in and chastised for misusing the system; the other was forced to resign. Both hired an attorney and filed a lawsuit for invasion of privacy. They lost on the grounds that they had been warned about such behavior and continued to misuse company facilities.

Love In Bloom

Then there's the story of the hapless e-mail user who inadvertently sent 100 copies of a romantic letter to 100 shocked coworkers. Romeo immediately realized what he'd done and called his provider to retrieve the letter. No dice. It was like dropping a letter in a mailbox, they told him. Once you've done it, it's on its way—nothing can stop its delivery. (Some providers do have an "unsend" button. This guy's didn't.)

If you receive an e-mail message that isn't intended for you, be polite and forward it to the intended recipient (if you know who he is) without reading any more than you have to. Also notify the sender that the message was sent to the wrong address. The error may be attributable to an incorrect e-mail address.

Reader's Responsibilities

Information overload is a term bandied about a lot. As a matter of fact, Chapter 18 deals exclusively with ways to cut overload. The writer is usually blamed for the overload, but the reader must share some responsibility. Here are a few ways the reader can help reduce information overload:

- ✔ Check your mailbox daily. It's rude to let mail sit in your mailbox unanswered.

- ✔ Delete unwanted messages; they take up disk space.

- ✔ Download files you want to keep; save them to a file.

- ✔ Routinely scan for viruses. Your computer is susceptible to bugs when you download files.

- ✔ When you reply to a message sent to a group, reply to the sender only, not to the entire group.

It's "geek" to me

Here are some cyberterms for the jargon-challenged:

@: The "at" sign separates the name of the user from the service provider.

Bandwidth: A measurement of the amount of data a network connection can transfer at a given time. For example 28.8 Kbps sends 28,800 bits of data per second. The greater the bandwidth, the faster data transfers. A large bandwidth is necessary to transfer large files, graphics, or sound.

Bits per Second (bps): How fast a modem can send and receive data. This used to be called "bauds per second."

Browser: A graphical software program that lets you view pages on the Internet. Examples are Netscape Navigator and Microsoft Internet Explorer.

Bulletin Board System (BBS): Any online or Internet area for posting messages.

Chat groups: The computer equivalent of going to a party. You can chat with people around the world by typing messages and receiving responses almost instantly. You can find hundreds of chat groups, some divided into special interest groups. This is a great opportunity to meet people who share your interests in sailing, skiing, gelatin wrestling, bungee jumping, or whatever.

Cracker (or hacker): A person who breaks into a computer system to cause harm or steal data.

Cyberspace: The metaphoric space where electronic communications take place.

Decrypting: Decoding a message that's been coded (encrypted).

Downloading: Electronically copying a file to your computer from another computer. Think of it as loading something *down* from cyberspace. (The opposite is uploading.)

Emoticons: Little faces made of punctuation marks that add body language to cyber-communications. They're also called *smileys* or *winkies*. See Chapter 13.

Encrypting: Coding messages so only the recipient can read it.

Flaming: Using explosive language in a e-mail message.

Home Page: The main page on a Web site. It give folks on the Internet an overview of what a company or person has to offer. It's somewhat like an extensive online brochure.

Internet (also referred to as the *Net*): The "network of networks" that connects hundreds of millions of computers. The Internet was launched in 1969 by the U.S. Department of Defense and has since become an information link between research laboratories, universities, and government agencies, businesses, and just-plain-folks.

Logging off: Signing off from your e-mail system or the Internet.

Logging on: Signing on to your e-mail system or the Internet.

Mailing list: A list of people, groups of people, departments, or companies to whom you're sending a message.

Modem: Stands for modulator/demodulator. It's a device that allows a computer's digital signals to travel through an analog phone line.

Netiquette: The unwritten guidelines for Internet behavior. See Chapter 14.

Newbie: A newcomer to the Internet.

Newsgroups: Internet-based discussion areas where users post comments and read messages posted by others.

Offline: Currently not connected to a network.

Online: Currently hooked up to a network (the opposite of offline).

Smiley: A little symbol used to show emotions. Do you know what emotion the following guy is showing? If you look sideways, you'll see it's a smile: **:)**. See Chapter 13.

Snail mail: A disparaging term for the U.S. Postal Service because it's slo-o-o-wer than e-mail.

Spam: Junk e-mail.

Surfing the Net: Navigating (getting around) the Internet.

Uploading: Sending a file from your computer to another computer. (The opposite of downloading.) Think of it as sending something *up* into cyberspace.

Web site: Multimedia electronic pages.

World Wide Web (WWW): In 1989, the Web was created by Tim Berners-Lee, in Switzerland, and is an attempt to organize all the information on the Internet. When you use the Web, you start anywhere you want and jump from one place to another to find what you're looking for.

Chapter 13

Electrifying Your E-Mail with the Six Steps

In This Chapter

▶ Six Stepping through e-mail

▶ Making your way through header fields

▶ Directing your message

▶ Composing meaningful subject lines

▶ Remembering your manners

▶ Using headlines effectively

▶ Drafting your message

▶ Closing graciously

▶ Highlighting tips for e-mail text

▶ Checking before sending

▶ Attaching separate files

▶ Communicating with e-symbols

E-mail should not to be used to pass on information. It should be used only for company business.

—Unnamed manager of a major corporation

E-mail is a vital and valuable business tool. It has done for writing what the telephone has done for voice. Your e-mail message can reach your reader in a matter of minutes, whether you're sending it across the building or across the globe.

 In this era of worldwide communications, you often send messages to people you don't know. Be sensitive to possible national and ethnic differences between you and your recipients. E-mail messages deliver more than words about you and your company.

Using electronic shorthand

E-mail shorthand is something you can have fun with when writing to a friend, relative, or others you know well. This form of shorthand and is very useful when you're trying to cram a lot of characters into a subject line. E-mail users are constantly making up new abbreviations, so no list is ever complete. The following lists a few popular abbreviations:

Use the abbreviation...	To say...
BRB	Be right back
BTW	By the way
EOM	End of message
F2F	Face to face
FWIT	For what it's worth
FYA	For your amusement
FYI	For your information
GMTA	Great minds think alike
IMHO	In my humble opinion
IOW	In other words
LOL	Laughing out loud
OBTW	Oh, by the way
OIC	Oh, I see
ROFL	Rolling on the floor laughing
CUL	See you later
SO	Significant other
TTFN	Ta-ta for now
TNK	Thanks
TIA	Thanks in advance
!!	Urgent
WTG	Way to go
WB	Welcome back
WRT	With respect to

Plugging In the Six Steps

If you haven't already done so, please read Part I, which introduces my Six Steps to successful business communication. The Six Steps can guide you through the entire writing process by helping you get started, create and sequence headlines, write your draft, hone your tone, spice up your document with design elements, and proofread like a pro.

Unless you're sending a casual let's-do-lunch message to an acquaintance, treat e-mail as a serious a business document.

E-Mail Headers: Up Close and Personal

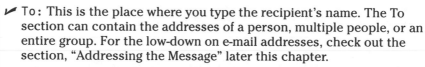

The *header* on the top of an e-mail message is much like the header on a memo. Although headers differ from one e-mail system to another, you'll likely see sections (or *fields*) of the header that say *To, Cc, Bc, Receipt,* or *Attachment.* Here's what these sections mean:

✔ To: This is the place where you type the recipient's name. The To section can contain the addresses of a person, multiple people, or an entire group. For the low-down on e-mail addresses, check out the section, "Addressing the Message" later this chapter.

Most e-mail software lets you store addresses in an electronic address book. Once you enter your recipient's e-mail address in your address book, you can click on her name within your address book and populate the To field. It's like using the speed dial on your telephone.

✔ Cc: The Cc field (which stands for *courtesy copy,* or to old timers, *carbon copy*) is the place where you indicate that you're sending the message as a courtesy to someone other than the recipient. Copy only those people who need to see the message, otherwise you're contributing to information overload. For more information on cutting information overload, check out Chapter 18.

✔ Bc: The Bc (or Bcc) field stands for *blind copy (or blind courtesy copy).* It's for situations when you don't want the addressee to know you're sending a copy to this third party.

Use the bc notation prudently. It's a clear indication you're sending something behind the recipient's back. And there's always the slight chance it may get into the hands of the wrong person.

✔ Receipt: Use receipt in much the same way as certified mail, return receipt requested. It assures that your message was received and read.

Use the Receipt feature with caution. The recipient may construe it as an insult. Your reader may take the receipt notification as a signal that you want proof that she's read your message so she has no excuses for doing, or not doing, whatever your message asks.

Receipt features usually only work within your own computer network. Getting the Reader Receipt feature to work outside your network involves both luck and technological savvy. Sometimes the feature simply is not available on your recipient's system.

✔ **Attachment:** Consider preparing long text messages in your word processor and then *attaching* the word-processing file to your e-mail message. You can attach files from most software packages available today (including spreadsheets like Excel and Lotus 1-2-3 and presentation software like PowerPoint). When you attach a document file, your e-mail message can then serve as a cover sheet. More about attachments later in this chapter.

Rather than sending an attachment, consider posting the information on the company's intranet.

Addressing the Message

To send someone an e-mail message you must know her *e-mail address*. Instead of the typical name, street, city, state, and zip code, an e-mail address has its own conventions. A simple e-mail address may look like the one in Example 13-1.

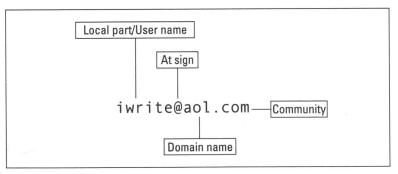

Example 13-1:
What an e-mail address may look like.

Here's what all this stuff means:

✔ **Local part or User name:** The local part is the electronic name of the addressee, which can be real or fictitious. (My teenage cousin Robin uses `iluvu` as her local part.)

✔ **At sign:** The at sign (@) appears in every message. It separates the local part (on the left) from the domain address (on the right).

✔ **Domain name:** The domain name is the e-mail service that transmits the message. In the Example 13-1, it's America Online.

✔ **Community:** The last part (after the period) is the community. (However, .com in Figure 13-1, .com doesn't stand for *community;* it stands for *commercial.*) Other commonly used communities are:

> .org = organization
>
> .gov = government agency
>
> .edu = educational facility
>
> .mil = military

Don't forget to let people know your e-mail address. Put it on your business cards, stationery, fax cover sheets, and everything else that has your name, address, and phone number.

If you don't know someone's address and can't find out by pestering everyone you know, check out *E-Mail For Dummies,* 2nd Edition, by John R. Levine, Carol Baroudi, Margaret Levine Young, and Arnold Reinhold (IDG Books Worldwide, Inc.) for some tips.

Don't confuse a *URL* (uniform resource locator) with an e-mail address. URLs are for finding Web sites and people on the Internet and usually have nothing to do with e-mail.

Crafting Seductive Subject Lines

The subject line is the most important piece of information in an e-mail message because it must seduce the reader to read the message. The subject line is her *first and only* hint as to what your message is about. If it doesn't grab the reader's attention, she may not read your message. For more information crafting subject lines, check out Chapter 3.

Example 13-2 shows an e-mail inbox with several messages. Do any of these subject lines jump out and shout: READ ME?

Counting characters

Some systems give you a finite number of characters you can use in the Subject field to get your reader's attention. They limit the Subject field to between 25 and 35 characters—including spaces and punctuation marks.

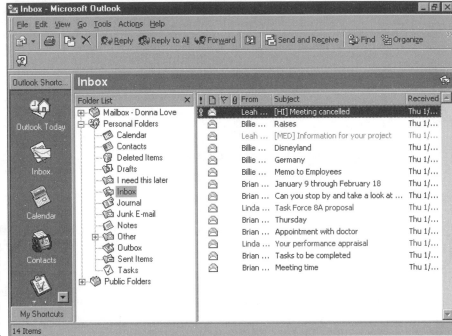

Example 13-2:
A screen full
of boring and
nonde-
scriptive
subject lines.

I recently viewed this subject line: `Sandy Kay's computer does`. The message lops off after 25 characters, leaving the recipient to ask: Sandy Kay's computer does what? Cartwheels? Sandy Kay wanted to broadcast that her computer wasn't working. Do you think anyone rushed to repair her computer? Sandy probably would have gotten action if she used the limited character count to make her subject line compelling. A subject line such as `Computer prblm. S.Kay` would have certainly conveyed Sandy's message and incited action.

Regardless of the number of characters your subject field can hold, short direct subject lines grab your reader's attention. Try to use as few words as possible to convey your message clearly and accurately.

Sounding compelling

The most important information should be the first part of your subject line. Look at the following subject lines. Ask yourself which would inspire you to read the message, then look at the reasoning that follows:

1. There's going to be a meeting of MI

2. MIS meeting

3. MIS: Urgent Mtg. 5/20

Subject line 1.	If the field allows for 35 characters, the "S" would be truncated. Even if the "S" were visible, this subject line doesn't give very much information. It wastes words.
Subject line 2.	This line is a little better; no wasted words. But it gives little information and isn't compelling.
Subject line 3.	This subject line gives you critical information. From reading just the subject line, you know that there's going to be an MIS meeting; it's an urgent meeting; and it's on May 20.

Signaling the importance of your message

Some e-mail programs have a check box or button that you can click to signal the importance of the message. Options may be "urgent" or "FYI"; "high, medium, or low"; a colored flag; or other designations. Also, your company may have an agreed upon system for signaling importance in subject lines.

If your company or e-mail program doesn't have a set of signals, consider starting the subject line with !! for urgent, or FYI for informational messages. If you're sending a message to more than one person, be careful how you use these signals. What's informational for one person may be urgent for another—and you don't want to be the little girl who cries wolf.

Using key words

Using a *key word* at the start of your subject line can be helpful when forwarding a message to someone else or trying to locate an old message on an important project. Some key word examples include: IT, Billing, Human Resources (HR), or anything else that can serve as a trigger. Key words can also be something specific such as "New products."

Simply add the key word to the start of the subject line. For example, you may use Billing: Hot April issues or HR: New vacation policy to get your message out.

People who get lots of e-mail message often look for key words to determine what to read.

Letting the subject line deliver your message

If the message itself can fit onto the subject line, let the subject line deliver your message. Type END at the end of your subject line to show that the subject line *is* the message. Here are a few scenarios showing how you can make the subject line deliver your message:

- ✔ The staff meeting scheduled for 6/2 is being moved to 6/3. All the other information (time and agenda) remains the same. Use the subject line Staff mtg chg to 6/3. All else same-END.

- ✔ You want to remind your team about the kick-off meeting on Friday, April 3, at noon, in the 4th floor conference room. Use the subject line 4/3, Kick-off mtg, noon, 4th flr conf rm-END.

- ✔ You're attaching a 15-page report that outlines the sales forecast for the second quarter. Even though you're sending an attachment, you use the subject line Sales to increase 15% Q2-END, which sums up the report. If the reader doesn't have time to read the report in its entirety, she's gotten the key piece of information she needs to know.

If your system won't send a message that doesn't have a "message," type a single character into the message section. The subject line will let the reader know that your message is complete, so she won't have to peek inside. It's just a way of tricking the system.

Sending Greetings 'n' Salutations

Rules of etiquette say you should always include a greeting when addressing someone. You do this in face-to-face contact and you do it in letters. You should also do it in e-mail messages, although your greeting can be less formal than in a letter. For more information about preparing salutations, check out Chapter 8.

For an informal message, try something like:

> *Informal:* Hi Guys,
>
> Don't forget to bring your notes to tomorrow's meeting.
>
> *Formal:* Dear Jason,
>
> I'd like to confirm that you'll be joining us at tomorrow's meeting. It will be from 3:00 to 4:30 in Conference Room B.

Telling the story with headlines

Just as when you're writing any business communication, use action-packed headlines and sequence them for your audience so they tell your story. For more information about crafting headlines and sequencing for impact, check out Chapter 3.

Example 13-3 shows an e-mail message with a compelling subject line and helpful headlines.

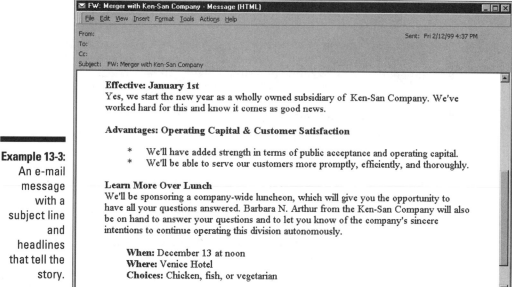

Example 13-3: An e-mail message with a subject line and headlines that tell the story.

Within the e-mail window:

FW: Merger with Ken-San Company - Message (HTML)

File   Edit   View   Insert   Format   Tools   Actions   Help

From: Sent: Fri 2/12/99 4:37 PM
To:
Cc:
Subject: FW: Merger with Ken-San Company

Effective: January 1st
Yes, we start the new year as a wholly owned subsidiary of Ken-San Company. We've worked hard for this and know it comes as good news.

Advantages: Operating Capital & Customer Satisfaction

* We'll have added strength in terms of public acceptance and operating capital.
* We'll be able to serve our customers more promptly, efficiently, and thoroughly.

Learn More Over Lunch
We'll be sponsoring a company-wide luncheon, which will give you the opportunity to have all your questions answered. Barbara N. Arthur from the Ken-San Company will also be on hand to answer your questions and to let you know of the company's sincere intentions to continue operating this division autonomously.

When: December 13 at noon
Where: Venice Hotel
Choices: Chicken, fish, or vegetarian

Writing the Draft

If you're sending someone a let's-do-lunch message, of course you don't need to prepare a draft. Otherwise, it's vital that you do so. If the business document is more than a few pages, consider preparing it in your word processor and sending it as an attachment or posting it on the company's intranet. For more information on writing a draft, check out Chapter 4.

The visual impact of your message is as important as the message itself. You must structure the message so the key information is up front. Following are a few tips for preparing short and long messages.

Structuring short messages

A short message can be delivered in one or two screens. Give your reader the who, what, when, where, why, and how (or whichever apply) on the first screen. The second screen may be for the supporting information. In Example 13-4 you see a message that does this.

Structuring long messages

If your message is three screens or more, you need to make a special effort to keep the reader interested. Here are a few things you may try:

✔ **Start with a table of contents (TOC).** The TOC can be as simple as a listing of the headlines. You're the subject-matter expert, so you be the judge. Here's an example of a simple listing of headlines:

> Subject: Preserving our Division's Reputation
>
> We're Losing Our Edge
>
> What's the Answer?
>
> Next Step

✔ **Include an executive summary.** The executive summary can include the purpose, scope, methods, results, conclusions, findings, recommendations, next steps, or whichever apply. Example 13-5 is an executive summary sequenced for unresponsive readers. For more information about sequencing for unresponsive readers, check out Chapter 3.

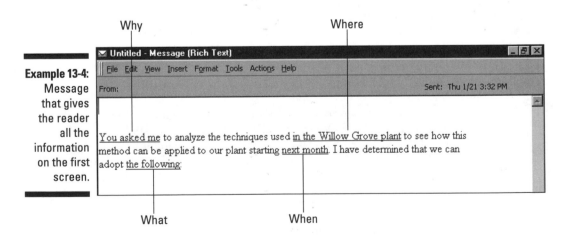

Example 13-4: Message that gives the reader all the information on the first screen.

Why — What — Where — When labels pointing to the message:

Untitled - Message (Rich Text)

File Edit View Insert Format Tools Actions Help

From: Sent: Thu 1/21 3:32 PM

You asked me to analyze the techniques used in the Willow Grove plant to see how this method can be applied to our plant starting next month. I have determined that we can adopt the following:

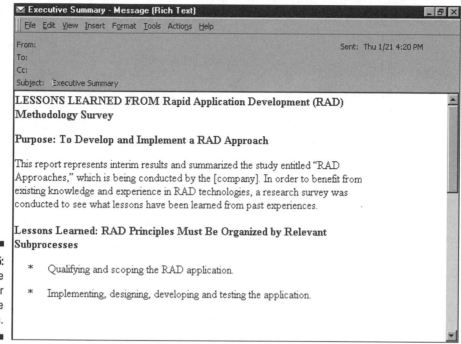

Example 13-5:
Executive
summary for
unresponsive
readers.

Use bullets, charts, or whatever is necessary to complete the executive summary on one or two screens. For more information about writing an executive summary, check out Chapter 9.

If your document is very lengthy, prepare it in your word processor and send it as an attachment or post it to the company's intranet. Use the message portion or your e-mail message for the TOC or executive summary.

Example 13-6 is an actual e-mail message I received. It's difficult to see the logical relationship between ideas because it's choppy. I had to print out the message and draw brackets around the bulleted items that related to each other. For more information about composing paragraphs and using bullets, check out Chapter 5.

If the writer of Example 13-6 had used the Six Step process, she would have written headlines and used them a framework to develop the draft. Notice in Example 13-7 that the headlines create a logical flow for the instructions. The numbered list outlines the sequence. Also, notice the difference between the subject lines. For more information about dynamic subject lines headlines, check out Chapter 3. And for more information about numbered and bulleted lists, check out Chapter 5.

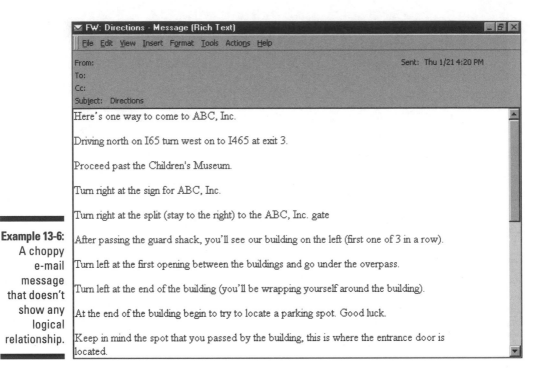

Example 13-6:
A choppy
e-mail
message
that doesn't
show any
logical
relationship.

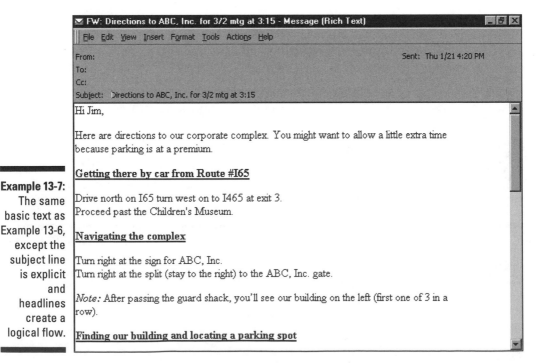

Example 13-7:
The same
basic text as
Example 13-6,
except the
subject line
is explicit
and
headlines
create a
logical flow.

Complimentary Closings

Would you ever hang up the telephone without saying "goodbye"? Of course not. So don't "hang up" your e-mail message without extending the same courtesy. Just as e-mail messages are less formal than letters, the closing of an e-mail message may be less formal. Instead of "Sincerely yours" or "Cordially," you may use "Thanks" or "Regards." You may even try the e-closing, THK (for *Thanks*). For more information about complimentary closings, check out Chapter 8.

ACSII and Ye Shall Receive

Many e-mail systems and programs use a limited character set (set of fonts), which can limit font capabilities. They're known as *ASCII* (pronounced *ass key*) characters. You can highlight text by

- ✔ Using asterisks or dashes.
- ✔ Leaving double spaces.
- ✔ Leaving lots of white space.
- ✔ Boxing or dividing information. For sophisticated e-mail systems, consider using a shadow box. For less sophisticated e-mail systems, consider blocking off sections of text with a line of asterisks or hyphens.

Always err on the side of simplicity. If you're sending a message to someone who's on another e-mail system, simplify your formatting because not all e-mail systems are created equal. If your system has all the bells and whistles and your reader's doesn't, your beautiful formatting and clearly expressed message may be garbled on her screen.

Are You Ready to Send?

Just because you've keyed in the closing, doesn't mean you're ready to send your e-mail message. Before you do, ask yourself:

- ✔ Is my subject line compelling and revealing?
- ✔ Is my document visually appealing?
- ✔ Have I established the right tone?
- ✔ Have I proofread, proofread, proofread?

Be certain your paragraphs are five to seven lines. A very common mistake people make when sending an e-mail message is to run their stream of consciousness into a single paragraph. If you don't break your message into visually pleasing coherent fragments, people won't read it. Example 13-8 is a real message someone forwarded to me.

Example 13-8:
An e-mail
message
cramming
the entire
stream of
consciousness
into a run-on
paragraph.

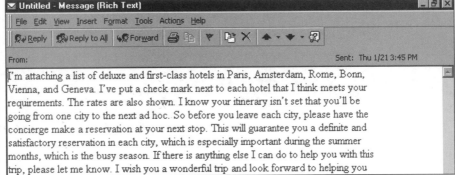

I'm attaching a list of deluxe and first-class hotels in Paris, Amsterdam, Rome, Bonn, Vienna, and Geneva. I've put a check mark next to each hotel that I think meets your requirements. The rates are also shown. I know your itinerary isn't set that you'll be going from one city to the next ad hoc. So before you leave each city, please have the concierge make a reservation at your next stop. This will guarantee you a definite and satisfactory reservation in each city, which is especially important during the summer months, which is the busy season. If there is anything else I can do to help you with this trip, please let me know. I wish you a wonderful trip and look forward to helping you

Before you hit the Send button, use the Editing Checklist featured on the Cheat Sheet for this book. Also, printing your document and reviewing the hard copy, may be a wise choice. It's easier to see errors and get continuity. For more proofreading tips and trade secrets, be sure to visit Chapter 7.

Sending Attachments

If you prepare your message in your word processor, spreadsheet, or graphics software, you can attach the file(s) to your e-mail message. Here are a few suggestions for attaching files:

- ✔ **Be sure your reader can receive the file.** Not all e-mail systems handle files in the same way. If you're unsure, send a test file to the reader to check for compatibility.

- ✔ **Let the reader know what file format you're sending.** Even with the same software vendor, files aren't *downwardly compatible*—which means an earlier version of a program can't read a file created with a newer version of the same program.

- ✔ **If an attached file is long, compress it.** Files compressed in programs like WinZip, StuffIt Expander, and ZipIt can speed up delivery and cut down on network traffic. Let the reader know what program you used to compress the document so that she can uncompress the file on her end.

If your message can't get through for any reason, it will bounce back with a notation, `MAILER-DAEMON`. *Daemon* is a Greek word meaning "spirit." Mailer daemons are good spirits because they can tell you what the problem is in sending.

Conveying e-motion

When you're engaged in conversation with someone, it's easy to convey emotions through tone of voice, inflections, and body language. It's not easy to understand these emotions via the written word. Here are a few tips to help clarify your emotions when using e-mail:

✔ Emphasize certain words using asterisks or all caps.

I *must* hear from you today.

I MUST hear from you today.

The following are some common emoticons:

✔ Consider conveying your emotions using *emoticons*—little cyber-symbols that display emotion. Avoid using them in formal business e-mail correspondence. In order to read or understand any of these emoticons, turn your head counterclockwise.

Bill, you did a great job :-)

Emotional State	Emoticon	Emotional State	Emoticon
Anger	:-II	Laughter	:-D
Apathy	:-I	No comment	<>
Brain dead	X-(	Sadness	:-(
Confusion	%-I	Shock	:-o
Crying	;-(	Sigh	<s>
Grin	<g>	Skepticism	:-/
Grinning	:-}	Smirking	:-]
Happiness	:-)	Tongue tied	:-&
Irony	<i>	Upset	:-<
Kidding	<k>	Wide eyed	8-)
Kiss	:-*	Winking	;-)
Laugh	<l>	Yelling	:-(O)

Chapter 14

Remembering Your E-Manners

· ·

· ·

A computer does not substitute for judgment any more than a pencil substitutes for literacy.

—Robert S. McNamara, *The Essence of Security*

There are few codified rules for the fledgling e-mail technology, and no one has written the decisive manual for e-mail etiquette (known as *netiquette*). The general rule is to remember what you learned as a pup: **Always be courteous and use common sense.**

Where's Amy Vanderbilt or Emily Post?

Neither Amy Vanderbilt nor Emily Post is around to guide us through the do's and taboos of e-mail etiquette. However, I doubt that either would have been comfortable using e-mail or surfing the net. (To them surfing was something you do in Hawaii.)

But, don't dismay. We have a new wave of "cybergurus" emerging—one is Ms. Etta Kitt. She's agreed to answer questions on netiquette. Perhaps one day she'll write the decisive manual and have an interactive Web site.

Angry Messages

Dear Etta:

The other day I received the following e-mail message from a coworker. It really made me angry:

> *I can't tell you what my reaction is. I'm fuming. Your suggestion is a bunch of garbage. I need time to digest this rot.*

How can we discourage people from sending "Rambograms"? You know the kind—rude, lewd, and crude.

Irritated in Iowa

Dear Irritated in Iowa:

In the world of cyberspace, you can easily forget that a human being is reading the message. Don't send angry messages. Each e-mail message is a permanent record of your words. If you feel compelled to let off steam, try the following:

- Compose the message on the word processor. Include the juicy insults if you feel the urge.
- *Don't send the message.* Save it to a file.
- Give yourself a cooling-off period . . . time to defuse the anger.
- Later, read the message and ask yourself: "Would I say this to the person's face?" If the answer is no, *don't send it.*

There's a term in the e-mail arena known as *flaming*—sending an "inflammatory" message. Before you flame someone, take a moment to cool down. Remember that once the message is sent, it can haunt you for all eternity.

Identify Yourself

Dear Ms. Kitt:

I'd like to remind your readers to identify themselves and their affiliations. When they're sending e-mail to people outside their company, there's no letterhead to make the identification.

Jane Doe

Dear Ms. Doe:

Thanks for the reminder. Are you related to John?

Did you know you can create a signature file that has your handwritten signature, your phone or fax number, and address? There's a great discussion of this in *E-Mail For Dummies* by John R. Levine, Carol Baroudi, Margaret Levine Young, and Arnold Reinhold (IDG Books Worldwide).

Libel and Copyright

Dear Ms. Kitt:

I'm having a debate with my wife and hope you'll cast the deciding vote. She says that libel and copyright laws do apply to e-mail, and I say she's wrong. I promised to fix dinner for the next month if you agree with her.

Will Cook

Dear Will Cook:

You certainly will! Dust off your chef's apron and get out your cheese grater. E-mail documents *are* subject to the same libel and copyright laws as paper-based documents. Treat e-mail messages with the same discretion you would if they were paper. *Bon appétit.*

Savvy Salutations

Dear Etta Kitt:

Is it appropriate to start your e-mail message with a salutation? I generally do, but most people don't.

Sir Harry Pape

Dear Sir Harry:

Do you say "hello" when you answer the telephone? An e-mail salutation is not only appropriate, it's expected. So you're doing the right thing. With any form of communication, you should always greet the person you're addressing. People who don't start with a greeting are the same ones who come into the office and bark out orders before they remove their coats.

P.S. Notice I didn't start my reply with *Dear Sir* because it's too impersonal, and I don't know you well enough to call you Harry. (For more information on salutations, see Chapter 8.)

Subject Line Quandary

Dear Ms. Kitt:

I never know what to say in the subject line. Can you offer some suggestions?

Ann Onymous

Dear Ms. Onymous:

The subject line determines whether the reader reads your message. If the subject line doesn't jump off the screen and shout READ ME, your message may not get read. So make your subject lines informative, direct, and brief.

```
SUBJECT: Tomorrow is JP's last day
```

Be mindful that some people share online access with coworkers, so avoid raising eyebrows with funky subject lines such as `Whips and chains`. For more information about composing subject lines, see Chapters 3 and 13.

About Abbreviations

Dear Etta:

Are abbreviations acceptable in e-mail?

A.B. Jones

Dear A.B. Jones:

Use abbreviations only if you're certain the reader will know what the abbreviation stands for. By the way . . . What's your name? Are you male or female? For more information about abbreviations, see Appendix C.

Toning Down the Tone

Dear Etta:

I use e-mail as a serious business communication and am uncertain how to deal with the tone of my messages. Many people are curt and don't treat e-mail as seriously as I do.

Uncertain Ulysses

Dear Uncertain Ulysses:

In every form of business writing, your tone is your personality on paper. E-mail is a serious business writing tool, and everyone should treat it as such. Here are some suggestions:

- ✔ Keep the message short and simple.
- ✔ Use the active voice.
- ✔ Select positive words.
- ✔ Be courteous, direct, and brief.

P.S. For more information about honing the tone, see Chapter 6.

ALL CAPS

Dear Miss Kitt:

I OFTEN GET MESSAGES DELIVERED IN ALL CAPITAL LETTERS. WHY DO PEOPLE DO THAT? HAVE THEY PRESSED THE CAPS LOCK KEY BY MISTAKE? WHEN I GET A MESSAGE IN ALL CAPS, I FEEL AS IF THE WRITER IS SHOUTING AT ME. AM I OVERREACTING?

HARRIET WITH A HEADACHE

Dear Harriet with a Headache:

No, you aren't overreacting. Typing a message in all capital letters is the e-mail equivalent of shouting. If you want to get someone's attention, don't shout at them. Plus caps are more difficult to read than the combination of upper- and lowercase. By the way, I hope your headache has subsided.

P.S. I'd like to add that the reverse is true. I recently got the following e-mail message from an e.e. cummings wannabe. He didn't use any capital letters. The effect was the opposite of shouting; it was weak and wimpy.

> *i won't be able to attend tomorrow's meeting because i'll be out of town. will call you when i get back. sam*

Creative with Color

Dear Etta:

I got a message the other day in fuchsia and green. The writer took advantage of his e-mail's color capabilities and his message got lost in the glare of the screen. I was tempted to put on my sunglasses.

Crazed by Color

Dear Crazed by Color:

You can be too creative with color. I personally reserve color for certain interoffice e-mails, such as announcing the annual Holiday party. Otherwise, the messages look like circus posters. If your program offers color capabilities, use colors that are easy on the eyes. Consider combinations of blue and white or yellow and black. If you select exotic color combinations (besides subjecting the reader to glare), people with certain types of color blindness may not be able to read your message at all.

And, before you spend time colorizing your message, make sure your recipient can view color. Not all systems are color compatible, and your message may be in black and white anyway.

P.S. For more information about the visual impact of color, see Chapter 5.

Urgency Overload

Dear Etta Kitt:

I'd like to offer a piece of advice to your readers. I have e-mail software that lets me designate priorities. I can designate FYI (for your information) or Urgent. I've always checked off Urgent because everything I send out is urgent to me. I didn't realize that people weren't reading my messages at all.

Last week I sent a message that was truly Urgent. I needed immediate feed-back, and no one responded. Without knowing it, I had become the "little boy who cried wolf." I learned two very valuable lessons:

1. *Unless a message is Urgent, don't tag it as such.*
2. *If something is truly urgent, consider phoning rather than risking that the recipient won't see the message in time.*

Frantic Fred

Dear Frantic Fred:

On behalf of harried e-mail users everywhere—thank you! And I want to emphasize your last comment. People generally listen to their voice messages after they've been away from their desks. But they don't necessarily check their e-mail messages that regularly. So if something is urgent, consider phoning the message.

Red in the Face

Dear Etta:

I attended a meeting recently where everyone was criticizing a manager who was out for the day. E-mail messages about the meeting—complete with negative comments about the manager—were sent from one person to another. And—as you may have guessed—one of those messages wound up in the manager's mailbox.

Embarrassed Enid

Dear Embarrassed Enid:

Never send anything you wouldn't want your mother or grandmother to see. Remember Murphy's Law: Assume the message will go to the worst possible recipient.

Chain Reaction

Dear Etta:

I keep getting chain letters and am not sure how to respond. The last one I got was supposedly from a dying boy seeking donations for a lifesaving operation. If I don't continue the chain, am I depriving this poor boy of a chance to live?

Sympathetic Sally

Dear Sympathetic Sally:

Wake up and smell the halibut; something's mighty fishy. Don't pass on chain letters. Although your heart may go out to this (alleged) boy, chances are this is a scam. Many chain letters offer get-rich-quick schemes and all sorts of wonderful things. They're not only annoying, they're often illegal.

Saving for a Rainy Day

Dear Ms. Kitt:

I'd like to advise readers to save copies of important messages they send and receive. It's so easy to hit the Delete key and loose valuable information. Diligent recordkeeping can come in handy one day. So be sure to cover your anatomy (CYA). Here's a little hint: Save important messages as a word-processing file on your hard drive or print them out. If it's something to share, put it on your company's intranet.

Dr. Kenneth A. Megill

Dear Dr. Megill:

I can't agree more.

International Savvy

Dear Etta:

I made a major blunder the other day. I sent an e-mail message to a gentleman in Europe to let him know about an urgent deadline of April 5, 1999. In order to save space, I wrote the date as 4/5/99. This important deadline was missed, and I was to blame. I'd forgotten that Europeans format dates differently. They put the day of the week before the month. So, April 5, 1999, to a European is 5/4/99. In essence, I gave the reader a deadline of May 4.

I also learned that the Japanese put the year first. So April 5, 1999, to a person in Japan is 99/4/5.

Miss Understood

Dear Miss Understood:

You offer a good piece of advice. It's good business practice to write out the month, date, and year *always* because you never know who may read your message. (Remember that e-mail can be forwarded around the world with the click of a button.) If you're compelled to use an abbreviation, use the written abbreviation like *Apr.* for April.

Part IV:
The Part of Tens

In this part. . .

No *...For Dummies* book is complete without a mother lode of tips. And, by coincidence, each of these chapters has ten tips in them.

You'll find tidbits on a variety of titillating topics here—everything from why letters fail and writing savvy sales letters to cutting information overload and working with a collaborative writing team.

Chapter 15
Ten Reasons Letters Fail

Writing [letters] when properly managed is but a different name for conversation.

—Laurence Sterne, *Tristram Shandy*

If you look at random business letters, you eventually see every mistake in the book. Here are the top ten on my hit parade:

1. Where's the Beef?

"Where's the beef?" is now a cultural catch-phrase. And many readers ask a similar question: "Where's the message?" Either the message is poorly written or the visual impact is so poor that the message is lost. Here are a few solutions:

✔ Create a subject line that delivers the message—the key issue. Why make the reader wade through scads of text to find out what she needs to know? For more information about subject lines, check out Chapter 3.

✔ Craft headlines that tell the story and are sequenced for the reaction of your reader. When headlines are well written and properly sequenced, the reader can get the big picture, just as she does when reading a newspaper. For more information about dynamic headlines and sequencing, check out Chapter 3.

✔ Make sure the body of the message is crystal clear and supports the headlines. For more information about drafting the body, check out Chapter 4.

✔ Create a visual impact that highlights your message. For more information about creating visual impact, check out Chapter 5.

Use your Start Up Sheet to determine your *audience, purpose,* and *key issue*.

2. Insensitive Salutations

When you walk into a room and someone shouts, "Hey, you!" do you consider that a welcoming greeting? I don't. If you want your letter to be well-received, start it off on the right foot.

"Dear Somebody" is better than "Dear Nobody"

Don't ever use the salutation *Dear Sir or Madam.* Instead, try to learn the person's name. If you can't find it, consider using the person's title—"Dear Vice President" or "Dear Marketing Director," for example.

When you use *Dear Sir,* you broadcast the fact that you're a dinosaur. Women are in the job market and don't like to be addressed as *Sir.* And if you use *Dear Madam,* that can have a negative connotation. . . "The best [little you know what] in [you know which Southern state]."

To Whom This May Concern:

On a scale of 1 to 10 (with 1 being the worst and 10 being the best), how do you think the salutation *To Whom This May Concern* rates? Perhaps a -2. It's as lazy and impersonal as you can get. *To Whom This May Concern* is an I-couldn't-bother-to-find-out-your-name-or-anything-about-you salutation.

3. I've Been Framed

People often try to squeeze a two-page letter into one page, forsaking the margins. Be sure to leave at least a one-inch margin on the top, bottom, and sides of your page. The white space serves as a frame around the words, giving the letter visual impact and making it easier to read. It's better to send a two-page letter that's visually appealing than a one-pager that's jam-packed.

4. Your "John Hancock" Please

It's amazing how many people forget to sign letters before sending them. This omission reaches the disastrous stage when the writer doesn't type her name at the bottom of the letter either. The reader may never know who sent the letter.

Even if you type your name at the end of a letter, make sure you sign it. A signature adds a personal touch—even when your handwriting is as dreadful as mine.

5. Spelling "Errers"

Make sure your letter doesn't have any spelling errors. Don't forget to go through the Editing Checklist on the Cheat Sheet. For more information about superb spelling, check out Appendix D. For tips on proofreading, check out Chapter 7.

I once received a letter from a job applicant who said she was well-suited for "writing and editting assignments." Do you think I trusted her to edit my valuable documents?

6. Grammatical Goofs

Ego sum rex Romanus et supra grammaticiam. Those are words spoken by Sigismund, Emperor of the Holy Roman Empire (HRE) in 1414. They mean "I am the Roman king and am above grammar."

Unless you're an Emperor of the HRE, you're not above grammar. Like the rest of us common folk, the way you communicate profoundly affects your success or failure in the business world. Don't let poor grammar ruin your chances for success. Grammar isn't grueling. For more information about those sticky grammatical issues, check out Appendix B.

The following is an excerpt that appeared in *The Boston Globe* recently. It's a response to a question that appeared on a national test to evaluate potential teachers. It was written by a person applying for a teaching position.

> ". . . In todays society it is very difficult to find a well-paid job to satisfy your income to buy a decent car to drive. A car is a very important machine to have in your posessions. . ." (Ouch! No wonder kids today aren't prepared for the business world.)

7. All About ME

Sigmund Freud believed that each child is born with a self-centered psyche called the *id*. Don't let your id hang out to the point that it overshadows the reader's point of view.

> *The id talking:* *I'm* happy to tell you that *we'll* be sending you. . .
>
> *The id stifled:* *You'll* be receiving. . .

Unless you're writing to a family member or friend, the reader doesn't really care about you. For more information about writing to the reader's needs, check out Chapter 6.

8. Kid in a Candy Shop

Some people have the urge to be creative and use a wide variety of fonts and colors. Documents with too much variety look like Web pages and should be avoided in business correspondence. Stick to one or two fonts and one or two colors. For more information about choosing fonts, check out Chapter 5.

9. Tinny Tone

If you clang in your reader's ear, she'll become tone deaf. For more information and examples to help you hone the tone, check out Chapter 6.

Ask yourself the following questions to judge your document's tone:

- ✔ Is my tone too formal and stuffy, sounding as if it were written by a veddy proper matron?

- ✔ Is my writing lean and pointed, or is it full of gobbledygook?

- ✔ Are the words I use positive, or is the glass half empty?

- ✔ Are my sentences active and engaging, or passive and drab?

10. The 500-Word Paragraph

Limit paragraphs to no more than seven lines. Limit sentences to no more than 25 words. For more information about paragraphs and sentences, check out Chapter 5.

Have you ever been overwhelmed by a paragraph that spanned the greater part of a page? When people see paragraphs that are too long, they tend to skip over them. The following paragraph contains a lot of useful information, but who'd read it?

> Be wary of giving out any information about an employee or former employee that's less than favorable. We've become a very litigious society and a number of employers have been sued for making unfavorable remarks. It's for this reason that many companies have adopted a policy of merely verifying a person's employment and length of employment. If you should be asked to have your name used as a reference and you don't feel that you can honestly give a favorable recommendation, you'd be wise to decline. However, if circumstances force you to terminate a valued employee, the employee may ask for a letter of recommendation to take with him. That's very appropriate and often done. When you're responding to a written request for information about a former employee, be certain to mark the response "Confidential." The reply should outline facts about the employee that will give a new employer an accurate picture. Try to separate opinions from facts.

Before you send any letter, be certain you go over the Editing Checklist that appears on the Cheat Sheet in the front of this book. You want your letter to stand out from the myriad of others—for the right reasons!

Chapter 16

Ten Tips For Writing Application Letters with a Hook

. . . .

In This Chapter

▶ Cover-lettering all the bases

▶ Being yourself

▶ Designing your own letterhead

▶ Personalizing each letter

▶ Focusing on the reader

▶ Including your key selling points

▶ Talking about money

▶ Finding the good

▶ Avoiding the bad

▶ Faxing and e-mailing

. . . .

Work is the curse of the drinking class.

— Oscar Wilde

Statistics show that Americans change jobs periodically and may have two, three, or more careers within a lifetime. Therefore, an application letter (also known as a cover letter) is a necessary part of your job-hunting arsenal. Employers can only interview a small number of candidates, so your application letter must do a great job of differentiating you from every other candidate. At the end of this chapter is a sample application letter that ties the ten tips together. (For more information on creating dynamite letters, check out Chapter 8.)

Don't forget to fill out the Start Up Sheet on the front of the Cheat Sheet. Your application letter may be one of the most important letters you ever write.

When you finish your letter, complete your Editing Checklist on the back of the Cheat Sheet. You want your letter to be memorable—for the right reasons.

1. Why You Write an Application Letter: A Résumé Isn't Enough

An application letter *must* accompany each résumé. The purpose of an application letter isn't to fatten up the envelope. It's to add strength to your résumé by giving the reader a capsulated view of who you are and what strengths you bring to the position. The time you invest in preparing your application letter is worth the effort. Exapmle 16-1 shows an application letter sent at the suggestion of a personal contact.

The goal of your application letter is to

- ✔ Grab the reader's attention
- ✔ Inspire him to turn to the résumé for more details
- ✔ Launch the interview process.

A great application letter doesn't make up for a poorly written résumé. Take the time to do both well. This book doesn't cover résumé writing, but t here are many books that do. You may want to check out *Résumés For Dummies* by Joyce Lain Kennedy (IDG Books Worldwide, Inc.).

2. Letting Your Personality Shine

Don't use someone else's application letter, no matter how wonderful and successful it may be. Wouldn't an employer be surprised to meet you and find out that you're an entirely different person from the one who wrote the letter? Write in your own style. An application letter should reflect *your* personality and *your* attitude toward *your* work and *your* life.

3. Preparing Letterhead

You can add a professional touch to your application letters by preparing letterhead. It doesn't have to be fancy or elaborate. Just create something on your word processor.

Use a font that's different from the text font. For example, if you're using Times New Roman for the text, consider using Arial for the letterhead, as Example 16-1 shows.

4. Personalizing Each Letter

Although it's often tempting to prepare a generic application letter and send it to many potential employers, this approach is ineffective because there is no generic job. Take the time to personalize each letter by researching the company and considering the skills needed to perform the position you're after. This strategy sets you apart from other candidates and increases your chances for an interview. Here are a few hints for personalizing:

- Match your strengths to the skills the job requires. If you're answering an ad, mention that you have the skills the employer is asking for.
- Show evidence that you understand the position and the company.
- Use some boilerplate (generic) phrases, but individualize each letter to meet the needs of the position you're after.

5. Keeping the Reader in Clear Focus

You want your letter to reflect your personal flavor, but always keep the audience and the industry you're targeting in focus. Pay close attention to the first item on your Start Up Sheet—targeting your audience. A clever and "catchy" letter may be appropriate for a position requiring imagination and creativity, but for more traditional employers stick to a more traditional format.

Conduct a trial run. Solicit feedback on the effectiveness of your letter from someone in the target industry or someone whose opinion you trust.

6. Building the Perfect Letter

The following sections offer pointers for the specific parts of your application letter.

The subject line

Make your subject line very specific. Consider using the position you're applying for or the person who referred you.

> ***Examples:***
>
> Subject: Position of Editor-in-Chief as advertised in *The Herald*
>
> Subject: Referred by Sally Jones

Although the subject line is your main headline, don't forget to use paragraph headlines to "walk" your reader through key pieces of information you want to highlight, as you see in Example 16-1 and other parts of this chapter.

The opening paragraph

Create an interesting opening paragraph that tells how you learned about this position. Did you learn of it a newspaper advertisement, from personal contact, or do you just know about the company (direct solicitation)? This paragraph mus get the reader's attention. You have a very short time in which to make an initial impression. This is your shot. Take a look at the following examples.

- ✔ **Answering a classified ad:** Your advertisement in *The Boston Globe* for a Process Engineer is of great interest to me. I have a Bachelor's Degree in Metallurgy and five years' experience in the semiconductor industry.

- ✔ **Responding based on a personal contact:** Mr. Tom Christensen, of your Training Department, brought to my attention your need for a top-quality Contracts Administrator. He's confident that my background and experience enables me to make a large contribution to Hanscom, Inc.

- ✔ **Sending out a letter of direct solicitation:** As a recent college graduate with a degree in mathematics, I want to make a contribution to the growth and high standards of Spring Valley High School.

Capture and use key phrases from any ads you answer. For example, if the ad calls for experience in *computer-aided drafting (CAD)* and you have it, mention it. If the ad asks for someone *flexible* and *creative,* use those terms to describe yourself. To really show that you have what it takes and more, try side-by-side headlines such as:

Your requirements	*My qualifications*
CAD	CAD/CAM
Flexible and creative	Flexible, creative, and people-oriented

The convincing middle paragraph(s)

After your opening, elaborate on your qualifications and explain how the company can benefit from them. Try to point out how you can do a superb job for the company because of your experience and/or the lessons you've learned throughout your career. Following are three different approaches.

I offer experience and leadership

My background includes 15 years in manufacturing and engineering. I'm experienced in the construction of production machinery and plant engineering requirements. I've been praised for my ability to direct and motivate others and have demonstrated the ability to meet very tight deadlines.

Saved $750,000 in one year

For five years I was the Manager of Marketing Communications at Sterling Corporation. I managed a $3.5 million budget, against which I saved $750,000 in one year. My responsibilities included overseeing a broad range of assignments for international audiences, including sales and customer training, newsletters, product brochures, advertising, news releases, user documentation and video productions.

I can increase sales and build goodwill

My employment with A&B Life Insurance Company and Delta Mutual Insurance Company taught me a great deal about human relations and the finer techniques of selling. As a result of this experience, I'm convinced that I can build sales and goodwill for Enterprise, Inc.

Your application letter determines whether the reader turns the page to read your résumé. Therefore, don't copy everything that's in your résumé. Just whet the reader's appetite by selecting the highlights that make you a strong candidate.

The closing paragraph

The final paragraph is your call to action. Request an interview. Include a telephone number where you can be reached if the number doesn't appear on letterhead. Following are three closing ideas:

When can we meet?

My résumé is merely a piece of paper. It doesn't reflect my enthusiasm, sense of humor, and team spirit. You'll need to evaluate those strengths for yourself. When can we get together?

Next step

I'd welcome the opportunity to meet with you so that you can evaluate the enthusiastic and creative contributions I can make to XYZ, Inc. You can reach me at (999) 123-4567 any afternoon after 2 o'clock.

Let's talk about how you can benefit from my background

I'm willing to travel or relocate. Please call me so that we can discuss how my qualifications can benefit or SalesForce, Inc.

7. Discussing Salary Requirements

Addressing your salary requirements in the application letter may weaken your bargaining power. If you come in too low, you devalue yourself. If you come in too high, you won't be considered. What the employer is trying to learn is if your salary requirements are in the ballpark. So, don't take yourself out of the game prematurely. Save salary discussions for the interview if at all possible. If an ad you're responding to forces the salary issue, however, how blunt should you be? Here are some suggestions:

- ✔ Ignore the salary issue completely. If you dazzle them with your qualifications, they'll probably get in touch with you anyway.

- ✔ Mention the range of salaries you've had in recent years, or state the range you expect the position to pay within.

- ✔ Give your current salary. (You can always try to justify at the interview that this position has greater responsibility.)

- ✔ State that you expect a salary commensurate with your experience.

The experts vary in their opinions of which option works best. Go with the option that makes you most comfortable.

8. Letter Do's

When you write an application letter, keep in mind the following points:

- ✔ Many resources can help you find information such as who heads a certain department. The company's receptionist usually can provide the names and titles you need; your local library has reference books you can use; and if the company has a Web page, it's always a good idea to check it out.

- ✔ Restrict your letter to three or four paragraphs.

- ✔ Select the highlights of your career and the qualifications that best sell your abilities. For example, consider listing projects you managed, money you saved the company, contributions you made, and anything else that made you a superior employee. If you're a recent graduate with little or no experience in the field, list relevant courses or volunteer work.

- ✔ Emphasize the contribution you can make to the company to which you're applying.

- ✔ It's okay to use "I" several times throughout the letter. After all, the letter is about you. However, try refer to yourself in other ways. For example, use "You can reach me at . . .", rather than "I can be reached at . . .".

- ✔ Mention that your résumé is enclosed or attached.

9. Letter Taboos

Here are some things to avoid:

- ✔ Don't reiterate everything in your résumé. Just sum up a few key selling points.

- ✔ Avoid egotistical or trite remarks such as "I have a good personality" or "I'm dependable." (Who's going to admit that their personality is lousy or that they're undependable?)

- ✔ Don't include a photo unless you're applying for a modeling job.

- ✔ Avoid statements about anything you can't back up, such as an award you won.

And never, never send a letter with food or coffee-cup stains. As obvious as this may be, you can't imagine how many application letters I've received knowing the person folded the letter while eating a Big Mac.

10. Sending Electronically

Fax and e-mail are now quite popular ways of sending application letters and résumés. These electronic alternatives offer the distinct advantage of going directly to the reader.

- ✔ Faxes are typically put in the reader's inbox or on his desk. They're not screened as letters from the post office often are.

- ✔ E-mail pops up on the reader's screen. With a great subject line, you can make your application letter and résumé shout "READ ME!" For more information on crafting great subject lines, check out Chapters 3 and 13.

Sending a fax

Prepare the application letter for a fax just as you would for sending through the mail. If you're launching a big job search and will be sending multiple faxes, think of all the money you save in envelopes and postage by sending during off-peak hours.

You don't have to use good stationery for the letter or résumé because you keep the original.

Sending an e-mail message

There are some slight differences when you send an application letter via e-mail. In e-mail, the address and subject line are part of the header, not part of the message, so when you write the message, include a salutation, body, complimentary closing, and your name. Don't repeat the address or the subject line. For more information on parts of an e-mail message, check out Chapter 13.

Send your résumé as an attachment.

Becki Gentry
10 John Place, Salem, MA 01970
(978) 562-3451

Letterhead prepared in Ariel

January 15, XXXX

Ms. Beth Wolf, President
Dillon Enterprises
11 Robert Street
Woburn, MA 01801

Sent to a specific person

Dear Ms. Wolf:

Position of Principal Engineer

Position applied for is the subject line

Ms. Kristen N. Stephen, Manager of your Finance Department, mentioned
that you're looking for a Principal Engineer for your new product line. She
suggested that I contact you.

My 25 years of experience

Strong headlines

My 25 years of engineering experience in advanced systems design have
earned me the following recognition, which I'm certain will be of benefit to
your company:

- Excalibur Award, Alcan's highest honor, for leadership in the
  MK 21 Fuze Product that enhanced the yield by 100% on major
  production contract.

- Alcan's individual recognition award for outstanding
  contribution in a lead engineering position in a military satellite
  program.

- Patent pending for high speed camera scoring, a project which
  was displayed at the Pentagon.

Next step

Mentions enclosed résumé and asks for an interview

After you have reviewed the enclosed résumé, I'd appreciate coming in for
an interview. I'll call you early next week to arrange for a convenient time.
Thank you.

Sincerely,

Becki Gentry
Enclosure

Example 16-1:
Application
letter using a
personal
contact.

Chapter 17

Ten Tips for Jazzy Sales Letters

> *Some of the sharpest traders we know are artists, and some of the best salesmen are writers.*
>
> —E.B. White, American writer

Sales letters are written sales calls. They're a terrific medium for getting your message out because they're a personal form of communication. You can send sales letters via snail mail (the post office), fax, or e-mail. Even when readers know that your letter is sent to thousands of people, they can still get the feeling that they're reading a personal note. People who are good at writing sales letters know this and use this medium to their advantage. They do their best to create a personal bond between the letter and the reader.

How long do you make your sales letter? This question inspires a lot of discussion and at least one more question: Do people really take the time to read multiple-page sales letters? Some experts feel that multipage sales letters are more effective than shorter ones—the theory being that people equate quantity with quality.

Even if you're working with a direct mail company, you still need to understand what constitutes a great sales letter. Not all the direct mail companies hit the mark.

Regardless of what you're selling, try to "talk" with your prospective buyer in your sales letter. Chat informally with short sentences and simple words. Make it easy for the reader to understand your offer and what you expect her to do. Most people only give your letter a three-second once-over before deciding whether to read further or toss the letter into the trash. For more information about honing your tone, check out Chapter 6. Chapter 5 discusses designing for visual impact.

Don't forget to fill out the Start Up Sheet featured on the Cheat Sheet in the front of the book. It's critical that you understand your audience, purpose, and key issue. Your livelihood depends on it.

1. The Envelope Please

Many people regard sales letters as junk mail and place them in the trash unread. So the key is to get the reader to look inside the envelope. A five percent response rate to an unsolicited mailing is considered good. Perhaps these hints can increase the odds.

- Handwrite the name and address of the addressee on the envelope and don't include a return address. Anonymity arouses the reader's curiosity.

- Use a postage stamp rather than a postage meter so that the envelope doesn't shout "junk mail." A stamp makes your letter look like a personalized mailing.

- Use a compelling tag line on the envelope. There are classic cases of people thinking they've won sweepstakes because the envelope read "You have already won a million dollars." Never be deceitful, but do be creative.

All the tips in this chapter apply to large and small mailings. If the mailing is large and some of these hints are too labor intensive, do what many companies do: Hire a temp to lick stamps, seal envelopes, sign letters, and the like.

Not all junk mail is "junque"

I recently received an envelope that looked like junk mail and threw it in the trash unopened. As my husband was emptying the trash, the envelope fell on the floor. Something compelled him to open it. He scratched his head and blurted out, "Are you so rich that you're throwing money away?" It was a royalty check for several thousand dollars. The publisher I had been writing for was acquired by another company, and I didn't recognize the return address. Since then, I never throw anything away until I've opened it. There may be a real treasure inside!

2. Attracting by Attaching

Attaching a simple object associated with your industry can be an effective attention-getter. A seaside resort may include a small bag of sand, or a lamination business may send a laminated copy of a couple's wedding announcement to them.

Examples:

This small bag of sand is just our way of reminding you that it's been a long time since we've had the pleasure of your company at the Sandy Beach Resort.

We've taken the liberty of permanently encasing in Plasticeen your recent engagement announcement that appeared in THE BOSTON GLOBE. As you can see, Plasticeen is . . .

Someone I know recently sent a resume to the Velcro company using—what else?—Velcro to attach pages one and two. What a creative idea. She was called for an interview and got the job!

3. Offering a Freebee

People love to get something for nothing. If it's appropriate, offer something for free—perhaps a coupon or a free demonstration. Or maybe there's a white paper on your Web site that's informational and can benefit the potential customer.

4. Starting Off with a Bang

Using a powerful opening is good old-fashioned psychology. Novelists call it a hook, journalists call it a lead, and writers call it an opening line. Whatever you call it, it makes all the difference. Here are some "bangers."

Questions, anecdotes, parables, and quotations

Asking a question gets your reader involved in mentally answering it. Opening with an anecdote, parable, or quotation is equally engaging. The following examples illustrate different approaches.

- **Question:** Can you use additional income?
- **Anecdote:** The other night I lay awake at night thinking about . . .
- **Parable:** As a documentation specialist, you undoubtedly spend a great deal of time focusing on the development of others. When was the last time you took a couple of days to focus on YOUR professional development?
- **Quotation:** "Don't wait for your ship to come in—swim out to it."

Stories

A story is longer than a question, anecdote, or parable but can be a great hook. Here's one that lured me into reading a technical manual:

> The door closed slowly as Jay entered the president's office and sank slowly into the dark leather chair in the far corner. Jay had been there many times but knew by the tone of the president's telephone conversation that she had another one of her "brainstorms."

5. Finding the Pain

One of advertising's classic sales techniques is finding the prospect's pain. You can see his approach used in marketing campaigns and commercials. The method goes like this: Direct the prospect's attention to a problem, and then proceed to make the problem seem even worse. After you establish the problem as a major impediment in your prospect's life, you can introduce your service or product as the perfect solution! The paragraph that follows applies this format succinctly and successfully.

Do your customers ever call your main number and get bounced from one representative to another while each one scurries around trying to be helpful? This level of frustration might be sending your customers flying into the arms of your competitor. We have your solution! Call 999-123-3445 to find out how you can keep your customers loyal and coming back for more.

6. Stressing Benefits, Not Features

Discuss how the benefits of your product or service can improve the customer's life, work situation, or bottom line. The benefits may be obvious to you, but don't leave it up to the reader to figure them out. Use headlines to link the benefits to the features. For more information about headlines, check out Chapter 3.

There's a major difference between a benefit and a feature. A *benefit* is about the reader. A *feature* is about the product or service. For example, a feature may be wider bandwith. A benefit is getting quicker access to information.

The following headlines stress the benefit to the readers. Notice that they all start with action words.

Examples:

Giving You the Lowest Total Cost of Ownership

Providing You Information Around the Clock—Around the World

Realizing a $500,000 Return on Investment in One Year

7. Concluding with a Call to Action

Always end by telling the reader what you expect her to do. You may want her to fill out an order blank, call a specific person, wait for your call, or attend a seminar. The following examples give you hints on wording your final paragraph.

Examples:

Act Now!

Remember, this offer is good through the week of June 1. After your order is in, you can be guaranteed continued service.

Next Step

All you need to do is sign your name at the bottom of this letter and fax it to me. Your additional coverage is effective immediately.

This is your last chance to make a strong impression. Of course, you must know your audience. Some readers can stand more warmth than others. In general, it's better to be too warm than too distant. Rather than the typical "Sincerely," or "Very truly yours," consider using any of the following:

- ✔ With best wishes,
- ✔ With confidence,
- ✔ Just to keep in touch,
- ✔ Warmest greetings,

Sign your letter legibly. One of the biggest mistakes people make is to send a letter with an illegible or missing signature, and/or no typewritten name below the signature. A sloppy signature may be construed as the sign of sloppy service. For more information about why letters fail, check out Chapter 15.

If your mailing is so large you're afraid you'll get carpal tunnel syndrome signing each letter, consider an electronic signature or having someone else sign your name.

8. Considering a Postscript

Studies show that most readers go directly to the postscript before looking at anything else! The P.S. can briefly restate the main point, mention something thought provoking, or be a final call to action. For more information about postscripts, check out Chapter 8.

9. Becoming a Junk-Mail Junkie

Do you save the junk mail that comes to your house or office? If not, perhaps you should—junk mail can be an education. Businesses spend hundreds of millions of dollars each year designing and sending direct mail pieces. Obviously, direct mailing works or companies wouldn't keep sending them. Look at the direct mail letters and envelopes delivered to you and ask some critical questions about them. Then use what you learn in your own sales letters.

- ✔ Are the letters amateurish or well done?
- ✔ Do they pull you in or turn you off?
- ✔ Are they fun to read or boring?

Collect your junk mail for a week or two. Look at it, study it, critique it, rewrite it, play with it. Try to incorporate what's exciting about each into your writing. If you can do that, you will write winning sales letters!

10. Taboos

The first nine hints have been do's, here are some don'ts:

- Don't be too palsy-walsy with the reader. She may get irritated and think you're insincere.
- Don't to be too cutesy. In this gotta-have-a-gimmick world, cute is overdone. It's inappropriate in most situations.
- Don't make idle statements such as, "You'll be sorry if you miss this opportunity."
- Don't make too many points in one letter. Concentrate on your strongest selling point—the key benefit(s).
- Don't bad-mouth the competition or make unwarranted claims. Let your product sell itself.
- Don't make claims such as "revolutionary," "incredible," "astounding," and other hyperbolic statements.

Don't forget to go through the Editing Checklist featured in the Cheat Sheet at the front of this book before you send the letter. Your first job is to sell the reader on your thoroughness and competence.

Chapter 18

Ten Ways to Cut Information Overload in the Electronic World

- -

In This Chapter

▶ Choosing the right delivery vehicle

▶ Filing efficiently

▶ Knowing when to write

▶ Filtering your incoming e-mail

▶ Forwarding messages with your own stamp

▶ Getting your message across quickly

▶ Crafting an easy-to-read message

▶ Responding appropriately

▶ Breaking the chains

▶ Using (not abusing) your company's system

- -

We are drowning in information but starved for knowledge.

—John Naisbitt, American writer
and social researcher

*W*hen computers first hit the marketplace, everyone was anticipating the paperless office. Well, that paperless office is about as likely as the paperless bathroom. Have you ever looked at the desk of a technoid and viewed stacks of green and white computer printouts piled to the ceiling? (I use the term *technoid* lovingly; my husband is one.)

I've seen people reprint a lengthy document because they changed one word on one page. If anything, computers have advanced the proliferation of paper. The trees are wincing. The modern era has turned into a quagmire of information—an *infobog!*

Add to that the e-mail explosion. While e-mail messages aren't on paper, they have to be read and dealt with. Some people I've spoken to receive hundreds of e-mail messages each day! But how many of these messages are really important? And, how many spark interest by many jumping off the screen and shouting "Read Me"?

Use the guidelines in this chapter to avoid contributing to the infobog or getting stuck in it yourself.

1. Optimizing Delivery and Sending Methods

When you're the sender, you're in full control. You can cut overload by asking yourself these questions before you send e-mail:

Is there a more appropriate way to deliver the message?

Before you send an e-mail message, consider other methods of delivery: You can telephone, fax, send traditional mail, visit your recipient, or share your information in a meeting. Take the time to decide which method is best for your message.

Table 18-1 shows my recommendations for how to get your message across in various situations.

Table 18-1	Choosing Your Message's Delivery Method
Situation	*Best Choice for Delivery*
It's noon and you learn that the meeting you scheduled for 3:00 needs to take place at 4:00. How do you notify the people scheduled to attend?	**Telephone** and leave a message if necessary or visit and leave a note on the computer of anyone not in his office. You can't assume that everyone will read an e-mail in time, but people tend to check telephone messages.
You decide that your harsh words to a coworker were unwarranted. How do you apologize?	**Visit** your colleague and apologize face to face. If a visit isn't feasible, **mail** a note—preferably a handwritten one. Check out Chapter 8 for situations such as this one. You may even borrow from the examples there.
A coworker earns a promotion. How do you send congratulations?	**E-mail** is great for congratulatory notes. You can also say it in person with a **visit** or by **telephone**.

Am I a selective sender?

Send messages only to those who need to receive them. There's a great tendency in an e-mail environment to broadcast your message to everyone you've ever met (an exaggeration, of course).

Are my mailing lists up to date?

Make sure you purge the names of employees who are no longer with the company and promptly delete the names of people who ask to be removed from your list. Send messages only to those people who need to read your pearly words.

2. Maximizing Filing Capabilities

You can do a lot to reduce information overload just by making the most of your filing capabilities. Ask yourself the following questions about your current filing system:

Do I use file folders effectively?

Do you clutter your metal file cabinet with papers that have no order? Or do you categorize the papers and place them in labeled file folders so you can retrieve them easily? (This assumes you have enough time to clean out your overflowing inbox.)

Rather than keeping all your e-messages in your inbox, create electronic file folders and label them as you do paper file folders so you can retrieve them easily. Filing electronically is so quick and easy (usually just dragging and dropping a message where you want it) that you have little excuse for chaos in your e-mail files.

Can I post this instead of sending it?

Many companies have intranet bulletin boards where you can post documents for electronic viewing. You can send a message to the site so other intranet users can access it when they need to. Intranet bulletin boards are useful for posting FYIs (such as information about the company picnic) and resource material (such as white papers and reports). Posting can eliminate paper reporting and create instant access to information resulting in people able to do their work more quickly and efficiently.

Talk to your network administrator or technology guru to find out what resources your company already has and how to use them.

3. Writing for the Sake of Visibility

People haven't heard from you in a while, and you feel it's time you earned some brownie points. Keep in mind that you don't get brownie points for adding to information overload. People who send e-mail for that purpose are abusing technology and should be given a life sentence in a chat room.

If you inundate people with nonessential messages, you run the risk of being stereotyped: Like the boy who cried wolf, no one will pay attention even when you have something important to say.

4. Using Bozo Filters

Some people use *bozo filters* (also know as *filters*) to zap out unwanted e-mail messages. Bozo filters demand that you preload the names of people from whom you want to receive mail, and the filters prioritize incoming messages from the names you entered. For example, a message from the president of the company will jump to the top of your screen. If you need information on bozo filters, chat with your computer guru or take a look at *E-Mail For Dummies,* 2nd Edition, by John R. Levine, Carol Baroudi, Margaret Levine Young, and Arnold Reinhold (IDG Books Wordwide, Inc.).

The downside to using a filter is that you risk blocking out valuable information from people you don't include on your list—others who may really have something to tell you. Keep in mind that information can change the course of your career, and opportunities may come from the most unexpected sources.

5. Changing the Subject Line of Forwarded Messages

Before you forward a message to someone else—think! Even though you didn't write the original document, you're still sending information that can add to overload. Be alert to situations where you can change the subject line, the headline, the sequence, or the key issue to meet the needs of the person(s) you're forwarding the message to.

Bob, a business associate, forwarded me an e-mail message whose subject line read: "Tomorrow's meeting canceled." Based on that subject line, I took the meeting Bob and I had scheduled for the next day off my calendar. I later found out that the message concerned a meeting Bob had with someone else. Bob forwarded the e-mail just for my information without bothering to change the subject line. Without realizing it, he sent me an inaccurate message. And I didn't show up at his meeting.

6. Crafting Subject Lines and Headlines to Cut Overload

Subject lines that deliver the message and headlines that tell the rest of the story are key factors in cutting overload. For more information about crafting subject lines and headlines, check out Chapter 3. Here's a brief overview:

Do my subject lines shout: Read me?

The subject line determines whether your message gets read. After you create a subject line, take a good look at it and ask yourself these questions:

- ✔ Does it get attention?
- ✔ Does it provide a key word(s)?
- ✔ Does it signal its level of importance?
- ✔ Does it deliver the message, if appropriate?

Are my headlines action packed?

Think about the way newspaper headlines direct your attention to key issues. You can have the same impact on readers by using headlines such as the following:

- ✔ Action requested (or recommended or required)
- ✔ Person to contact [Name]
- ✔ Deadline [Date]
- ✔ How to . . .
- ✔ Next step(s)

7. Creating Visual Impact: Getting the Message Across

Strong visual impact helps the reader organize information and emphasizes what's important. Keep the opening paragraph short so it's inviting. When the opening paragraph is too long, the reader may groan and not bother to read the rest of the message. For more information about designing for visual impact, check out Chapter 5.

Is my formatting effective?

Many e-mail systems can use only the ASCII character set, which means your font choices and styles are limited. As I describe in Chapter 13, you do have other ways to highlight text, namely by:

- ✔ Using asterisks or dashes
- ✔ Leaving double spaces
- ✔ Leaving lots of white space
- ✔ Boxing information

Err on the side of simplicity. If you're sending a message to someone who's on another e-mail system, simplify your formatting because not all e-mail systems are created equal. If your system has all the bells and whistles and your reader's doesn't, your beautifully formatted and clearly expressed message may be garbled on his screen.

Is my message concise?

The essence of good business writing (and remember that e-mail is business writing) is to remove any needless words. You don't want to force your reader to read long-winded, visually unappealing documents. Strip messages down to their bare essentials. For more information about keeping it short and simple, check out Chapter 6.

Concise: I understand the criteria for the computer engineering position.

Wordy: This message is to inform you that I understand what you indicated would be the criteria for determining the qualifications for the newly created position of computer engineer.

Is my message in an easy-to-read sequence?

Readers must be able to scan the document to find what's important. For more information about sequencing, check out Chapter 3.

Short documents

If your document is longer than one screen, put all the key information, such as who, what, where, when, why, and how, on the first screen.

Long documents

To make long documents reader-friendly, consider one of the following tips:

✔ Include a table of contents or executive summary on the first screen.

✔ Send the document as an attachment if it's longer than three screens.

✔ If you use a compression program, tell your recipient which program it is and make sure he can decompress it.

✔ Post the document to an intranet bulletin board and send an e-mail message letting folks know how to find it.

8. Double-Checking Reply Lists

Many novice users reply to messages by responding to everyone rather than to just the sender. This is annoying to receivers who have to wade through messages that don't interest them. This is particularly troublesome when sending broadcast messages.

Reply only to the person(s) who needs to receive your response. And consider deleting the original message unless you need it for clarity or a (virtual) paper trail.

Scenario: A coworker invites 50 company employees to an awards dinner. He requests an RSVP.

Problem: Some e-mail systems automatically send replies to everyone on the original list. Imagine 50 people cluttering each other's mailboxes with these replies.

Solution: Encourage people to double check their response lists before sending a reply.

9. Ignoring Chain Letters and Scams

Chain letters and scams are rampant in the electronic world; they contribute dramatically to information overload. Big companies aren't giving free trips to Bora Bora; there's no organ donor theft ring in Kalamazoo; Colonel Sanders isn't selling his chicken recipes; and the sky isn't falling. Even if there were a rocket disaster that contained plutonium and it spread over the entire northern hemisphere, do you really think this information would reach the public in a chain letter?

If you're absolutely, positively, and emphatically compelled to forward that 15th generation message you get, at least have the decency to trim the 25 miles of headers showing everyone else who's received the message in the last several years. And it's a good idea to get rid of all the > symbols that begin each line—they're a tip-off that the message has been around the e-world a gazillion times.

10. Using Your Business System for Business Messages Only

Some companies allot space on their intranets to post nonwork-related announcements, such as: "I'm having a garage sale this weekend" or "Please stop by my office; I'm selling cookies for my daughter's soccer league." Otherwise, don't overload your company's e-mail with such notices.

Chapter 19

Ten Hints for Writing Savvy Speeches

It usually takes me more than three weeks to write a good impromptu speech.

—Mark Twain

Two of the things people fear most are the dentist's drill and the podium. Speaking is truly one of life's terrors. If you resist speaking before a group because you fear you'll drop dead from "stage fright," you're not alone. Many people—even well-known TV and stage personalities—suffer from stage fright. Believe it or not, stage fright is actually healthy. The sudden rush of the hormone adrenaline is a form of positive energy that makes you appear excited about your talk.

Public speaking may be anything from a talking head behind a podium to a presentation with all sorts of visual aids. To ensure that you deliver a presentation with panache, check out Chapter 11 where you find out about the pros and woes of visuals and handouts.

Even though the draft of a speech isn't writing someone else will read, you must still identify your reader, purpose, and key issue in order to write an effective speech. The Start Up Sheet on the Cheat Sheet in the front of this book can help you deal with these critical issues.

1. Asking the Four Questions

(These four questions have nothing to do with a Passover seder.) Before you begin writing a speech, try this exercise: Write the answer to each of these questions in one sentence.

1. What's my topic?

Generally, the topic is obvious, but on occasion it isn't.

Obvious: You're asked to speak at a professional conference on a special process you developed. The process, of course, will be your topic.

Not obvious: You're a member of the Rotary Club and are invited to speak at the March meeting because the group is having trouble getting a speaker for that meeting. You have to speak on something that will interest your audience. If you're unsure, discuss it with the person who asked you.

2. What's my message?

 Question 7 on your Start Up Sheet concerns getting your key point across. If you can distill your key point in one sentence, you can deliver a clear message to your audience.

3. What's my purpose?

Question 6 on your Start Up Sheet talks about your purpose for writing or, in this case, speaking. Your purpose is what you want the audience to think, feel, or do. You purpose isn't what will benefit you personally.

4. What's in it for me?

Are you tooting your own horn? Does the speech mean exposure and a boost to your career? Is it an opportunity to speak before a live audience? Any of these motivations are valid, just know what they are.

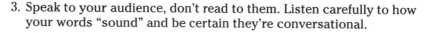

Briefer is better (or at least healthier)

Contrast the following tidbits:

✔ George Washington delivered his second inaugural address in just 135 words.

✔ William Henry Harrison delivered his inaugural address in 9,000 words; it lasted

two hours. The following day Harrison came down with a cold, and a month later he died of pneumonia. Long live brevity!

2. Thinking Lean and Mean

Limit your speech to no more than 20 minutes. People have short attention spans, and their minds tend to drift after 20 minutes. (If you have an interactive exercise, you'll keep their attention longer.) Stick to your topic and tell the audience what they need to know.

We live in a "wristwatch" society and people operate on time schedules. If you're scheduled to speak for a limited period of time, be certain to stick to the time frame.

3. Speaketh, not Readeth

The key to good speechwriting is to keep in mind that your words will be spoken, not read. Here's an approach that works for me:

1. Write the speech out.

2. Tape record it.

3. Speak to your audience, don't read to them. Listen carefully to how your words "sound" and be certain they're conversational.

Writing a speech gives you a chance to break some of the laws of grammar—single-word sentences and idiomatic expressions reflect the way people speak in casual conversation, and are often acceptable in a speech. You must appear to be speaking to your audience, not reading to them.

Speaking: I was working on the Smith v. Smith file when I had a sudden revelation.

Reading: The Smith v. Smith file, on which I was working for the last few months, presented me with a sudden revelation. (This even reads poorly as text, but you get the point.)

4. Faking Spontaneity

To sound spontaneous, rehearse in front of a mirror or in front of people who are willing to be guinea pigs. You'll probably speak a little faster during the "real thing" because of the adrenaline. Even though you think that certain people are naturals when it comes to public speaking, very few are; they work at it.

Always use notes or your fully written speech, and highlight your crucial points, so that they catch your eye when you glance down. Do try to memorize key sections. Make lots of eye contact with your audience and make a point of pausing. Spontaneity doesn't just happen—it takes practice. (Keep in mind the Twain quote at the beginning of this chapter.)

5. Timing Is Everything

Here's how the experts (whoever the experts are) recommend you divide your time:

- **Opening Remarks.** Limit your opening remarks to one or two minutes. As George Jessel once said, "If you haven't struck oil in your first two or three minutes, stop boring." Do what works for your personal style. Make sure your opening is appropriate for the topic.
  - Relate a story.
  - Ask a question.
  - Use a quotation.
  - Cite a statistic.
  - Tell a joke.
- **Body.** Limit the body of your speech to no more than two to five key issues. Tell your audience about your theme and capture the major points. Don't state the obvious or give inconsequential data.
- **Closing Remarks.** Take one to two minutes to wrap things up. A good speech ends with a bang. Recap your theme and major points. Or end with an appeal, illustration, inducement, quote, or summary.

Write your speech out; not word-for-word necessarily, but at least point-by-point. The main thing is to catch the audience's interest quickly, share something of value, and leave the audience with something memorable.

6. Introducing a Speaker

If you introduce a speaker, avoid the tiresome openers you hear much of the time.

- ✔ "Ladies and gentlemen, this is a person who needs no introduction." (Then why bother?)

- ✔ "Ladies and gentlemen, h e e r r e's [name]." (This line worked for Ed McMahon, but it won't work for you.)

- ✔ "We are truly honored to have with us. . ."

- ✔ "Without further ado. . ."

- ✔ "It is indeed my privilege to introduce. . ."

Consider a quick anecdote about the speaker or a few highlights of the speaker's career that make her worth listening to.

7. Getting the Right Tone

Use language that's clear, concise, and conversational. **Keep It Short and Simple (KISS).** Use positive words and the active voice. Be sensitive to word associations, sarcasm, and sexist language. For more information about getting the right tone, check out Chapter 6.

There are three specific ways to get the right tone and stress your message:

1. **Phrase your sentences so that they're strong and have impact.**

   Strong: Financial planners believe that the market will continue to rise.

   Weak: There's a belief among financial planners that the market will continue to rise.

2. **Use your voice to stress words or phrases you want to punctuate.**

   The goldgoldfish is in the sink. (Simple statement of fact. Nothing is stressed.)

   The *goldfish* is in the sink. (As opposed to the shark.)

   The goldfish *is* in the sink. (In case you doubted it the first time.)

   The goldfish is *in* the sink. (As opposed to in the fish tank.)

   The goldfish is in the *sink*. (As opposed to the bathtub.)

3. Use statements and pauses.

Here's how that works: Make a bold statement. Pause. Then say, "Think about that for a moment." Then pause again.

I generally put two slash marks (/ /) in my notes where I want to pause.

Be aware of your speech patterns

When you listen to your recorded speech on tape, pay attention to speech patterns that may distract the audience from what you're saying. Many people speak each sentence with the same vocal pattern. They start in the lower register, work up to the emphasized word in the sentence, and then trail down until they reach the end of the sentence. This pattern can literally rock an audience to sleep: Try to vary where the emphasis falls in your sentences.

Avoid *umm*-ing. After a speech Robert Kennedy, Jr. gave recently, a news commentator pointed out that Kennedy used about 20 *ums*. Now, whenever I hear Kennedy speak, I find myself counting his *um's* and don't concentrate on what he's saying.

Use repetition for emphasis

Repetition can give strength to your ideas.

Strong: Why should we adopt this policy? We should adopt it because it will give us the competitive edge. And we should adopt it because it will give us a 50 percent profit.

Weak: Why should we adopt this policy? Because it will give us the competitive edge and a 50 percent profit.

Include alliterations or rhymes

These are often memorable parts of your talk.

Alliteration: Really rigid requirements!

Rhyme: I'm sure you remember the famous rhyme that came out of the O.J. Simpson trial: "If it doesn't fit, you must acquit."

8. Phrases to Leave at the Office

The following includes some phrases you should omit from your talk because your audience may perceive them incorrectly (or correctly).

If you say . . .	Your audience may think . . .
I'm really not prepared.	Why should I waste my time listening to you?
I don't know why I was asked to speak here today.	Am I being victimized by someone's poor judgment?
As unaccustomed as I am . . .	Thanks for sharing that. I should've stayed away.
I won't take up too much of your time.	The speaker doth protest too much. This is going to be a sleeper.
I don't want to offend anyone, but . . .	Oh, no. Here comes an insult.
Have you heard the one about . . .	Jerry Seinfeld she's not.
Just give me a few more minutes.	It's already been too long.

9. On the Foreign Front

It's a small world and shrinking quickly. International travel is commonplace. If you have occasion to speak before a foreign audience (even if they're foreigners visiting or living in your own country) you must display international savvy. Here are a few suggestions when speaking to people from foreign countries or cultures.

Do's

Here are a few audience enticers:

- ✔ Start your talk by expressing your sincere honor at being able to address the group.

- ✔ Deliver a powerful line or phrase in the audience's native language.

  I can remember when John F. Kennedy brought the house down (so to speak) when he delivered a speech in Germany. He gave a very emphatic hand gesture and bellowed out, *"Ich bin ein Berliner!"* Some Germans loved his words. But the sentiment backfired, however, with some Germans. Why? There was a double meaning to JFK's famous words. In addition to stating, "I am a Berliner," he also said, "I am a jelly doughnut." (Yes, *Berliner* is the German word for "jelly doughnut.")

- Be aware of current events that surround the country or culture and be sensitive to those issues.

- Quote a well-known person from your audience's country or culture. Make sure that person is someone your audience can admire.

- Bolster the need for international communication. Use statistics, anecdotes, or stories.

  "We are greatly indebted to [host country] for . . ."

  "The majority of [your company's] foreign investments are in [host country]."

- If you're talking about measurements, use metric terms. The United States is one of the few places in the universe that doesn't use the metric system.

If you have occasion to give out business cards, here's a way to win points: Write your name, company, and address on the reverse side of your card in the language of the host country. Offer it with the native-language side showing.

Taboos

Here are ways to avoid shooting yourself in both feet:

- Never (inadvertently) insult your audience with cute remarks that can be interpreted as social blunders.

- Never tell off-color stories or use profanities.

- Avoid idiomatic expressions your audience may not understand.

Tricky translations

When you say something in a foreign language, be sure it translates properly. Following are some signs translated into English to accommodate English-speaking visitors.

Bangkok dry cleaners: "Please drop your trousers here for best results."

Acapulco hotel: "The manager has personally passed all the water served here."

Budapest zoo: "Please do not feed the animals. If you have any suitable food, give it to the guard on duty."

Paris elevator: "Please leave your values at the front desk."

Paris boutique: "Dresses for street walking."

Czech tourist agency: "Take one of our horse-driven carriage tours. We guarantee no miscarriages."

10. Learning from the Experience of Others

Don't be like the Michigan football coach (nicknamed Hurry-Up Yost). He gave an inspirational speech during halftime. After the final appeal, he led his team on the run through the wrong locker room door, into the swimming pool.

If you're delivering a speech you've made before, be sure it sounds timely. I attended my son's graduation from chiropractic college in the month of June. At the close, the master of ceremonies—reading from his notes—wished everyone a "joyous holiday and happy new year."

Chapter 20

Ten Hints for Collaborative Writing

Our team is well balanced. We have problems everywhere.

—Tommy Prothro, American football coach

A collaborative writing team exists any time two or more people are involved in writing and/or approving a document—whether the document is for an internal or external audience. The team may be a writer and reviewer; a group of writers, editors, and one or more reviewer(s); or any combination of people with some level of responsibility in the overall project.

Some people enjoy being part of a collaborative team; others don't. If you're one of those who don't, try to view the experience as an opportunity to benefit from the wisdom and talents of others.

Don't forget the Six Steps that I discuss in Part I. It's vital to the success of any collaborative writing project that everyone be on the same page (so to speak).

The following are ten (somewhat sequential) hints for projects such as brochures, reports, proposals, presentations, and so forth. It may not be your responsibility to undertake all these steps, but someone needs to.

1. Knowing What Role You Play

A team usually consists of a combination of the following: a leader, delegator, writer, editor, and reviewer. And people often assume more than one role. For example, you may be a lead writer and delegate sections to other writers. Your role may differ from project to project or within a project. You may write one chapter, and then be asked to edit someone else's chapter. All team members should have a clear understanding of their roles and the pecking order. Although this sounds basic, it's often the area where people trip over each other.

2. Preparing a "Who's Doing What" List

Prepare a "Who's Doing What" list that identifies the task, leader, responsibilities, and procedures. Feel free to pick and choose from the checklist shown in Example 20-1. After the team agrees to each member's responsibilities, every member should sign the agreement and receive a copy.

3. Generating a Production Schedule

Team members don't always realize the impact of not meeting a target date and, as the leader, you may have to stress its importance. Ideally, your production schedule (or milestone chart) builds in extra time. Make sure it includes columns for both the target date and the actual date completed. Example 20-2 shows a Production Schedule you may want to use.

Take a look at the Production Schedule to identify projects that may be worked on concurrently. For example, the artwork can be prepared while the text is being written.

I've always found it helpful to plan a project backward. After I identify the due date, I know how much time I have to reach each milestone. Then I can fill in the Production Schedule in reverse order.

Who's Doing What

Team Leader

> Who is responsible for keeping the team on task, leading meetings, and coordinating communication?

Team Responsibilities

> What specific tasks must be completed to finish the project?

> Who is responsible for each task?

Working Procedures

> When, where, and how often will the team meet?

> What procedures will be followed in the meetings?

> How will decisions be made (majority or consensus?)

> How will team members communicate? (E-Mail? Phone? Face to face?)

Example 20-1:
Collaborative
checklist
of who's
doing what.

Production Schedule

[Name of Project]

Milestone	Target Date	Actual Date	Person Responsible
Fill out Start Up Sheet			
Brainstorming Session			
First Draft Delivered			
Prepare Visuals			
Comments Due			
Final Draft Submitted			
Final Visuals Submitted			
Final Draft Approval			
Final Visuals Approved			
Mechanicals (if reqd.)			
Proofs			
Print			

Example 20-2:
Production schedule listing each milestone.

4. Completing the Start Up Sheet

Fill out the Start Up Sheet when the entire team is assembled so you have everyone's participation. Too often the people responsible for signing off don't get involved until the end. If everyone isn't on the same page from the beginning, the results can be disastrous.

If you can't assemble the entire team, fill out the Start Up Sheet with as many people as you can round up. Before going further, get approval from those who aren't present.

5. Brainstorming: Generating Ideas and Outlining as a Team

Brainstorming is a great getting-started strategy for collaborative writing. It's an opportunity for the entire team to give and get input on content and structure. For more information about brainstorming, check out Chapter 2. If you can't assemble the entire team, get written approval for the outline from those who weren't there before you go further.

Example 20-3 is text from an actual memo I sent. Feel free to borrow from it. The situation was that I was the only writer on a project team for the company's annual report. There were three reviewers: the CEO, the VP of Marketing, and the Director of Marketing.

6. Drafting Collaboratively

If more than one person is doing the writing, break the project into manageable chunks and assign sections accordingly. Each writer can draft a chapter, section, or whatever makes sense. Ultimately the document must sound as if it were written by one person. But that's generally the job for a good editor.

7. Organizing a Peer Review

For a large project, a peer review is appropriate after the first draft is complete. It's the time to get everyone's input on general content, formatting, and any other sticky-wickets. If you can't assemble everyone, gather as many people as possible.

Date: September 9, XXXX
From: Sheryl Lindsell-Roberts
To: Wile E. Coyote, Chip N. Dale, and Polly Purebred
Re: Outline for Annual Report

The following is the outline I'm proposing for this year's annual report:

No. of Pages	Content
2	Letter to Shareholders.
6	Testimonials from customers with photos. (A bulleted list of companies whose testimonials I am pursuing.)
4	About the products. Testimonials from analysts and the press.
2	Year in Review.

Total pages: 14

Note: The financials portion—about 20 pages—will be printed separately and inserted into a pocket in the back of the report. This will allow the annual report to double as a corporate capabilities brochure.

Deadline for Approval: September 19, XXXX

Please indicate your approval of the outline or note any changes. Thank you.

_____   _____
Wile E. Coyote   Date   Polly Purebred   Date

_____
Chip N. Dale   Date

Example 20-3:
A memo detailing the outline for a collaborative project.

Photocopy the document (single-sided) on 11-x-17-inch paper. This size gives reviewers room to make notes in the margins. If you only have standard 8 ½-x-11-inch paper, reduce the document size slightly so there's ample room in the margins for editing. Different colored inks work well, too. Assign each editor a different color pen.

Make sure *all* the reviewers go through the Editing Checklist featured on the Cheat Sheet in the front of this book, either separately or together.

8. Using Group Writing Tools

When several writers are using the same software, learn to annotate text without destroying the original. Here are a few suggestions:

- ✔ Use the strikethrough feature or a different typeface or color. Some software accommodates proofreading marks.

- ✔ Use a split screen to display the original copy and the edited copy with the changes highlighted. And, keep in mind that even though reviewers make comments, the author owns the final alterations.

- ✔ Ask the reviewer(s) to use revision marks found on the Tools menu in Word.

9. Signing Off

The sign-off involves getting the approval of those who are ultimately responsible for the project.

I always try to get the signature of upper-level management because they're the ones who must yea or nay the document.

10. Putting Your Ego Aside

Two heads may be better than one, but two egos are worse. Typically, everyone who reviews a document feels compelled to comment. That's just human nature. It isn't necessarily a reflection on your writing or your style; it's just part of the process. Never take this personally.

Part V:
Appendixes

In this part. . .

The English language is certainly strange. Have you ever wondered. . .

- ✔ Why you drive *on* a parkway and park *in* a driveway?
- ✔ Why Hawaii has Interstate highways?
- ✔ Why you put a "u" in *four* and *fourth,* but not in *forty?*
- ✔ Why *abbreviation* is such a long word?

No wonder English can be such a struggle. But don't fret. All you need is a knowledge of eighth-grade English (or so the "experts" say) and a quick way to deal with the persnickety little nuances you often stumble on. This part covers the most common stumbling blocks, including punctuation, grammar, abbreviations, and spelling.

Appendix A
Punctuation Made Easy

· ·

I'm glad you came to punctuate my discourse, which I fear has gone on for an hour without any stop at all.

—Samuel Taylor Coleridge, English Poet

*P*unctuation is one of the most significant tools you can use to create documents in your own voice. When you speak aloud, you constantly punctuate with your voice and body language. You also make a sound in the reader's head when you write. Your "writing voice" can be a dull, sleep-inducing mumble (like a tedious, unformatted document) or it can be a joyful sound, a shy whisper, a throb of passion. It all depends on the punctuation you use.

General Guidelines

If you omit a mark of punctuation or place it incorrectly, you can dramatically alter the meaning of your sentence. In the following sentences, you can see the differences in meaning.

Woman without her man is a savage.

Woman: without her, man is a savage.

I present the punctuation marks in the order in which they're most commonly used and confused.

We're hungry let's eat mom

How would you punctuate the headline sentence it to make its meaning clear? Check out the possibilities below.

We're hungry. Let's eat, mom.

We're hungry; let's eat mom.

This stresses the importance of punctuation. I'm sure your mother would agree.

Different (key) strokes for different folks

The following three sentences are worded identically. Yet, the different marks of punctuation give each a unique sound:

Dashes: The Ace Chemical Company—winner of the Service Award—just introduced its new product line. (The emphasis is on what's enclosed in the dashes.)

Parentheses: The Ace Chemical Company (winner of the Service Award) just introduced its new product line. (This construction plays down what's enclosed in the parentheses.)

Commas: The Ace Chemical Company, winner of the Service Award, just introduced its new product line. (What's enclosed in the commas is neutralized.)

Commas

Commas are the most used (and misused) punctuation mark. While a period indicates a *stop* in thought, a comma acts as a *slow sign*—something like a speed bump. Commas let you know which items are grouped together, what's critical to the meaning of the sentence, and more.

  ✔ Use commas to separate three or more items in a series. A comma before the final *and* or *or* is optional. It can, however, increase the clarity. The choice is yours, but be consistent.

  ✔ Use a comma before a conjunction *(and, but, or, nor, for, so, yet)* that joins two sentences.

> *Complete sentences:* Joe recognized the four delegates, but he can't recall their names.

> *Second clause not a sentence:* Joe recognized the four delegates but can't recall their names.

  ✔ Don't place a comma before *because.*

  ✔ Use commas to separate items in an address or date. (But don't use any punctuation before a zip code.)

> As of Saturday, September 16, 1998, Barbara's address becomes One Adam Street, Marlborough, MA 01752.

  ✔ Use commas to set off an expression that explains, modifies, or emphasizes the preceding word, name, or phrase.

> Main Street, our town's main thoroughfare, will be closed to traffic tomorrow.

✔ Use commas to set off a word(s) that directly addresses the person to whom you're speaking by name, title, or relationship.

> Please let me know, Senator, if you can add anything to that.

✔ Use a comma after an introductory phrase if it's followed by a complete sentence. This type of clause may include introductory words such as *when*, *if*, *as*, and *although*.

> If we advertise in that magazine, our sales should increase.

✔ Use commas around a phrase that isn't necessary to the meaning of the sentence.

> My older son, the one you met last Monday, is an architect. (He is an architect regardless of when you met him.)

✔ Don't place commas around information that makes the sentence clear.

> The person who meets all our qualifications will never be found.

✔ Use commas to set off expressions that interrupt the natural flow of the sentence. These expressions can include: as a result, in fact, therefore, however, consequently, for example, in fact, and on the contrary.

> We will, therefore, continue with the project.

✔ Use commas to show contrast.

> The assignment is long, but not difficult.

✔ Use commas to identify a person quoted directly.

> In 1981, Bill Gates said, "640K ought to be enough for anybody."

✔ Use commas to set off designations, titles, and degrees that follow a name.

> Max Lorenz, CPA, will be our guest speaker.

✔ Use a comma to divide a sentence that starts as a statement and ends as a question.

> I can't think of anything further, can you?

✔ Use commas to separate items in reference material.

> You can find an area code map in *The Office Professional's Quick Reference Handbook,* by Sheryl Lindsell-Roberts, Fourth Edition, page 224.

✔ Use a comma to separate words when the word *and* is omitted, and to separate adjectives.

> Please include a stamped, self-addressed envelope.

> It may be a long, long time before we see him again.

Ending Punctuation

Ending punctuation refers to periods, question marks, and exclamation points.

Periods

The period is the stop sign of punctuation. It slows you down and makes you take a breath before you go into the next thought.

- ✔ Use a period after a statement, command, or request.
- ✔ Use a period after words or phrases that logically substitute for a complete sentence.

    Okay.

    No, not at all.

- ✔ As a general rule, use periods when writing abbreviations, acronyms, or initialisms. Although a number of dictionaries cite many abbreviations without periods—YMCA, FDIC, and CPA, for example. When in doubt, check it out. For more information about abbreviations, acronyms, or initialisms, see Appendix C.

Question marks

A question mark, like a period, serves as a stop sign—a break in thought—with an added air of mystery. Although you probably use question marks correctly, there are a few tricky situations, which I hope these guidelines can demystify.

- ✔ Use a question mark after a direct question.
- ✔ Use a question mark after a short, direct question that follows a statement.

    You saw the requisition, didn't you?

- ✔ Use a question mark after each item in a series of questions within the same sentence.

    Which of the candidates has the most experience? Mary? Joe? Jeff?

    For this sentence, is the correct punctuation mark a period? A comma? A question mark?

One space, not two

In the olden days of typewriters it was sound advice to space twice after a punctuation mark. It was the only way to separate one sentence from another clearly. With computers, there's a clear distinction between sentences because of proportional spacing.

Therefore, you should space once—not twice—after a period, colon, exclamation point, question mark, quotation mark, or any other mark of punctuation that ends a sentence.

✔ Use a question mark enclosed in parentheses to express doubt.

He said the contract is due on April 8 (?).

Exclamation points

Exclamation points are reserved for words or thoughts that show strong emotion.

Please try to do better!

That was an inspiring talk. Congratulations!

Colons and Semicolons

A semicolon is a separator that's stronger than a comma and weaker than a period. A colon directs the reader's attention to what follows. This section shows you how to use both of them correctly.

Colons

A colon is a mark of anticipation. It serves as an introduction and alerts you to a close connection between what comes before and after it.

> ✔ Use a colon after an introduction that includes or implies *the following* or *as follows*.
>
> ✔ Use a colon to introduce a long quotation.
>
> ✔ Use a colon to separate hours and minutes.

Semicolons

Consider semicolons a cross between periods and commas. They create more impact than commas, yet less than periods. Following are some rules about when to use them.

> ✔ Use a semicolon in place of a conjunction *(and, but, or, nor, for, so, yet),* to join complete sentences.
>
>> The raw material is supplied by our Georgia plant; the finished product is made in our Chicago plant.
>
> ✔ Use a semicolon before expressions that can be removed without changing the meaning of the sentence, as when a parenthetical word or phrase introduces a separate sentence.
>
>> The project came to a standstill during the strike; however, we did eke out a small profit.
>
> ✔ Use a semicolon to separate items in a series when the items themselves have commas.
>
>> The three most important dates in our company's history are January 15, 1937; April 8, 1952; and July 30, 1994.

Dashes and Parentheses

Dashes and parentheses affect how the reader understands information. Dashes highlight the text; parentheses play down the text.

Dashes

Dashes (often considered strong parentheses) are vigorous and versatile, and have several uses. They can stand alone or be used in pairs. Just don't overdo dashes or they lose their impact.

In Microsoft Word you have two ways to form an em dash (—). An em dash gets its name from the capital *M,* which is the same width.

1. Type two hyphens. If you don't space between the second hyphen and the word that follows, the two hyphens magically become an em dash.

2. Click Insert, and highlight Symbols in the drop-down list that appears.

And speaking of spaces—some writers leave one space before and after the em dash, others leave no spaces. It's dealer's choice.

Use the following rules to help you with your dashing dashes.

✔ Use dashes to set off expressions you want to emphasize.

> This brand of software—as unbiased tests have disclosed—is more powerful than what you're currently using.

✔ Use a dash before a word that sums up preceding text as an option to a colon. (Be consistent in your style.)

> The dishwasher, the washing machine, the dryer—items that eventually need repair.

✔ Use a dash to indicate a strong afterthought that disrupts the sentence.

> I know you're looking for—and I hope this helps—a list of qualified people.

✔ Use a dash before the name of an author or work that follows a direct quote.

> *You can turn painful situations around through laughter. If you can find humor in something, you can survive it.*
>
> —Bill Cosby

Parentheses

Parentheses (often considered weak dashes) are like a sideshow; they're used to enclose a word or words that aren't integral to the meaning of the sentence. A parenthetical expression is one that doesn't change the meaning of the sentence (removing the expression doesn't alter the gist).

Some examples of when to use parentheses follow.

✔ Use parentheses around an expression that you want to de-emphasize.

> This brand of software (as unbiased researchers have established) is more powerful than what you're using.

- Use parentheses around references to charts, pages, diagrams, authors, and so on.

  Please read the section on fossils (pages 36-52).

- Use parentheses to enclose numerals or letters that precede items in a series.

  We are hoping to (a) meet the Mayor, (b) express our views, and (c) submit our petition.

- When you enclose a sentence in parentheses, punctuate it as a sentence.

Other Punctuation

Last, but not least, are quotation marks, apostrophes, hyphens, ellipses, slashes, and brackets.

Quotation marks

Quotation marks are reserved for those occasions when you cite something verbatim.

If you're paraphrasing, don't use quotation marks.

> *Quoting:* Mr. Schultz said, "Please come to the meeting at 2:00."

> *Paraphrasing:* Mr. Schultz asked her to come to the 2:00 meeting.

Follow these general guidelines for using quotation marks.

- Place commas and periods inside quotation marks.

  The most desired response is "yes."

- Place semicolons and colons outside quotation marks.

  The person being sued is the "defendant"; the person suing is the "plaintiff."

- Place question marks and exclamation points inside the quotes only when they apply to the quoted material.

  "What's the circulation of that newspaper?" he asked.

- Place question marks and exclamation points outside the quotes when they apply to the entire sentence.

  Did he say, "Our circulation is over a million"?

✔ Use quotation marks to enclose direct quotes.

> "Our industry is vital to the economy," said the CEO.

✔ Use quotation marks to enclose articles from magazines, songs, essays, short stories, one-act plays, sermons, paintings, lectures, and so on.

> *Loony Laws & Silly Statutes,* by Sheryl Lindsell-Roberts, has a chapter entitled, "Sorry, My Dance Card's Full."

✔ Use quotation marks to set off words or phrases introduced by expressions such as *the word, known as, was called, marked, entitled,* and so on. (Italics serve the same purpose, just be consistent.)

> *Quotes:* The phrase "each and every" should always have a singular verb.

> *Italics:* The phrase *each and every* should always have a singular verb.

✔ Use quotation marks to set off words used in an unconventional manner. (Again, you can use italics instead.)

> That clue was a real "red herring."

✔ Use single quotation marks around a quotation within a quotation.

> The consultant said, "You would do well to heed Mr. Smith's advice: 'Give the public what it wants and you will be in business for a long time.'"

Apostrophes

Apostrophes show possession or omissions. They're not flying commas.

Possession

Possession refers to ownership, authorship, brand, kind, or origin. These guidelines demonstrate how to use apostrophes to show possession:

✔ Apostrophes are most commonly used with nouns to show possession.

> The host called the guests names when they arrived.

> The host called the guests' names when they arrived.

> (Which host would you prefer?)

✔ Form the possessive case of a singular noun by adding an apostrophe.

✔ Form the possessive of a regular plural noun (one ending in *s*) by adding an apostrophe after the *s*.

> The Murphys' home is being painted.

✔ Form the possessive of an irregular plural noun (one not ending in *s*) by adding an apostrophe and *s*.

> The salespeople's territories are being divided.

✔ To show joint ownership, add the apostrophe and *s* after the last noun. To show single ownership, add the apostrophe and *s* to each noun.

> ***Joint ownership:*** Jim and Pat's locker is near the lounge.

> ***Individual ownership:*** Jim's and Pat's lockers are near the lounge.

✔ In hyphenated words, put the apostrophe at the end of the possession.

> He borrowed his brother-in-law's car.

✔ To make an abbreviation possessive, put an apostrophe and *s* after the period. If the abbreviation is plural, place an apostrophe after the *s*.

> The Smith Co.'s sale starts next month.

> Two M.D.s' opinions are needed.

✔ Express time and measurement in the possessive case.

> We'll have an answer in one week's time.

✔ Use an apostrophe to show possession of initialisms or acronyms. Some writers eliminate the apostrophe when there's little chance of misreading.

> I used AAA's towing service last week.

The names of companies and publications are often written without apostrophes. When in doubt, check it out.

Omission

Everyday contractions are the most obvious example of apostrophes used in place of a letter or letters. Basic guidelines follow:

If you want to highlight a negative statement, consider a contraction. *Don't* is more noticeable than *do not*.

✔ Use an apostrophe to show that letters (as in contractions) or numbers (as *the '70s*) are missing.

✔ Use an apostrophe to form the plural of a number, letter, or symbol, or a word.

> Sally doesn't always pronounce her r's at the end of a word.

> No if's, and's, or but's.

Some companies frown on using contractions and prefer the more formal style. Defer to the style of the company.

Hyphens

Don't confuse hyphens (-) with em dashes (—). They're different species. Hyphens function primarily as spelling devices.

- ✔ Use a hyphen to join a unit of two or more words modifying a noun.

    The bank extended the family a 30-day note.

    The bank extended the note for 30 days. *(Comes after the noun.)*

- ✔ Use a hyphen for compound numbers and written-out fractions.

    One hundred fifty-two people attended the meeting.

    This is three-fourths the annual revenue.

- ✔ Use a hyphen to join *ex-* and *-elect* to a title.

    Did ex-President Carter return to his farm after he left office?

- ✔ Use a hyphen to add to the clarity of the word.

    I re-sent the message yesterday.

- ✔ Use a hyphen between a prefix that ends with a vowel and a word beginning with the same vowel. (When in doubt, check it out.)

    The television station pre-empted my favorite program.

    The beach ball sank because it was only semi-inflated.

Ellipses

Ellipses show that words or names are omitted in a quotation. Place the ellipses where the omission occurs. Ellipses are formed by typing three periods, with a space between each.

When ellipses end a sentence, you don't need a period. Here's what ellipses show:

- ✔ Omission at the beginning:

    ". . . Conference calls are used to allow people in remote locations to conduct business meetings without being face to face."

- ✔ Omission at the end:

    "Cables interfaced with computers allow you to get information on your bank accounts, query your local library. . ."

- ✔ Omission at the somewhere in between:

    "Cables interfaced with computers allow you to get information on your bank accounts, query your local library, and . . . are used to allow people in remote locations to conduct business meetings without being face to face."

Slashes

These critters go by a variety of names: slant line, virgule, bar, or shilling line. They separate or show an omission, such as in care of (c/o) or without (w/o).

- ✔ Use slashes in and/or expressions.

    The sales/advertising departments are deciding on the issues.

- ✔ Use slashes in Internet addresses.

    ```
    http://www.dummies.com
    ```

Brackets

Brackets aren't substitutes for parentheses. They have their own place in the world, as the following guidelines explain:

- ✔ Use brackets to enclose words you add to a direct quote.

    He said, "The length of the trial [from early June to late July] was entirely too long."

- ✔ Use brackets as parentheses within parentheses.

    Your order (including one dozen blue pens [which aren't available], three dozen green pens, and five dozen red pens) will ship on Monday, September 8.

Appendix B
Grammar's Not Grueling

. . . .

This is sort of English up with which I will not put.

> —Winston Churchill (A comment against clumsy avoidance of a preposition at the end of a sentence, from E. Growers *Plain Words*)

You may remember when you were a kid, asking your mother, "Mom, can Pat and me go to the movies?" Your mother replied," That's Pat and I," and she didn't give you the money until you corrected your grammar. Although you didn't think so then, your mother was doing you a favor. Poor grammar didn't get you far with your mother, and it doesn't get you far in the business world.

I don't get into the nitty-gritty details of every part of speech because I don't want to bore you to tears. Rather, I touch upon the most troublesome areas in alphabetical order.

Adjectives

An adjective adds pizzazz to a sentence. It's a word, phrase, or clause that modifies, describes, or limits the noun or pronoun it's describing. You can use adjectives to transform an ordinary sentence into a tantalizing one.

> *Ordinary:* The steak cooked on the grill.

> *Tantalizing:* The darkly charred steak—its top beaded with red-hot juices—cooked on the grill.

An adjective answers at least one of the following questions: What kind? Which? What color? How many? What size?

Quickie quiz

Take a look at the following sentences and see what errors you notice, if any. (Turn the book upside down for the answers.) If you find all the mistakes, tear this chapter out of the book and share it with a deserving coworker.

And, if you're so grammatically correct, feel free to skip this appendix entirely.

1. A group of 50 people are waiting to see the president.

2. With most of the votes counted, the winner was thought to be her.

3. Everyone in the room, including the president and vice president, is being asked to do their share.

4. What was the name of the speaker we had yesterday?

5. James, who enjoys this type of assignment, would certainly be interested if he was here now.

6. The Jones Company is celebrating their 50th anniversary.

Answers

1. A group of 50 people *is* waiting to see the president. (*Group is* a singular subject and takes a singular verb.)

2. With most of the votes counted, the winner was thought to be *she*. (*She was* thought to be the winner. The nominative case is used when the pronoun is the subject of the sentence or it follows any form of the verb *to be*.)

3. Everyone in the room, including the president and vice president, is being asked to do *his or her* share. (*Everyone* takes a singular verb, even if you throw in specific people. After all, the president and vice president are part of everyone.)

4. What *is* the name of the speaker we had yesterday? (The speaker's name hasn't changed. Why use the past tense?)

5. James, who enjoys this type of assignment, would certainly be interested if he *were* here now. (Not a statement of fact. He isn't here now.)

6. The Jones Company is celebrating *its* 50th anniversary. (The Jones Company is a singular subject and takes a singular verb.)

Forms of adjectives

Adjectives take different forms, depending on the noun or nouns they're modifying.

Use a *positive* adjective when you're not comparing anything.

> It's *cold* today.

Use a *comparative* adjective when you're comparing two things.

> It's *colder* today than it was yesterday.

Use a *superlative* adjective when you're comparing three things or more.

> It's the *coldest* day we've had all week.

Several adjectives have irregular comparatives and superlatives; they don't end in *er* or *est*. The following table illustrates a few:

Adjective	Comparative	Superlative
good	better	best
little	less	least
bad	worse	worst

Absolute adjectives

Some adjectives are absolute; they either *are* or *aren't*. For example, one thing can't be more complete than something else. Either it's complete or it's not. Following are some adjectives considered absolute:

complete	correct	dead	empty
genuine	parallel	perfect	right
round	stationary	unanimous	wrong

Express the comparative and superlative forms of absolute adjectives by adding "more nearly" or "most nearly."

> Jason's assumption was more nearly correct than Jim's.

Compound adjectives

In many cases, you use a hyphen to join together two adjectives so they form a single description. Use a hyphen only when the compound adjective comes before the noun, not after.

> ***Before the noun:*** a part-time job; a two- or three-year lease

> ***After the noun:*** a job that's part time; a lease of two or three years

Here are two exceptions:

1. Eliminate the hyphen when you generally think of the words as a unit; for example, *post office address* and *life insurance policy*.

2. Don't put a hyphen between adjectives if the first one ends in *est* or *ly;* as in *newly elected officer* and *freshest cut flowers*.

Articles

Use *the* to refer to a specific article and *a* or *an* to a nonspecific item. Use *a* when a consonant sound follows the *a* (*a* hot dog, *a* three-week trip); use *an* when a vowel sound follows (*an* onion, *an* illness; and *an* heir, *an* X-ray).

Adverbs

Just as an adjective can add pizzazz to a noun, an adverb spices up a verb. An adverb modifies a verb, an adjective, or another adverb. An adverb answers one or more of these questions: How? When? Why? How much? Where? To what degree? Adverbs take different forms for the positive, comparative, and superlative, just as adjectives do.

Adjectives ending in *ly* may also function as adverbs—depending on what they're modifying.

> ***Adjective:*** Her handwriting is legible.

> ***Adverb:*** She writes legibly.

> ***Adjective:*** The professor's talk was brief.

> ***Adverb:*** The professor spoke briefly.

Double negatives

If you've ever said, "I don't want no liver," what you said is that you do want liver. Two negatives equal a positive. Never use two negative words to express one positive idea.

> ***Correct:*** I can hardly believe what I just heard.
>
> ***Incorrect:*** I can't hardly believe what I just heard.

Conjunctions

A conjunction connects two or more words, phrases, or clauses that are equal in construction and importance. Common conjunctions are *and, or, for, so, but, nor,* and *yet.*

For information about punctuating sentences that contain conjunctions, see Appendix A.

Nouns

The noun—although critical to every sentence—is probably the least sexy part of speech. The noun doesn't create any emotion or add flair to your thoughts; it's merely a *person, place,* or *thing*.

A proper noun is specific and is capitalized. A common noun isn't specific and isn't capitalized.

> ***Proper nouns:*** New York City; Marlborough High School; Main Street
>
> ***Common nouns:*** the city; the school; the street

A collective noun is a group. When the group is acting as a unit (company, council, audience, faculty, union, team, jury, committee, and so on), use a singular verb. When members of the group are acting independently, use a plural verb.

> ***Acting collectively:*** The family is going on vacation.
>
> ***Acting individually:*** The family are going on separate vacations.

Prepositions

A preposition shows the relationship between words and sentences. Here are some common prepositions:

above	about	across	after	along
among	around	at	before	behind
below	beneath	beside	between	beyond
by	down	during	except	for
from	in	inside	into	like
near	of	off	on	since
to	toward	through	under	until
up	upon	with	within	without

Pronouns

A pronoun is a word that substitutes for a noun. Do you recall being unkind to a substitute teacher? Treat your pronouns well, and you'll atone for all the substitute teachers you made cry.

A pronoun substitutes for a noun. Use a pronoun to eliminate awkward wording. The pronoun must agree with the noun it replaces in person, number, and gender.

Singular pronouns

Certain pronouns are always singular and take singular verbs and pronouns, including: anybody, anyone, anything, each, either, everybody, everyone, everything, much, neither, nobody, nothing, one, somebody, someone, something.

> *Everyone*, including Pete and Jane, has *his* and *her* problems.
>
> *Neither* Gary's nor Bob's proposals *is* acceptable.

Who and whom

Who-and-whom cowards can mumble these words hoping the listener won't notice their indecision. Writers don't have that luxury. But it is possible to think of *who* and *whom* in easy terms!

When you can substitute he/she/they, use *who*. And when you can substitute her/him/them use *whom*.

> The company needs a person *who* knows the new software. (*He/she* knows the new software.)

> Are you the person to *whom* I spoke yesterday? (I spoke to *her/him*.)

Verbs

The verb is the most important part of a sentence because it expresses an action, condition, or state of being. The verb makes a statement about the subject and can breathe life into dull text.

Dangling participles

If your participles dangle, it's nothing to be ashamed of. The condition's curable. A *dangling participle* is nothing more than a verb that doesn't clearly or logically refer to the noun or pronoun it modifies. Participles can dangle at the beginning or end of a sentence. The following shows how to undangle a participle:

> *Dangling:* While attending the meeting, the computer malfunctioned. (*Who* attended the meeting?)

> *Correct:* While James attended the meeting, the computer malfunctioned.

Were and was

Have you ever fantasized about being someone else? The English language provides a verb for those fantasies. "I wish I *were*. . ." The verb *were* is often used to express wishful thinking or an idea that's contrary to fact. *Was,* on the other hand, indicates a statement of fact.

She acts as if she *were* president of the company. (Wishful thinking.)

If Charles *was* at the airport, I didn't see him. (He may have been there.)

Was is the past tense of is. Why am I mentioning the obvious? Because people mistakenly use *was* for the present tense when referring to something that's already happened.

> *Correct*: I thoroughly enjoyed the book—even though it *is* 950 pages long.

> *Incorrect*: I thoroughly enjoyed the book—even though it *was* 950 pages long.

Split infinitives

The present tense of a verb preceded by *to* is called an infinitive. Don't put a modifier between *to* and the verb or you split the infinitive and sometimes confuse and distract your reader.

> *Correct:* The instructor wants *to read* all the papers carefully.

> *Incorrect:* The instructor wants *to* carefully *read* all the papers.

It's a good thing I wasn't asked to proofread Gene Roddenberry's original *Star Trek* script or we'd never have heard "To boldly go. . ."

Subject and verb agreement

One of the most basic rules in grammar is that the subject and verb of a sentence must agree. Both must be singular or both must be plural. Although most situations are pretty straightforward, the following demonstrate situations that may be a little tricky:

- Don't be fooled by interrupting phrases.

  > *Correct:* The software, despite the new installation manuals, still takes several days to install.

  > *Incorrect:* The software, despite the new installation manuals, still take several days to install. (The subject is *software*.)

- *Many a, many an, each* and *every* always take a singular verb.

  > Each and every computer *has* a modem.

  > Many a man *is* denied this chance.

✔ *None, some, any, all, most,* and *fractions* are either singular or plural, depending on what they modify.

> Half the shipment was misplaced. (The subject, *shipment*, is singular.)

> Half the boxes were misplaced. (The subject, *boxes*, is plural.)

✔ When referring to the name of a book, magazine, song, company, or article, use a singular verb even though the name may be plural.

> *Little Women* is a great classic.

> Wanderman & Greenberg is a fine team of attorneys.

✔ When referring to an amount, money, or distance, use a singular verb if the noun is thought of as a single unit.

> I think *$900 is* a fair price.

> There *are 10 yards* of fabric in that dress.

✔ When *or* or *nor* is used to connect a singular and plural subject, the verb must agree in number with the person or item closest to the verb.

> Neither Jim nor his *assistants were* available.

> Neither the assistants nor *Jim was* available.

Gerunds

A gerund is a word or phrase whose root is a verb and which ends with *ing.* Gerunds start out as verbs, but act as nouns. When a gerund is preceded by a noun or pronoun, the noun or pronoun takes the possessive form.

> I don't like *your giving* me such short notice.

> *Ted's yelling* is quite irritating.

Commonly Confused Constructions

Figuring out the correct usage for phrases that include prepositions can often mangle the mind. Table B-1 can help straighten you out.

Table B-1	Confusing Phrases
Phrase	*Example*
accompany by (a person)	The teacher was *accompanied by* her student.
accompany with (an object)	The bicycle was *accompanied with* assembling instructions.
account for (something or someone)	I can't *account for* Peter's behavior.
account to (someone)	The cashier had to *account to* the manager for the error.
compare to (show similarity)	You can *compare* this restaurant *to* any one with four stars.
compare with (examine for similarities and differences)	She *compared* his writing *with* Poe's.
convenient for (suitable)	Will Sunday be *convenient for* you?
convenient to (close)	The new theater should be *convenient to* you.
correspond to (agree with)	The merchandise doesn't *correspond to* what was advertised.
correspond with (write letters)	I *correspond with* Aunt Raye.
differ about (something)	We *differ about* ways to accomplish that project.
differ from (be unlike)	I *differ from* you in many ways.
differ with (someone)	I *differ with* you over the outcome of the project.
different from (never use *different than*)	This computer is not too *different from* my last one.
talk to (address)	The speaker *talked to* the audience for two hours.
talk with (discuss)	I *talked with* the speaker after he finished.

Appendix C
Abridged Abbreviations

• •

A lot of fellows nowadays have a B.A., M.D., or Ph.D. Unfortunately, they don't have a J.O.B.

—Antoine "Fats" Domino, singer

Abbreviations are useful for a variety of reasons: to avoid repetition, save space, or conform to conventional usage. Leading authorities can't agree on the capitalization or punctuation for many abbreviations; therefore, there are few set rules. For the most part, it's wise not to abbreviate unless you have a reason to do so. Having said that, here are some guidelines to cover variations, exceptions, and peculiarities.

I present the abbreviation guidelines in alphabetical order.

Acronyms and Initialisms

An *acronym* is a combination of the first letters of several words which you pronounce as a word itself; laser (light amplification by stimulated emission or radiation) and OPEC (Organization of Petroleum Exporting Countries) for example. An *initialism* is also a combination of the first letters of words, but you pronounce an initialism as separate letters, like I - B - M (International Business Machines) and F - D - I - C (Federal Deposit Insurance Corporation).

In business, industry, education, and government, acronyms and initialisms are often used among people who work together. That's fine, as long as your reader can easily understand your frame of reference. Keep in mind that the reference may not be comprehensible to those outside your magical kingdom. And, certain acronyms can mean different things to different people. For example, the ABA to an attorney is the American Bar Association; to a banker, the American Banking Association; to a bowler, the American Bowling Association; and to a bookseller, the American Booksellers' Association.

My son's friend used to impress his classmates by telling them that his father was head of the CIA. Everyone was awed. His dad was the head of the Culinary Institute of America, not the Central Intelligence Agency.

Alphabet soup

Don't feed your readers alphabet soup. I attended a meeting recently with what I refer to as the alphabet people. Those attending were the CEO; COO; CFO; VP of HR; VP of MIS; and, oh yes, B.J., the Pres.

Writing Acronyms and Intialisms

Abbreviate acronyms and intialisms after you spell them out the first time. (unless you're absolutely sure that your reader will understand your reference).

The National Association of Manufacturers (NAM) will hold its annual meeting in July. At that time, NAM will outline its agenda for the year.

The FDA did not give its approval to the drug you mentioned. (Most people know what FDA means.)

Companies and Organizations

Styling varies widely in organizational names. Treat the name as the company or organization treats it. Check the company's Web site or letterhead for an accurate picture. If you can't check it out, write it out.

Compass Points

Abbreviate compass points when they appear after street names. Spell them out when they appear before street names.

Latin Words and Phrases

Words derived from Latin are commonly abbreviated. Use lowercase and don't italicize them. Here are some you commonly see:

c. or ca.	*(circa)* about
etc	
e.g.	*(exempli gratia)* for example
et al.	*(et alii)* and others
etc.	*(et cetera)* and so forth
ibid.	*(ibidem)* the same
i.e.	*(id est)* that is
pro tem	*(pro tempore)* for the time being
ss.	*(silicet)* namely (often used in affidavits)
viz.	*(videlicit)* namely

I suggest that people refrain from using Latin abbreviations because they're often written or read improperly. For example, many people confuse *i.e.* and *e.g.* They're not interchangeable.

Laws and Bylaws

Write the complete law or bylaw at first mention: "The reference appears in Article I, Section 2." Thereafter, use the abbreviation: "See Art. I, Sec. 2."

Periods

To use a period or not to use a period: That is the question. Here are the answers.

- In general, use periods for academic degrees, but not for professional references.

    Thomas Greenberg, Ed.D.; Richard L. Hodge, CPA

- Use a period after most abbreviations formed by omitting all but a few letters of a word.

    mfg. (for manufacturing); avg. (for average)

- Omit the period from abbreviations made up of initial letters that constitute an acronym, initialism, or compound word.

    ROI (return on investment) and GNP (gross national product); but f.o.b. (free on board) and a.k.a. (also known as)

Postal Abbreviations

The United States Postal Service requests that the two-letter state abbreviations—without periods—be used on all mail. Table C-1 gives the abbreviations for U.S. states and territories.

Table C-1	U.S. Postal Service Abbreviations		
Location	*Abbreviation*	*Location*	*Abbreviation*
Alabama	AL	Missouri	MO
Alaska	AK	Montana	MT
Arizona	AZ	Nebraska	NE
Arkansas	AR	Nevada	NV
California	CA	New Hampshire	NH
Canal Zone	CZ	New Jersey	NJ
Colorado	CO	New Mexico	NM
Connecticut	CT	New York	NY
Delaware	DE	North Carolina	NC
District of Columbia	DC	North Dakota	ND
Florida	FL	Ohio	OH
Georgia	GA	Oklahoma	OK
Guam	GU	Oregon	OR
Hawaii	HI	Pennsylvania	PA
Idaho	ID	Puerto Rico	PR
Illinois	IL	Rhode Island	RI
Indiana	IN	South Carolina	SC
Iowa	IA	South Dakota	SD
Kansas	KS	Tennessee	TN
Kentucky	KY	Texas	TX
Louisiana	LA	Utah	UT
Maine	ME	Vermont	VT
Maryland	MD	Virginia	VA
Massachusetts	MA	Virgin Islands	VI
Michigan	MI	Washington	WA
Minnesota	MN	West Virginia	WV
Mississippi	MS	Wisconsin	WI
		Wyoming	WY

Scientific Terms

Scientific terms are often used in technical writing. However, people who read technical documents don't always have technical backgrounds, so follow these guidelines in order to be clear:

> ✔ Write out scientific terms at first mention. Thereafter, use the abbreviated form.
>
> > At first mention use *escherichia coli*; thereafter, use *e. coli.*
>
> ✔ Abbreviate the names of chemical compounds, medical, mechanical, and electrical equipment or processes without periods.
>
> > CPU for central processing unit; EKG for electrocardiogram.
>
> ✔ Don't use periods with the symbols for chemical elements.

Metric System

The United States is probably the only country in the universe that isn't using the metric system. Some of the more popular metric abbreviations are shown in Table C-2.

Table C-2	Metric Abbreviations
km	kilometer
hm	hectometer
dam	dekameter
m	meter
dm	decimeter
cm	centimeter
mm	millimeter
l	liter
cl	centileter
ml	millileter
MT or t	metric ton
kg	kilogram
hg	hectogram
dag	dekagram

(continued)

Table C-2 (continued)

g or gm	gram
dg	decigram
cg	centigram
mg	milligram

Write out metric measurements unless you're certain your reader will understand your abbreviated form.

Appendix D
Spelling Superbly

. . . .

Nothing you can't spell will ever work.

—Will Rogers

1f you're frustrated with English language spelling, be glad we don't have words such as *Wirtschaftstreuhandgesellschaft,* the German word for "business trust company." Perhaps that's no consolation because English certainly has its own perplexities. For example, check out some of the words in the English language that end with the "er" sound and see how differently they're spelled: burgl*ar,* writ*er,* aviat*or,* glam*our,* ac*re,* murm*ur,* inj*ure,* mart*yr.* It is any wonder we all scratch our heads when it comes to spelling?

If you remember a few basic rules, you can overcome many of the spelling difficulties you may have. Just keep in mind that there are exceptions to every rule.

Butt, eye half Spill-Czech

Now that we have spell checkers, why worry about spelling?

I have a spelling checker.

It came with my PC.

It plane lee marks four my revue

Miss steaks aye can knot see.

—Author Unknown

Despite all the advances in technology, the need to spell is alive and kicking. Spell checkers don't identify all spelling errors. They can't discriminate between homophones (they're, their, there) or commonly confused words (proceed, precede). And they can't know that you mean *our* instead of *out.* Only humans can do that.

Plurals

How simple things would be if we could walk around like befuddled children saying, "My feets hurt." Plurals aren't that simple.

The list below demonstrates different ways to make plurals by adding *s* or *es*.

> ✔ Form the plurals of most nouns by adding an *s:* automobil*es*, flower*s*, leg*s*.
>
> ✔ Pluralize words ending in *s, x, z, ch,* or *sh* by adding *es:* bunch*es*, business*es*, Sanchez*es*.
>
> ✔ Pluralize words ending in *y* when *y* is preceded by a vowel by adding an *s:* chimney*s*, journey*s*, kidney*s*.
>
> ✔ Pluralize words ending in *y* when *y* is preceded by a consonant by changing the *y* to *i* and adding *es:* academ*ies*, arm*ies*, beneficiar*ies*.

Handle words ending with *o* like so:

> ✔ Pluralize words ending in an *o* preceded by another vowel by adding an *s:* cameo*s*, studio*s*.
>
> ✔ Pluralize words ending in an *o* preceded by a consonant by adding *es:* veto*es*, hero*es*, echo*es*.
>
> ✔ Pluralize musical terms ending in *o* by adding an *s:* piano*s*, soprano*s*, solo*s*.

When compound words aren't hyphenated, they work as regular words. For example, just add *s* to make *letterheads* and *handfuls*. With a hyphenated compound word, make the main part of the word plural, as in *sisters-in-law* and *editors-in-chief*.

Making some words plural requires changing the vowel and/or the form, like child*ren*, g*ee*se, and ox*en*. Other words require no change at all because singular and plural forms are the same—deer, mathematics, news, sheep, and series.

You usually pluralize words ending in *f* or *fe* by changing the *f* to a *v* and adding *s* or *es: knives* and *lives,* for example.

You pluralize many foreign words with origins in Greek or Latin by changing the ending. Check out the table below for the most common examples.

Change	This	To this
sis to *ses:*	analysis	analyses
um to *a:*	datum	data
us to *i:*	radius	radii
on to *a:*	criterion	criteria

Pluralisms

We'll begin with a box and the plural is boxes, But the plural of ox is oxen, not oxes.

Then one fowl is a goose, but two are called geese, Yet the plural of mouse should never be meese.

You may find a lone mouse or a whole set of mice, But the plural of house is houses, not hice.

If the plural of man is always called men, Shouldn't the plural of pan be called pen?

If I speak of a foot and you show me your feet, And I give you a boot, would a pair be called beet?

If one is a tooth and the whole set are teeth, Why shouldn't the plural of booth be called beeth?

Then one may be that and three would be those, Yet hat in the plural wouldn't be hose. And the plural of cat is cats, and not cose.

We speak of a brother and also of brethren, But though we say mother, we never say methren.

Then the masculine pronouns are he, his, and him, But imagine the feminine she, shis, and shim.

So English I fancy that, I'm sure you'll agree, Is the funniest language you ever did see.

Note: The author of this poem is anonymous. If you can identify him or her, you may win a copy of Webster's original dictionary signed by him shortly after his death.

The Final E

To e or not to e, that is the question.

- ✔ Drop a final *e* preceded by a consonant when the suffix starts with a vowel. Excuse becomes *excusable;* argue, *arguable;* and desire, *desirous.*
- ✔ Retain the final *e* when the suffix begins with a consonant. Move becomes *movement;* care, *careless;* and resource, *resourceful.*

The Final Y

If you want to know y, here's y.

- ✔ Retain the final *y* when the *y* is preceded by a vowel, so that employ becomes *employs* and attorney becomes *attorneys.*
- ✔ When the final *y* is preceded by a consonant, change the *y* to *i* and add the suffix. Easy becomes *easily;* salary becomes *salaries;* and angry becomes *angrily.*

IE and EI

Perhaps Old MacDonald had the right idea: E I E I O. He didn't need to learn this jingle. If you learn it, however, you'll be able to spell most of the *ie* and *ei* words.

Put *i* before *e*, (yield, field)
Except after *c*, (deceit, receive)
Or when sounded like *a*,
As in *neighbor* or *weigh*.
And except *seize* and *seizure*,
And also *leisure*.
Weird, height, and *either*,
Forfeit and *neither*.

Doubling the Final Consonant

This section answers that ageless question: To double, or not to double.

✔ Double the final consonant if the word has one syllable or has its accent on the last syllable. The table shows some common verbs.

crop	cropped	cropping
admit	admitted	admitting
plan	planned	planning

✔ Double the final consonant in a word ending in a single vowel followed by a single consonant.

allot	allotted	allotting
prefer	preferred	preferring
transfer	transferred	transferring

✔ Don't double the final consonant if the word has three or more syllables: congealed, benefited.

Then there are words where the consonant may be either singled or doubled: canceled, traveller.

Super Stumpers

These super stumpers are the way they are—just because they are. Table D-1 lists the correct spelling and usage of some tricky words and expressions. The abbreviations in the table are fairly standard ones: *n* for noun, *v* for verb, *adj* for adjective, *adv* for adverb, *conj* for conjunction, *prep* for preposition, and *pron* for pronoun. In addition, letters or words in **boldface** indicate common letter(s) that can help you remember both the correct spelling and correct usage.

Table D-1	Use the Word You Really Want
Word	*Usage*
accept (v)	to take
except (prep)	other than
ad (n)	short for advertisement
add (v)	to increase
addition (n)	something added
edition (n)	published work
adverse (adj)	hostile
averse (adj)	unwilling
advice (n)	recommendation
advise (v)	to give an opinion
affect (v)	to influence
effect (n/v)	result/to bring about
already (adv/adj)	previously
all ready (adj)	all prepared
alright	slang for *all right*
all right	entirely correct
altar (n)	part of church
alter (v)	to chang**e**
altogether (adv)	entirely
all together (adv)	everyone in one group
among (prep)	comparison of three or more
between (prep)	comparison of two
amount (n)	refers to things in bulk or mass

(continued)

Table D-1 *(continued)*

Word	Usage
number (n)	refers to countable items
appraise (v)	to estimate
apprise (v)	to notify
assistance (n)	help
assistants (n)	those who help
bare (n)	naked; no more than
bear (v)	to carry
beside (prep)	alongside
besides (prep)	in addition to
biannual (adj)	twice a year
biennial (adj)	every two years
brake (n/v)	device for stopping motion/to stop
break (n/v)	fracture/to breach
canvas (n)	course cloth
canvass (v)	to solicit
choose (v)	to select
chose (v)	past tense of choose
coarse (adj)	rough
course (n)	direction, series of studies
complement (n/v)	that which completes/to complete
compliment (n/v)	expression of praise/to praise
correspondence (n)	letters
correspondents (n)	those who write letters
device (n)	a plan
devise (v)	to plan
disburse (v)	to pay out
disperse (v)	to scatter
dual (adj)	double
duel (n)	formal fight
elicit (v)	to draw out
illicit (adj)	illegal

Word	Usage
eminent (adj)	well-known
imminent (adj)	**imm**ediate
ensure (v)	to make certain
insure (v)	to protect against
farther (adj)	greater distance
further (adv)	to a greater degree
faze (v)	to embarrass
phase (n)	stage of development
fewer (adj)	modifies plural nouns
less (adj)	modifies singular nouns
formally (adv)	in a **formal** manner
formerly (adv)	at a **former** time
forth (adv)	forward
fourth (n)	follows third
forward (adv)	ahead
fore**word** (n)	preface in a book
incite (v)	stir to action
insight (n)	clear understanding
knew (v)	past tense of know
new (adj)	not old
know (v)	to understand
no (adj)	not any
lay (v)	to place an object down
lie (v/n)	to recline/untruth
lead (n/v)	heavy metal/to guide
led (v)	past tense of lead
maybe (adv)	perhaps
may be (v)	might be
miner (n)	one who works in a mine
minor (n)	person under legal age
moral (n)	lesson relating to right and wrong
morale (n)	spirit

(continued)

Table D-1 *(continued)*

Word	Usage
over**do** (v)	**do** to excess
over**due** (adj)	past **due**
passed (v)	past tense of pass
past (n)	time gone by
patience (n)	endurance
patients (n)	persons receiving treatment
peace (n)	state of calm
piece (n)	portion
peer (n)	equal
pier (n)	wharf
persecute (v)	oppress
prosecute (v)	institute legal proceedings
personal (adj)	private
personnel (n)	staff
principal (n/adj)	sum of money; school official/ main, first in rank
principle (n)	rule
respectfully (adv)	in a **respect**ful manner
respectively (adv)	in the order listed
role (n)	part in a play; function
roll (n)	register or list, small bread
should of	improper English
should have	proper English
stationary (adj)	fixed in pl**a**ce
station**ery** (n)	pap**er** products

SHERYL SAYS

I went to a recently opened supermarket looking to buy a package of envelopes. I spotted an aisle marked "stationary," and an *oops!* went off in my head. I found the manager and asked him if that was the only aisle in the store that doesn't move. He looked at me as if I had two heads. (So much for being a smart aleck.)

than (conj)	comparison expressing exception
then (adv)	at that time, next
undo (v)	open; render ineffective

Word	Usage
undue (adj)	improper; excessive
waive (v)	forego
wave (n)	gesture; surge of water
weather (n/v)	atmospheric condition/to come through safely
whether (conj)	if; in case
who's (contraction)	who is; who has
whose (pron)	possessive of who
your (pron)	belonging to you
you're (contraction)	you are
adapt (v)	to adjust
adept (adj)	skilled
adopt (v)	take as your own
access (n)	right to enter, admittance
assess (v)	to set a value
excess (n/adj)	extra
capital (n/adj)	official city of a state, money/ serious, chief
capitol (n)	building which houses state legislature
Capitol (n)	building in Washington, DC
cite (v)	to summon
sight (n)	that which is seen
site (n)	location
council (n)	assembly
counsel (n/v)	attorney/to advise
consul (n)	foreign representative
its (pron)	belonging to it
it's (contraction)	it is
its'	no such word
loose (v)	to set free
lose (v)	to suffer a loss, to mislay
loss (n)	something lost

(continued)

Table D-1 *(continued)*

Word	Usage
right (adj/n)	correct/just privilege
rite (n)	formal ceremony
write (v)	to inscribe
suit (n/v)	clothes/to please
suite (n)	set of rooms
sweet (adj)	having a sugary taste
their (pron)	belonging to them
there (adv)	in that place
they're (contraction)	they are
to (prep)	toward
too (adv)	also
two (adj)	numeral

Booby Traps

Table D-2 presents the "spelling demons" hit parade.

Table D-2 Lollapaloozas

abbreviation	absence	accept	accessible
accommodate	accompanied	acknowledge	acquaintance
across	advantageous	affect	affiliated
a lot	already	ambiguity	anonymous
apparent	appreciate	appropriate	argument
arrangement	attendance	bankruptcy	beginning
believable	beneficial	benefited	benign
bookkeeping	bulletin	business	calendar
campaign	cancel	cannot	category
cemetery	changeable	clientele	coming
committee	competition	concede	confident
conscientious	controversy	convenience	corroborate
criticism	defendant	depreciate	description

desirable	difference	disappoint	disbursement
discrepancy	dissatisfactory	dissipate	effect
eligible	embarrass	endeavor	endorsement
enthusiastic	environment	equipped	especially
exceed	excellent	except	exercise
exhaust	existence	experience	explanation
extension	extraordinary	familiar	feasible
February	foreign	forty	government
grateful	guarantee	handwritten	height
immediate	inasmuch as	incidentally	independence
independent	insistent	interpret	jeopardize
jewelry	judgment	knowledge	laboratory
leisure	library	license	lien
likable	litigation	loose	lose
maintenance	mandatory	mediocre	mileage
minimum	miscellaneous	misspell	municipal
necessary	occasion	occurred	omission
opportunity	opposite	original	paid
pamphlet	parallel	paralyze	perseverance
persuade	physician	possession	practical
precede	preferred	procedure	prosecute
privilege	psychology	pursue	questionnaire
really	receive	reference	repetition
separate	sheriff	similar	sincerely
subpoena	succeed	successful	sympathy
techniques	unanimous	unnecessary	until
vacuum	Wednesday	withheld	yourself

Just for Fun

1. Can you name a word in the English language that has three consecutive double letters?

2. Can you think of a word with four consecutive vowels?

3. Can you think of a word that has 28 letters?

Answers

1. Bookkeeper or bookkeeping 2. Sequoia or queue 3. Antidisestablishmentarianism

Index

Discover Dummies™ Online!

The *Dummies* Web Site is your fun and friendly online resource for the latest information about *...For Dummies*® books on all your favorite topics. From cars to computers, wine to Windows, and investing to the Internet, we've got a shelf full of *...For Dummies* books waiting for you!

Ten Fun and Useful Things You Can Do at www.dummies.com

1. Register this book and win!
2. Find and buy the *...For Dummies* books you want online.
3. Get ten great *Dummies Tips*™ every week.
4. Chat with your favorite *...For Dummies* authors.
5. Subscribe free to *The Dummies Dispatch*™ newsletter.
6. Enter our sweepstakes and win cool stuff.
7. Send a free cartoon postcard to a friend.
8. Download free software.
9. Sample a book before you buy.
10. Talk to us. Make comments, ask questions, and get answers!

Jump online to these ten fun and useful things at
http://www.dummies.com/10useful

For other technology titles from IDG Books Worldwide, go to
www.idgbooks.com

Not online yet? It's easy to get started with *The Internet For Dummies*®, 5th Edition, or *Dummies 101*®: *The Internet For Windows*® *98*, available at local retailers everywhere.

Find other *...For Dummies* books on these topics:

Business • Careers • Databases • Food & Beverages • Games • Gardening • Graphics • Hardware
Health & Fitness • Internet and the World Wide Web • Networking • Office Suites
Operating Systems • Personal Finance • Pets • Programming • Recreation • Sports
Spreadsheets • Teacher Resources • Test Prep • Word Processing

IDG BOOKS WORLDWIDE
BOOK REGISTRATION

Register This Book and Win!

We want to hear from you!

Visit **http://my2cents.dummies.com** to register this book and tell us how you liked it!

✔ Get entered in our monthly prize giveaway.

✔ Give us feedback about this book — tell us what you like best, what you like least, or maybe what you'd like to ask the author and us to change!

✔ Let us know any other *...For Dummies*® topics that interest you.

Your feedback helps us determine what books to publish, tells us what coverage to add as we revise our books, and lets us know whether we're meeting your needs as a *...For Dummies* reader. You're our most valuable resource, and what you have to say is important to us!

Not on the Web yet? It's easy to get started with *Dummies 101*®: *The Internet For Windows*® *98* or *The Internet For Dummies*®, 5th Edition, at local retailers everywhere.

Or let us know what you think by sending us a letter at the following address:

...For Dummies Book Registration
Dummies Press
7260 Shadeland Station, Suite 100
Indianapolis, IN 46256-3945
Fax 317-596-5498

BESTSELLING BOOK SERIES